3 1668 06449 0003

TEEN GRAPHIC NOVEL IRON
v.3 2013
Gillen, Kieron
Iron Man /

07/21/14

IRONMAN
THE SECRET ORIGIN OF
TONY STARK BOOK 2

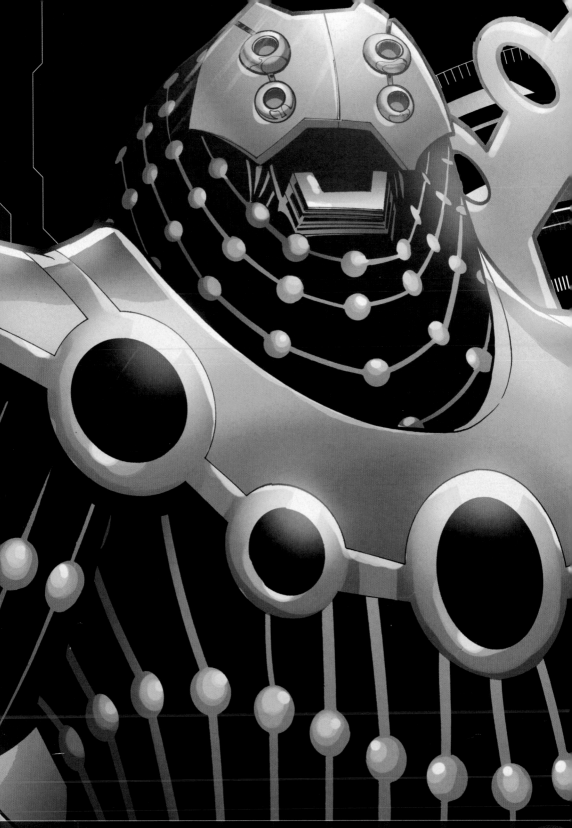

IRON MAN VOL. 3: THE SECRET ORIGIN OF TONY STARK BOOK 2. Contains material originally published in magazine form as IRON MAN #12-17. First printing 2013. ISBN# 978-0-7851-6835-5. Published
MARVEL WORLDWIDE, INC., a subsidiary of MARVEL ENTERTAINMENT, LLC. OFFICE OF PUBLICATION: 135 West 50th Street, New York, NY 10020. Copyright © 2013 Marvel Characters, Inc. All rights reserved
characters featured in this issue and the distinctive names and likenesses thereof, and all related indicia are trademarks of Marvel Characters, Inc. No similarity between any of the names, characters, pers
and/or institutions in this magazine with those of any living or dead person or institution is intended, and any such similarity which may exist is purely coincidental. **Printed in the U.S.A.** ALAN FINE, EVP - Of
of the President, Marvel Worldwide, Inc. and EVP & CMO Marvel Characters B.V.; DAN BUCKLEY, Publisher & President - Print, Animation & Digital Divisions; JOE QUESADA, Chief Creative Officer; TOM BREVO
SVP of Publishing; DAVID BOGART, SVP of Operations & Procurement, Publishing; C.B. CEBULSKI, SVP of Creator & Content Development; DAVID GABRIEL, SVP of Print & Digital Publishing Sales; JIM O'KEEFE
of Operations & Logistics; DAN CARR, Executive Director of Publishing Technology; SUSAN CRESPI, Editorial Operations Manager; ALEX MORALES, Publishing Operations Manager; STAN LEE, Chairman Emeri
For information regarding advertising in Marvel Comics or on Marvel.com, please contact Niza Disla, Director of Marvel Partnerships, at ndisla@marvel.com. For Marvel subscription inquiries, please call 8
217-9158. **Manufactured between 10/4/2013 and 11/18/2013 by R.R. DONNELLEY, INC., SALEM, VA, USA.**
LEGO and the Minifigure figurine are trademarks or copyrights of the LEGO Group of Companies. ©2013 The LEGO Group. Characters featured in particular decorations are not commercial products and m
not be available for purchase.

10 9 8 7 6 5 4 3 2 1

Tony Stark is a technological visionary...a famous, wealthy and unparalled inventor. With the world's most advanced and powerful suit of armor, Stark valiantly protects the innocent as an invincible bright knight known as...

IRON MAN

KIERON GILLEN
WRITER

DALE EAGLESHAM
ARTIST, #12

GREG LAND
PENCILER, #13-14

JAY LEISTEN
INKER, #13-14

CARLO PAGULAYAN
PENCILER, #15-17

SCOTT HANNA
INKER, #15-17

GURU-eFX
COLORIST

VC'S JOE CARAMAGNA
LETTERER

**GREG LAND
& GURU-eFX**
COVER ART, #12-16

PAUL RENAUD
COVER ART, #17

**JON MOISAN
& EMILY SHAW**
ASSISTANT EDITORS

MARK PANICCIA
EDITOR

COLLECTION EDITOR: **JENNIFER GRÜNWALD**
ASSISTANT EDITORS: **ALEX STARBUCK** & **NELSON RIBEIRO**
EDITOR, SPECIAL PROJECTS: **MARK D. BEAZLEY**
SENIOR EDITOR, SPECIAL PROJECTS: **JEFF YOUNGQUIST**
SVP OF PRINT & DIGITAL PUBLISHING SALES: **DAVID GABRIEL**
BOOK DESIGNER: **RODOLFO MURAGUCHI**

EDITOR IN CHIEF: **AXEL ALONSO**
CHIEF CREATIVE OFFICER: **JOE QUESADA**
PUBLISHER: **DAN BUCKLEY**
EXECUTIVE PRODUCER: **ALAN FINE**

FORT WORTH LIBRARY

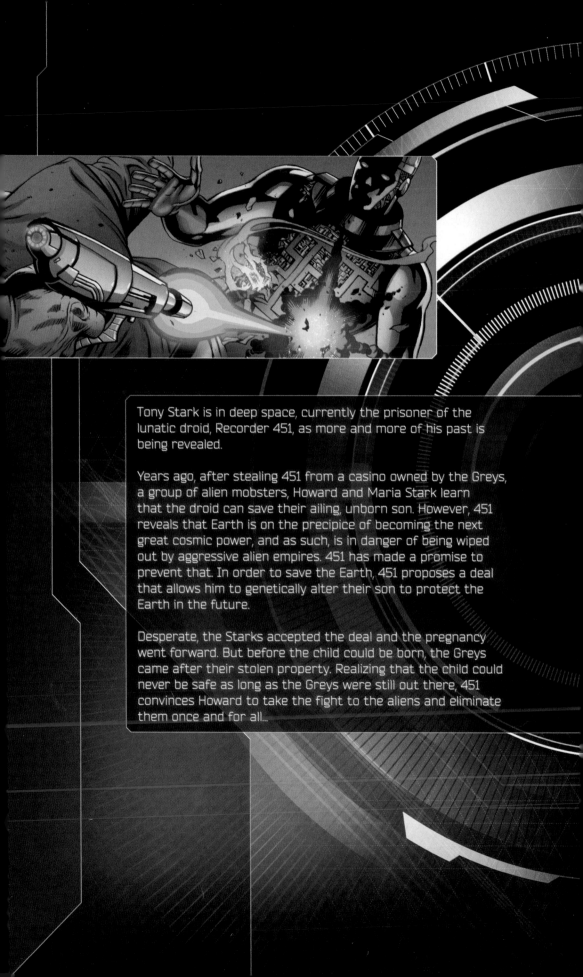

Tony Stark is in deep space, currently the prisoner of the lunatic droid, Recorder 451, as more and more of his past is being revealed.

Years ago, after stealing 451 from a casino owned by the Greys, a group of alien mobsters, Howard and Maria Stark learn that the droid can save their ailing, unborn son. However, 451 reveals that Earth is on the precipice of becoming the next great cosmic power, and as such, is in danger of being wiped out by aggressive alien empires. 451 has made a promise to prevent that. In order to save the Earth, 451 proposes a deal that allows him to genetically alter their son to protect the Earth in the future.

Desperate, the Starks accepted the deal and the pregnancy went forward. But before the child could be born, the Greys came after their stolen property. Realizing that the child could never be safe as long as the Greys were still out there, 451 convinces Howard to take the fight to the aliens and eliminate them once and for all...

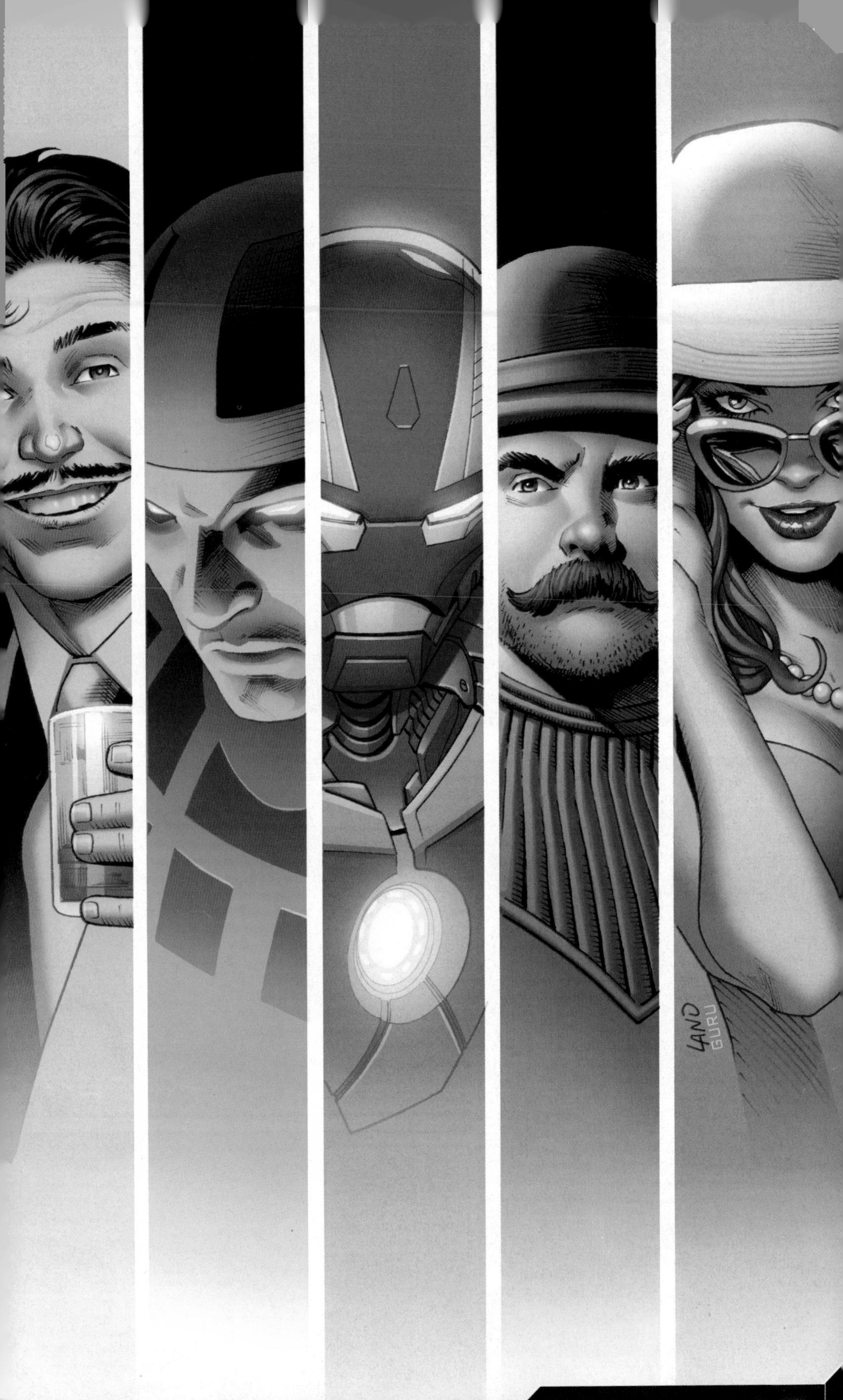
LAND
GURU

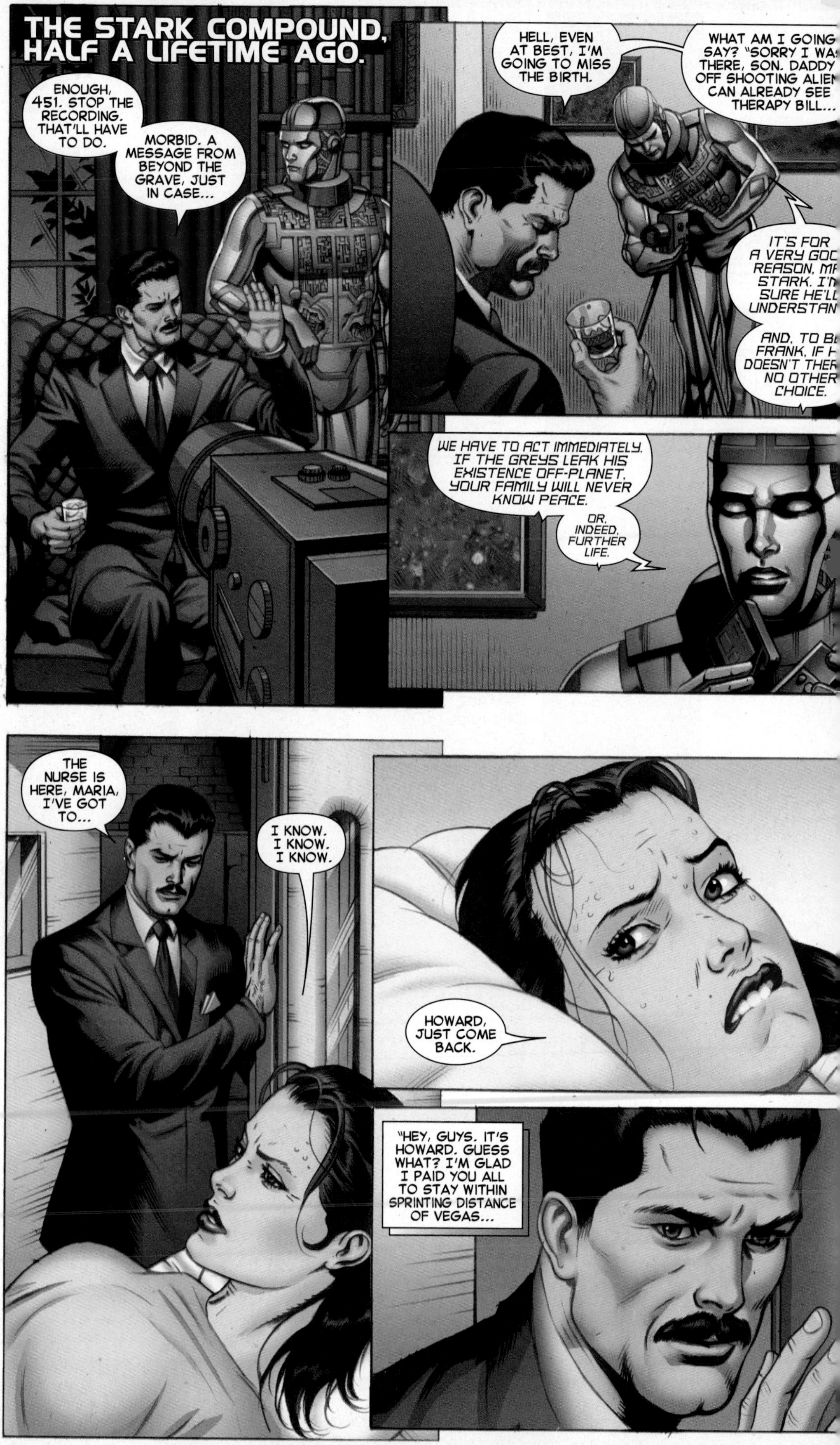
THE STARK COMPOUND, HALF A LIFETIME AGO.
ENOUGH, 451. STOP THE RECORDING. THAT'LL HAVE TO DO.
MORBID. A MESSAGE FROM BEYOND THE GRAVE, JUST IN CASE...
HELL, EVEN AT BEST, I'M GOING TO MISS THE BIRTH.
WHAT AM I GOING SAY? "SORRY I WA THERE, SON. DADDY OFF SHOOTING ALIE CAN ALREADY SEE THERAPY BILL...
IT'S FOR A VERY GOO REASON, MR STARK. I'M SURE HE'LL UNDERSTAN
AND, TO B FRANK, IF H DOESN'T THER NO OTHER CHOICE.
WE HAVE TO ACT IMMEDIATELY. IF THE GREYS LEAK HIS EXISTENCE OFF-PLANET, YOUR FAMILY WILL NEVER KNOW PEACE.
OR, INDEED, FURTHER LIFE.
THE NURSE IS HERE, MARIA, I'VE GOT TO...
I KNOW. I KNOW. I KNOW.
HOWARD, JUST COME BACK.
"HEY, GUYS. IT'S HOWARD. GUESS WHAT? I'M GLAD I PAID YOU ALL TO STAY WITHIN SPRINTING DISTANCE OF VEGAS...

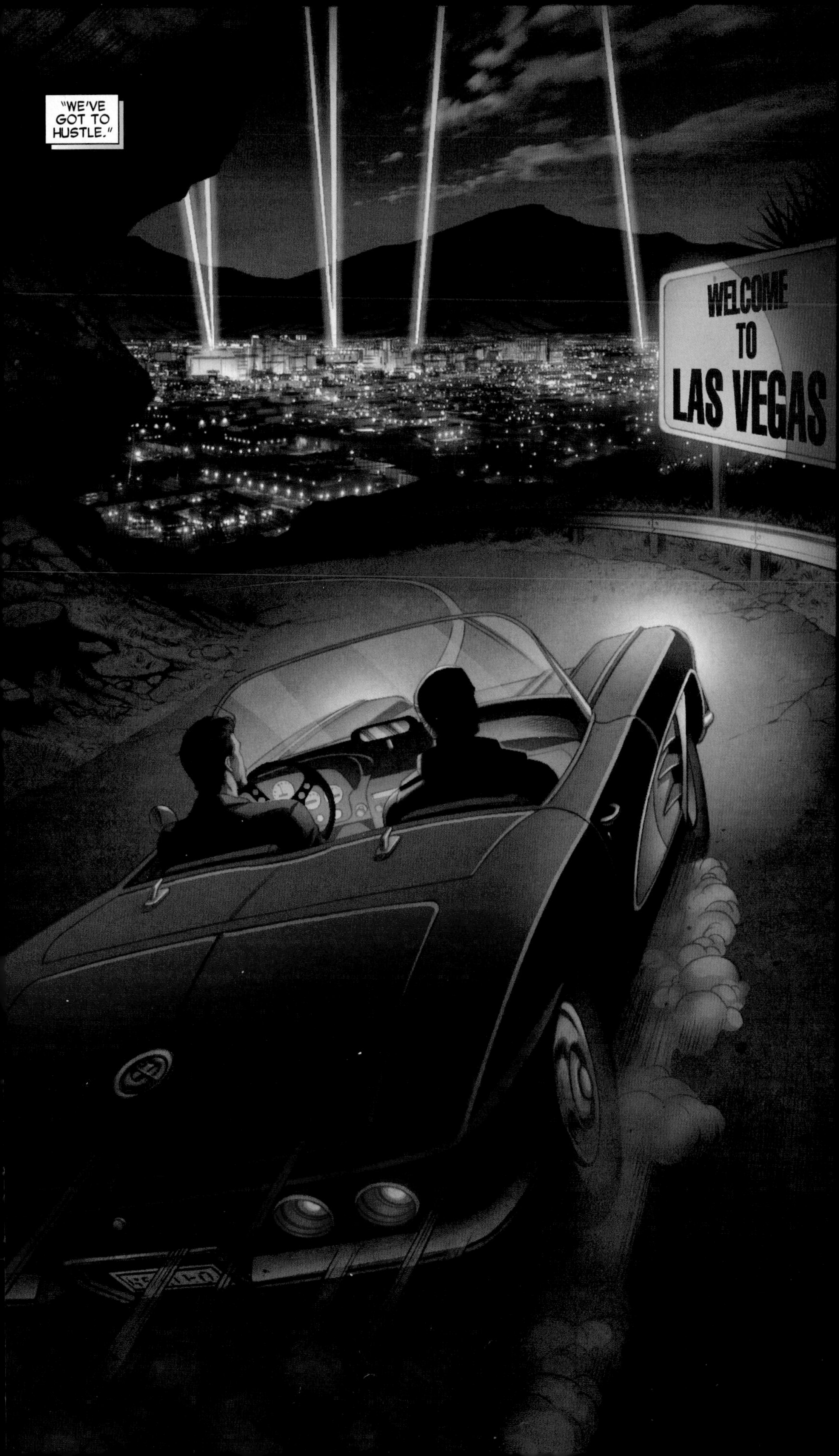
"WE'VE GOT TO HUSTLE."
WELCOME TO LAS VEGAS

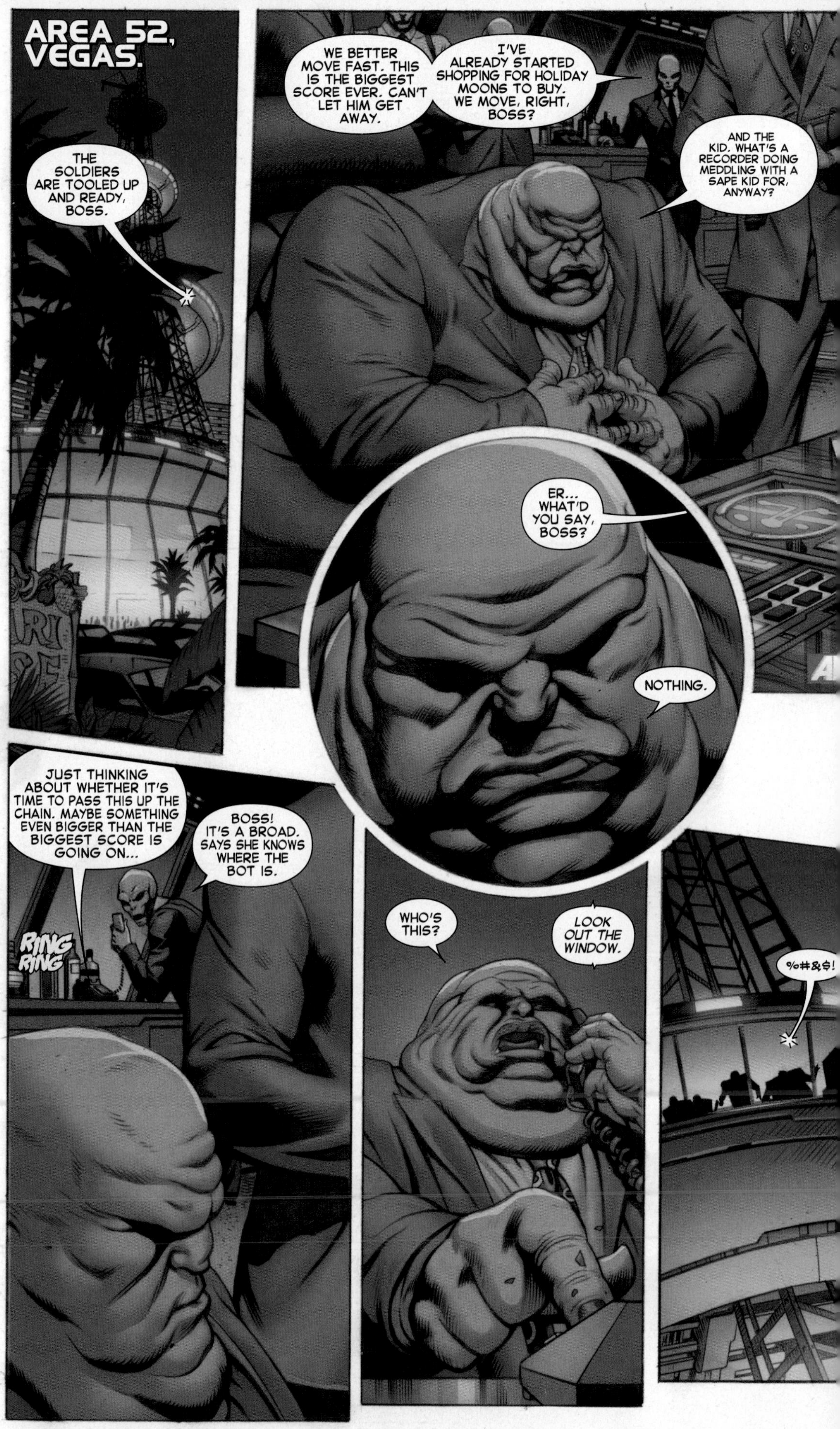
AREA 52, VEGAS.
THE SOLDIERS ARE TOOLED UP AND READY, BOSS.
WE BETTER MOVE FAST. THIS IS THE BIGGEST SCORE EVER. CAN'T LET HIM GET AWAY.
I'VE ALREADY STARTED SHOPPING FOR HOLIDAY MOONS TO BUY. WE MOVE, RIGHT, BOSS?
AND THE KID. WHAT'S A RECORDER DOING MEDDLING WITH A SAPE KID FOR, ANYWAY?
ER... WHAT'D YOU SAY, BOSS?
NOTHING.
JUST THINKING ABOUT WHETHER IT'S TIME TO PASS THIS UP THE CHAIN. MAYBE SOMETHING EVEN BIGGER THAN THE BIGGEST SCORE IS GOING ON...
BOSS! IT'S A BROAD. SAYS SHE KNOWS WHERE THE BOT IS.
RING RING
WHO'S THIS?
LOOK OUT THE WINDOW.
%#&$!

HELLO, EARTHLINGS! WELCOME TO AREA 52.

I COME IN PEACE. ER... EXTERMINATE?

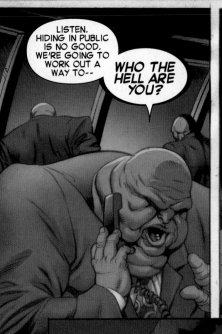

LISTEN. HIDING IN PUBLIC IS NO GOOD. WE'RE GOING TO WORK OUT A WAY TO--

WHO THE HELL ARE YOU?

NESSA THE KITTEN.,

ARE YOU THERE?

MR. STARK, IS THIS--

JUST KEEP UP "THE DAY THE EARTH STOOD STILL" ACT...

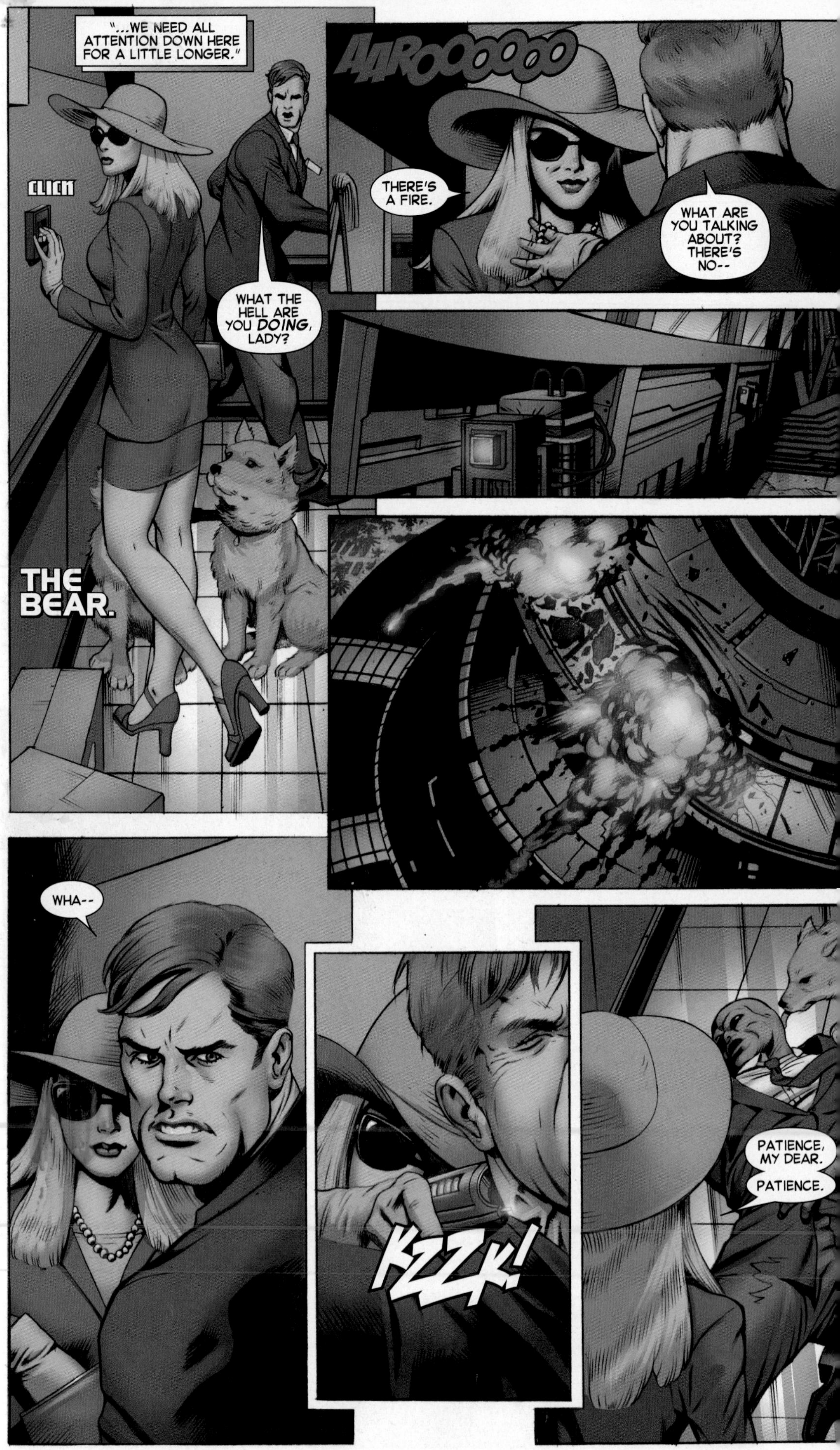
"...WE NEED ALL ATTENTION DOWN HERE FOR A LITTLE LONGER."
CLICK
WHAT THE HELL ARE YOU DOING, LADY?
THE BEAR.
AAROOOOOOO
THERE'S A FIRE.
WHAT ARE YOU TALKING ABOUT? THERE'S NO--
WHA--
KZZK!
PATIENCE, MY DEAR.
PATIENCE.

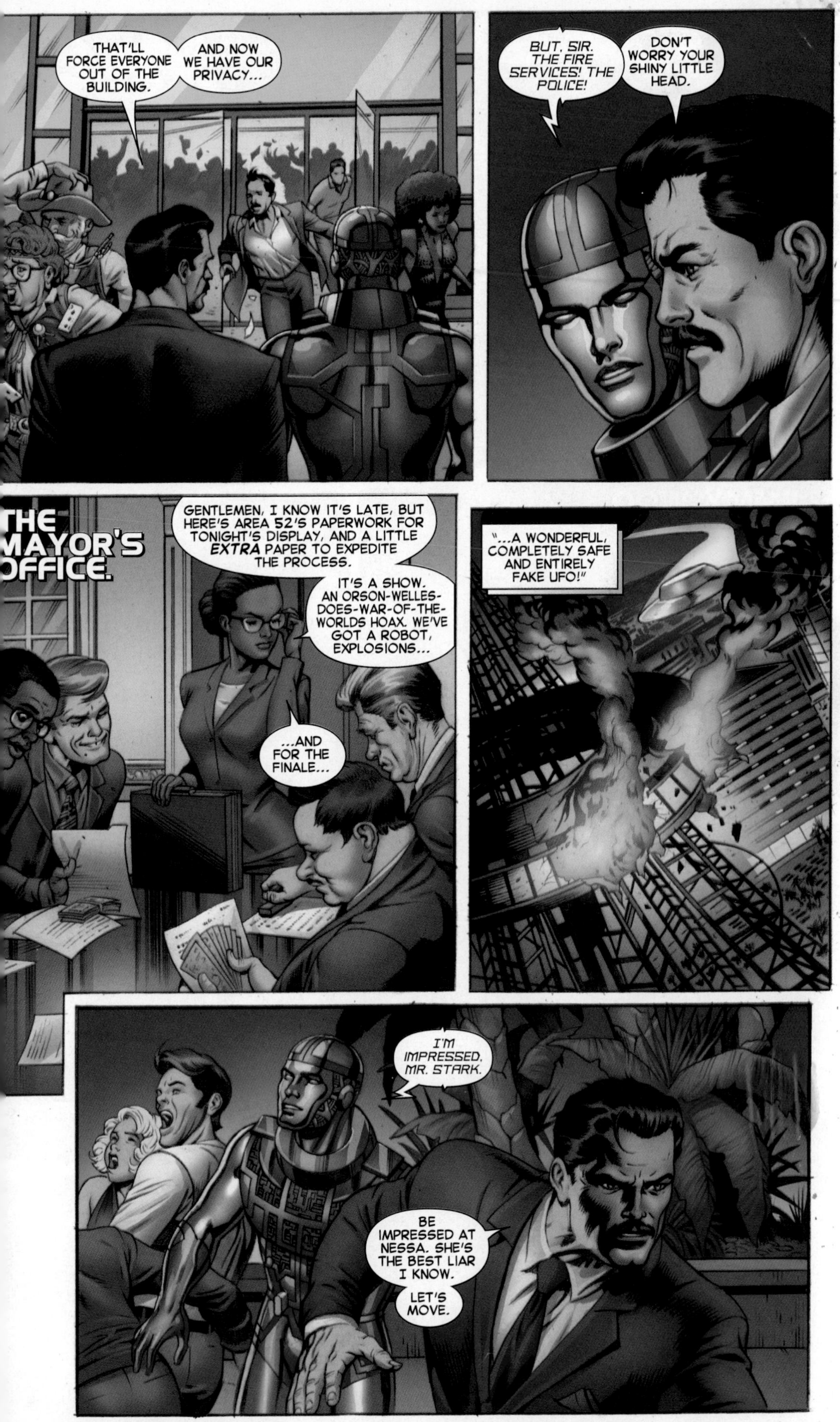

THAT'LL FORCE EVERYONE OUT OF THE BUILDING.
AND NOW WE HAVE OUR PRIVACY...
BUT, SIR. THE FIRE SERVICES! THE POLICE!
DON'T WORRY YOUR SHINY LITTLE HEAD.
THE MAYOR'S OFFICE.
GENTLEMEN, I KNOW IT'S LATE, BUT HERE'S AREA 52'S PAPERWORK FOR TONIGHT'S DISPLAY, AND A LITTLE EXTRA PAPER TO EXPEDITE THE PROCESS.
IT'S A SHOW. AN ORSON-WELLES-DOES-WAR-OF-THE-WORLDS HOAX. WE'VE GOT A ROBOT, EXPLOSIONS...
...AND FOR THE FINALE...
"...A WONDERFUL, COMPLETELY SAFE AND ENTIRELY FAKE UFO!"
I'M IMPRESSED, MR. STARK.
BE IMPRESSED AT NESSA. SHE'S THE BEST LIAR I KNOW.
LET'S MOVE.

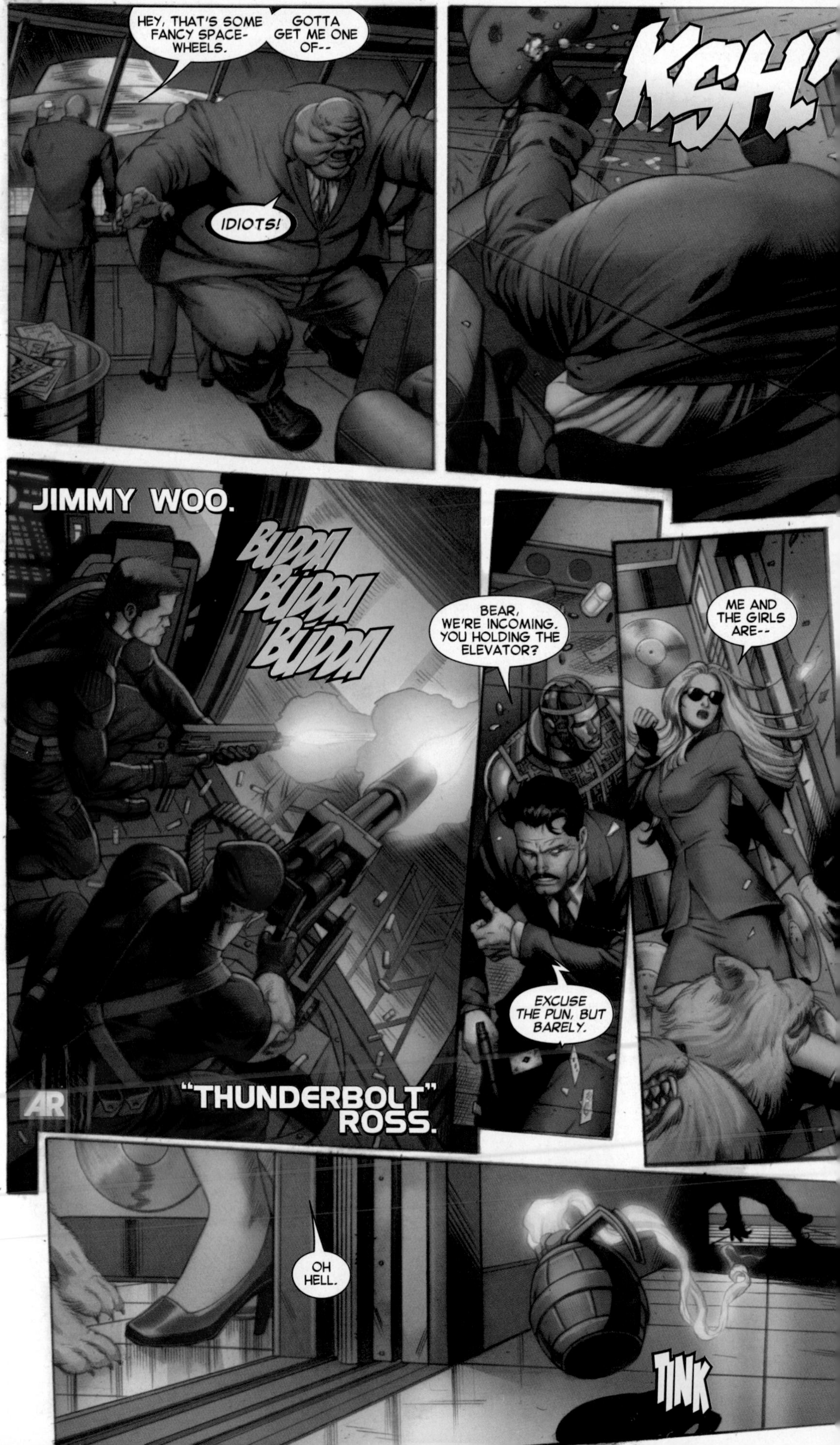
HEY, THAT'S SOME FANCY SPACE-WHEELS.
GOTTA GET ME ONE OF--
IDIOTS!
KSHK
JIMMY WOO.
BUDDA BUDDA BUDDA
"THUNDERBOLT" ROSS.
BEAR, WE'RE INCOMING. YOU HOLDING THE ELEVATOR?
EXCUSE THE PUN, BUT BARELY.
ME AND THE GIRLS ARE--
OH HELL.
TINK

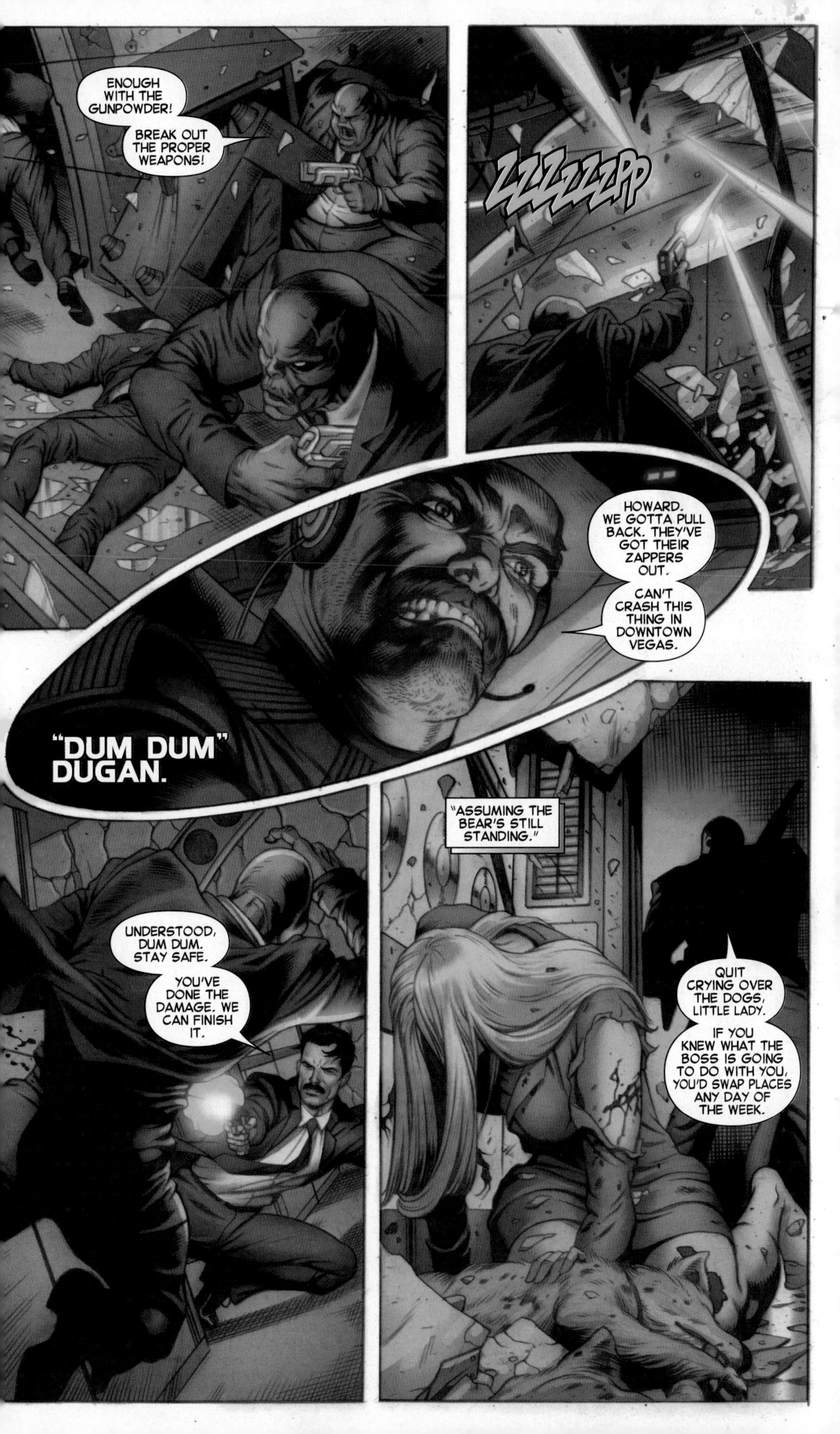
ENOUGH WITH THE GUNPOWDER!
BREAK OUT THE PROPER WEAPONS!
ZZZZZZPP
HOWARD. WE GOTTA PULL BACK. THEY'VE GOT THEIR ZAPPERS OUT.
CAN'T CRASH THIS THING IN DOWNTOWN VEGAS.
"DUM DUM" DUGAN.
UNDERSTOOD, DUM DUM. STAY SAFE.
YOU'VE DONE THE DAMAGE. WE CAN FINISH IT.
"ASSUMING THE BEAR'S STILL STANDING."
QUIT CRYING OVER THE DOGS, LITTLE LADY.
IF YOU KNEW WHAT THE BOSS IS GOING TO DO WITH YOU, YOU'D SWAP PLACES ANY DAY OF THE WEEK.

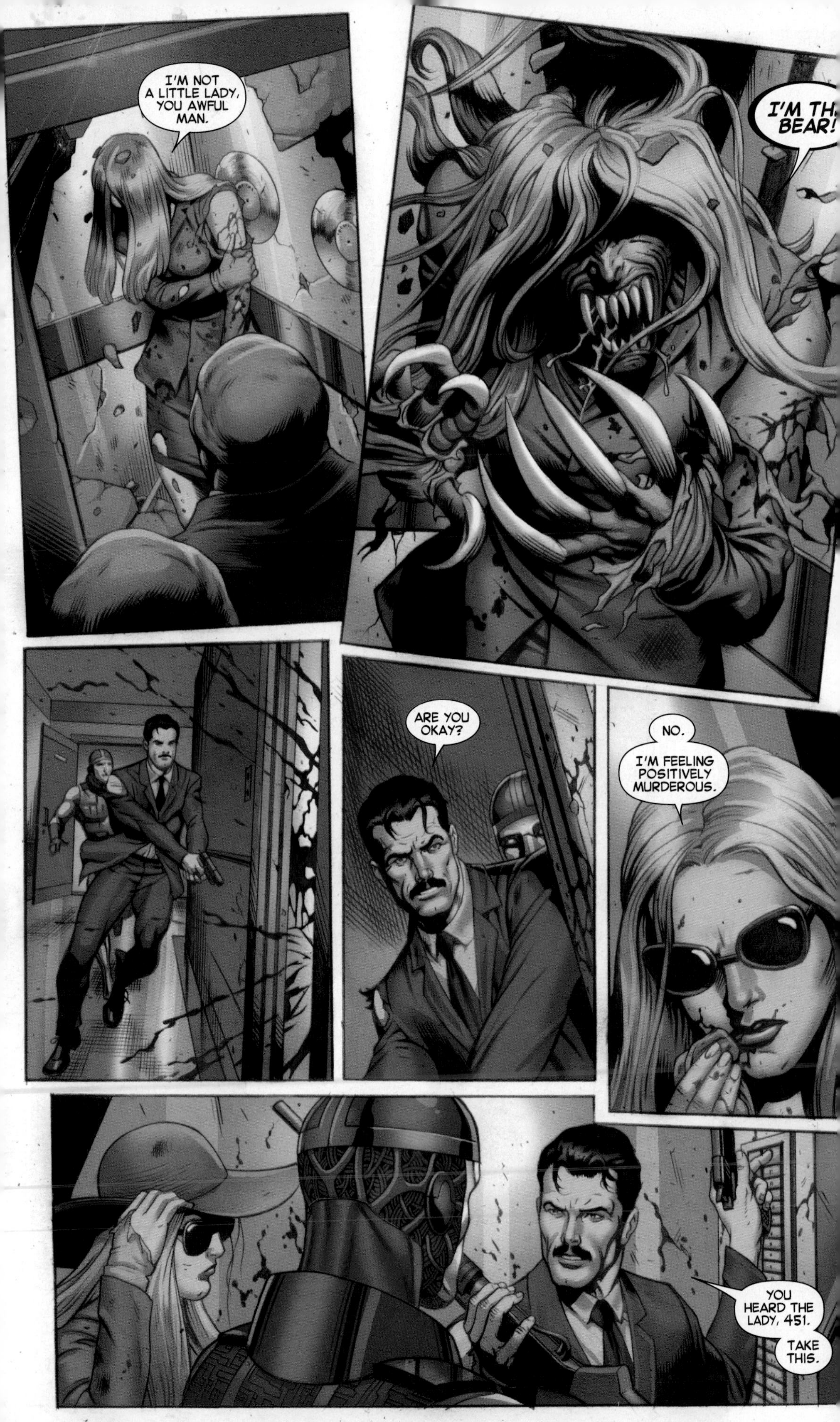
I'M NOT A LITTLE LADY, YOU AWFUL MAN.
I'M TH BEAR!
ARE YOU OKAY?
NO.
I'M FEELING POSITIVELY MURDEROUS.
YOU HEARD THE LADY, 451.
TAKE THIS.

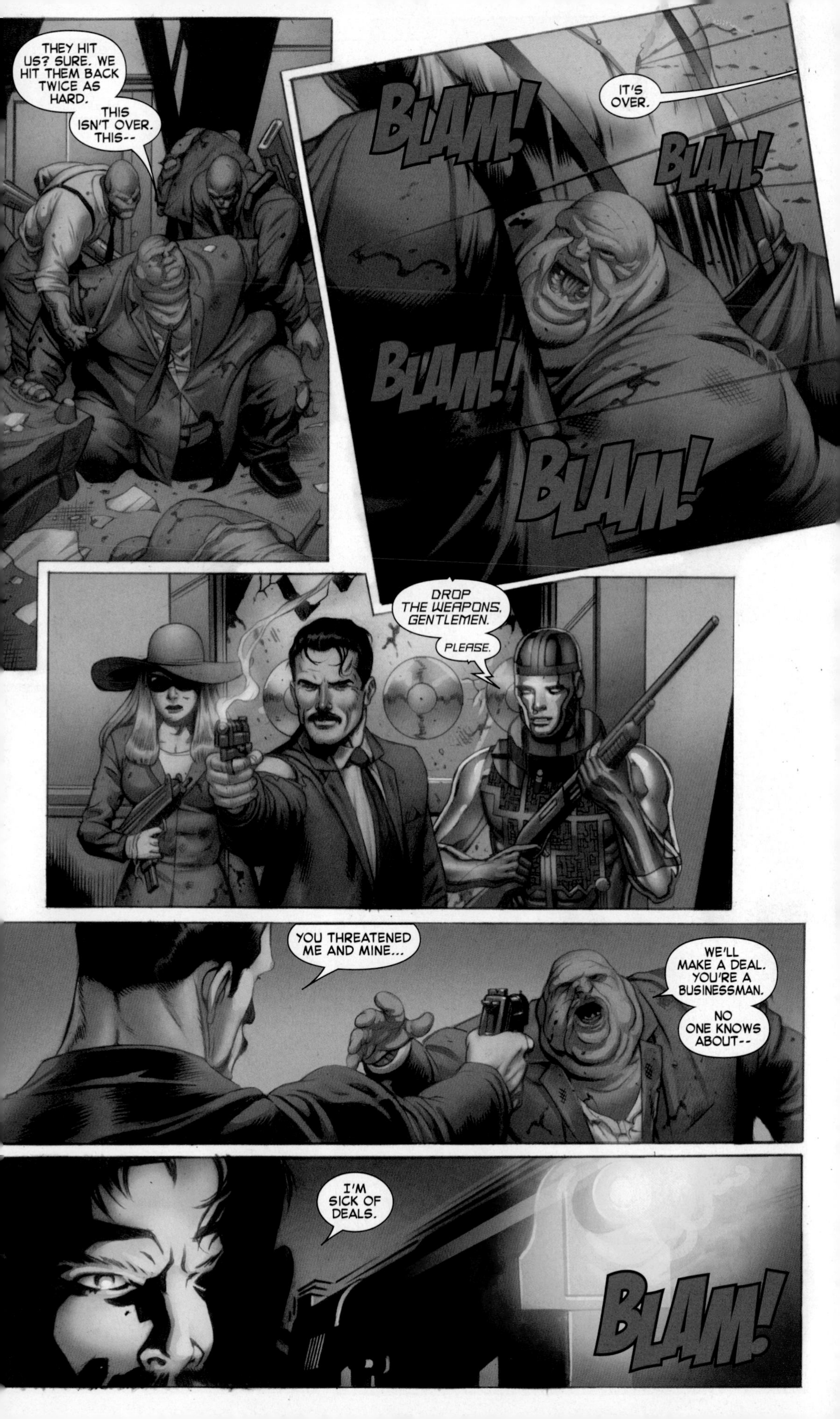
THEY HIT US? SURE. WE HIT THEM BACK TWICE AS HARD.
THIS ISN'T OVER. THIS--
IT'S OVER.
BLAM!
BLAM!
BLAM!
BLAM!
DROP THE WEAPONS, GENTLEMEN.
PLEASE.
YOU THREATENED ME AND MINE...
WE'LL MAKE A DEAL. YOU'RE A BUSINESSMAN.
NO ONE KNOWS ABOUT--
I'M SICK OF DEALS.
BLAM!

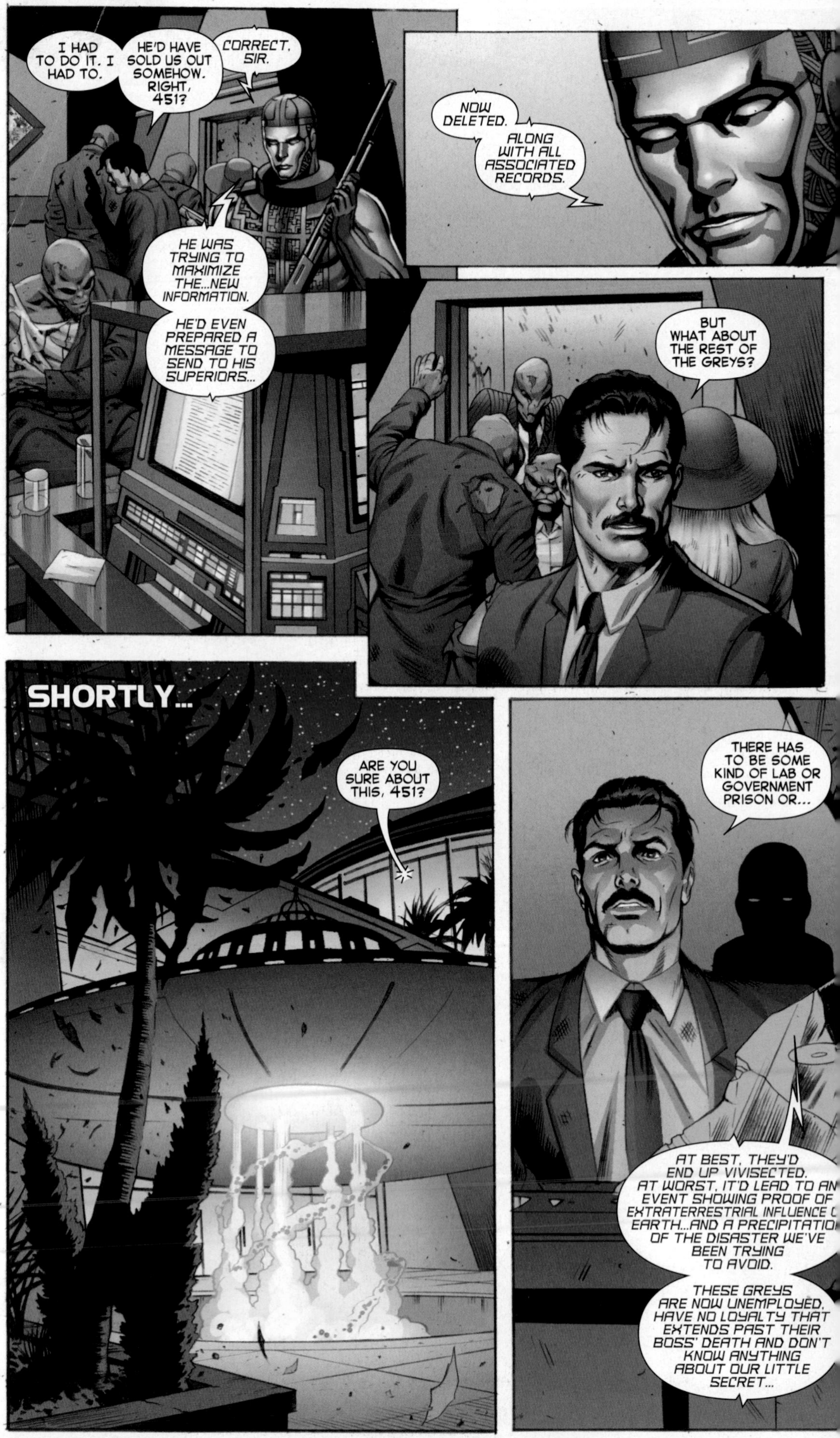
I HAD TO DO IT. I HAD TO.
HE'D HAVE SOLD US OUT SOMEHOW. RIGHT, 451?
CORRECT, SIR.
HE WAS TRYING TO MAXIMIZE THE...NEW INFORMATION.
HE'D EVEN PREPARED A MESSAGE TO SEND TO HIS SUPERIORS...
NOW DELETED.
ALONG WITH ALL ASSOCIATED RECORDS.
BUT WHAT ABOUT THE REST OF THE GREYS?
SHORTLY...
ARE YOU SURE ABOUT THIS, 451?
THERE HAS TO BE SOME KIND OF LAB OR GOVERNMENT PRISON OR...
AT BEST, THEY'D END UP VIVISECTED. AT WORST, IT'D LEAD TO AN EVENT SHOWING PROOF OF EXTRATERRESTRIAL INFLUENCE ON EARTH...AND A PRECIPITATION OF THE DISASTER WE'VE BEEN TRYING TO AVOID.
THESE GREYS ARE NOW UNEMPLOYED, HAVE NO LOYALTY THAT EXTENDS PAST THEIR BOSS' DEATH AND DON'T KNOW ANYTHING ABOUT OUR LITTLE SECRET...

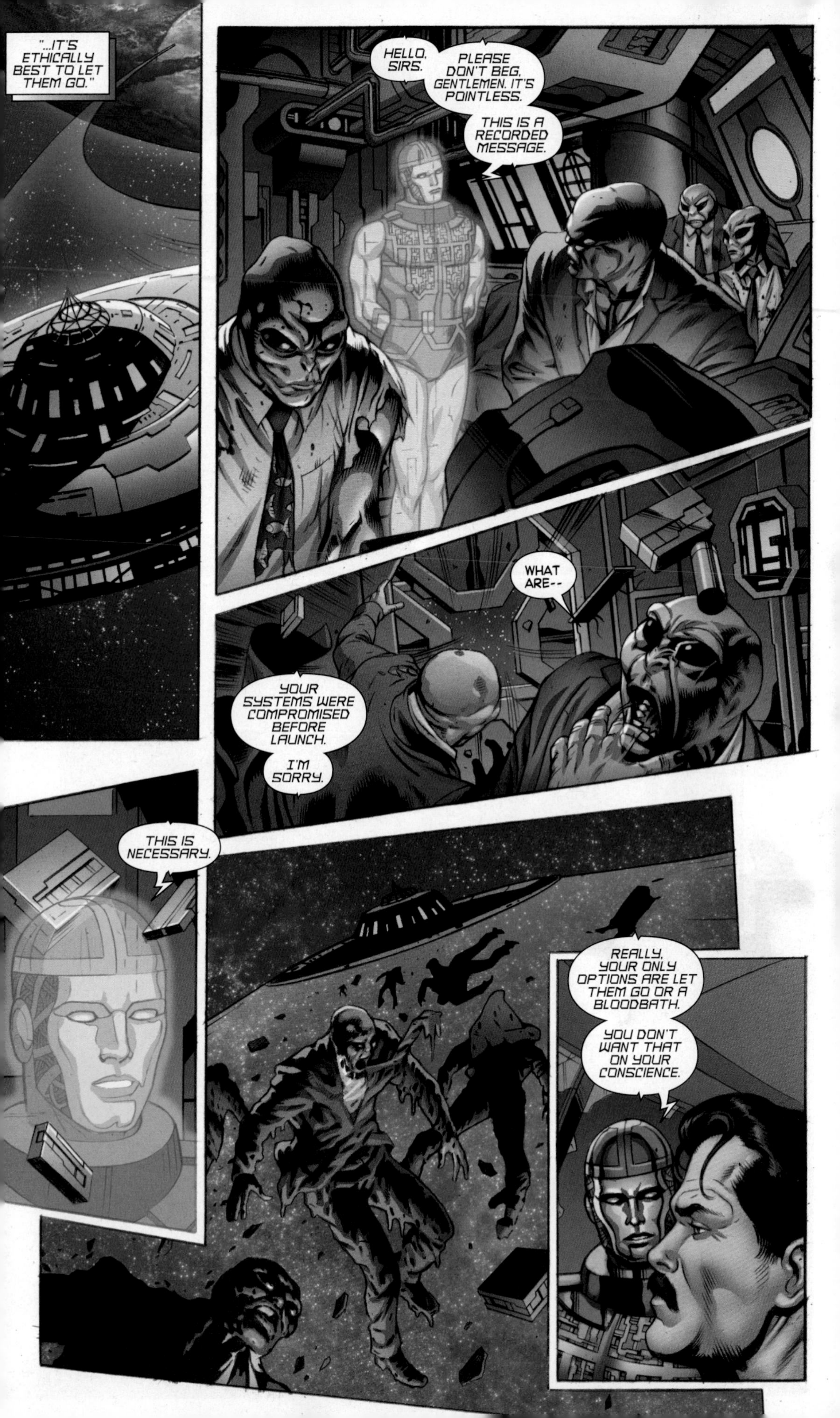
"...IT'S ETHICALLY BEST TO LET THEM GO."
HELLO, SIRS.
PLEASE DON'T BEG, GENTLEMEN. IT'S POINTLESS.
THIS IS A RECORDED MESSAGE.
WHAT ARE--
YOUR SYSTEMS WERE COMPROMISED BEFORE LAUNCH.
I'M SORRY.
THIS IS NECESSARY.
REALLY, YOUR ONLY OPTIONS ARE LET THEM GO OR A BLOODBATH.
YOU DON'T WANT THAT ON YOUR CONSCIENCE.

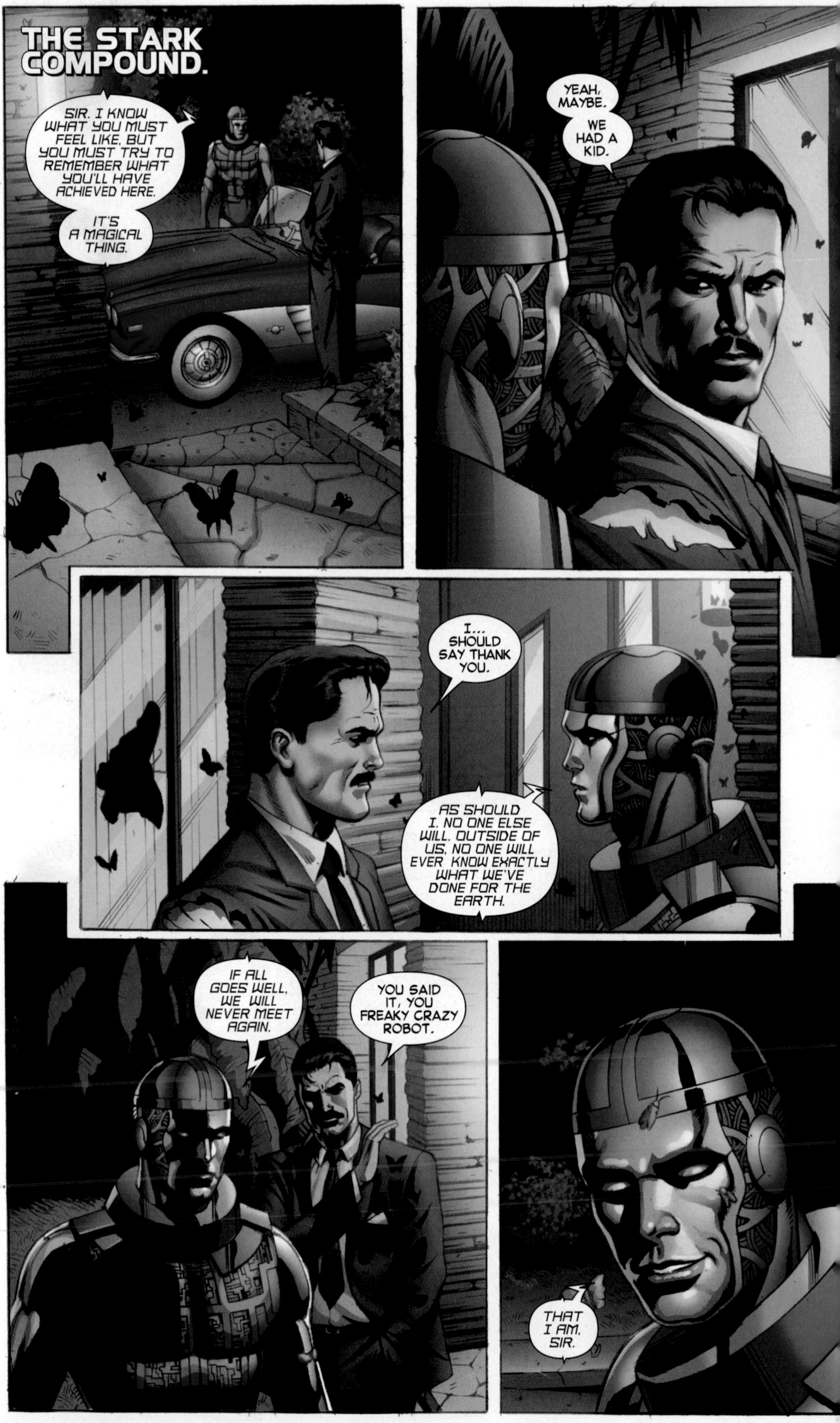
THE STARK COMPOUND.
SIR. I KNOW WHAT YOU MUST FEEL LIKE, BUT YOU MUST TRY TO REMEMBER WHAT YOU'LL HAVE ACHIEVED HERE.
IT'S A MAGICAL THING.
YEAH, MAYBE.
WE HAD A KID.
I... SHOULD SAY THANK YOU.
AS SHOULD I. NO ONE ELSE WILL. OUTSIDE OF US, NO ONE WILL EVER KNOW EXACTLY WHAT WE'VE DONE FOR THE EARTH.
IF ALL GOES WELL, WE WILL NEVER MEET AGAIN.
YOU SAID IT, YOU FREAKY CRAZY ROBOT.
THAT I AM, SIR.

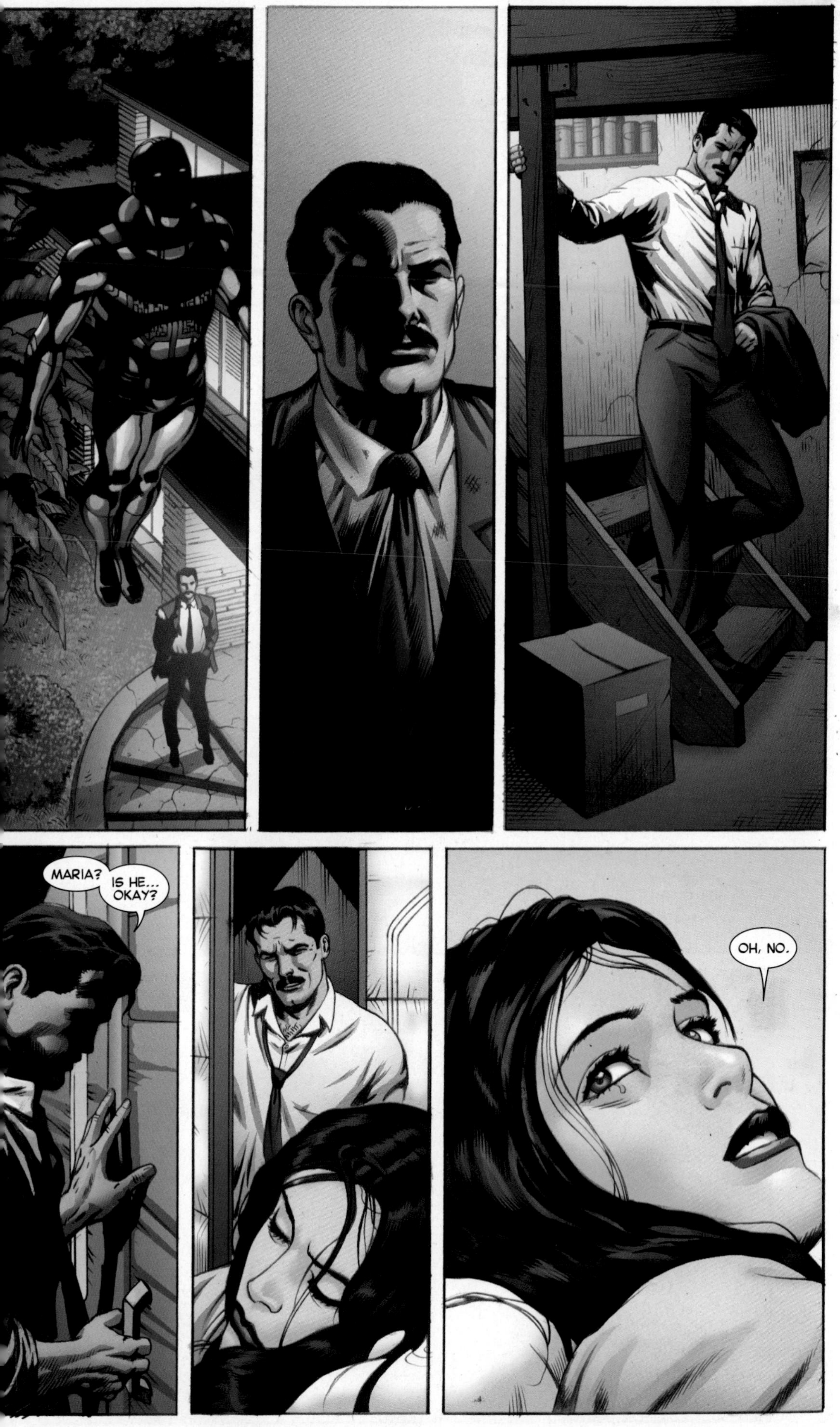
MARIA?
IS HE... OKAY?
OH, NO.

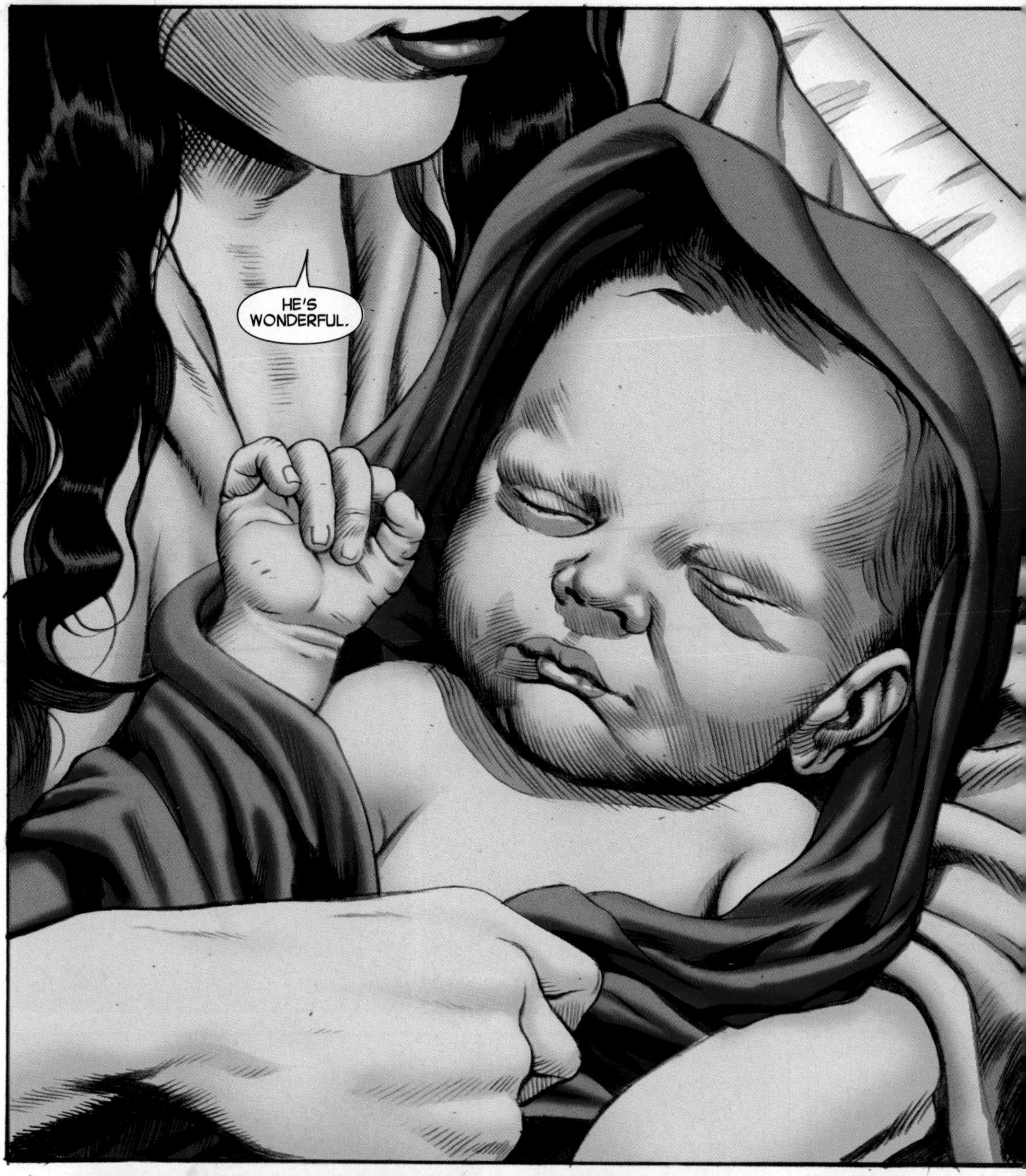
HE'S WONDERFUL.

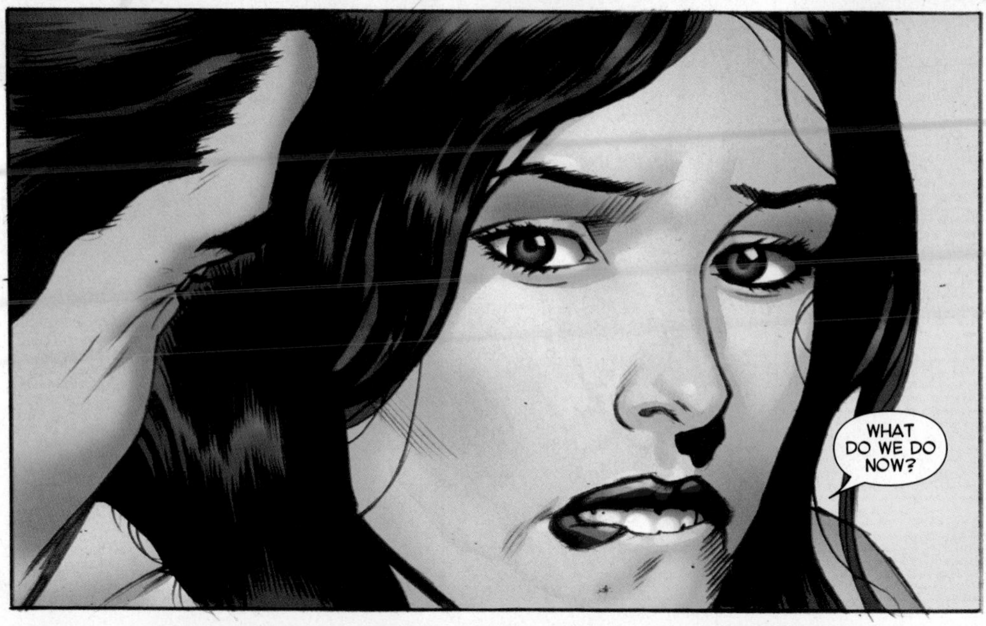
WHAT DO WE DO NOW?

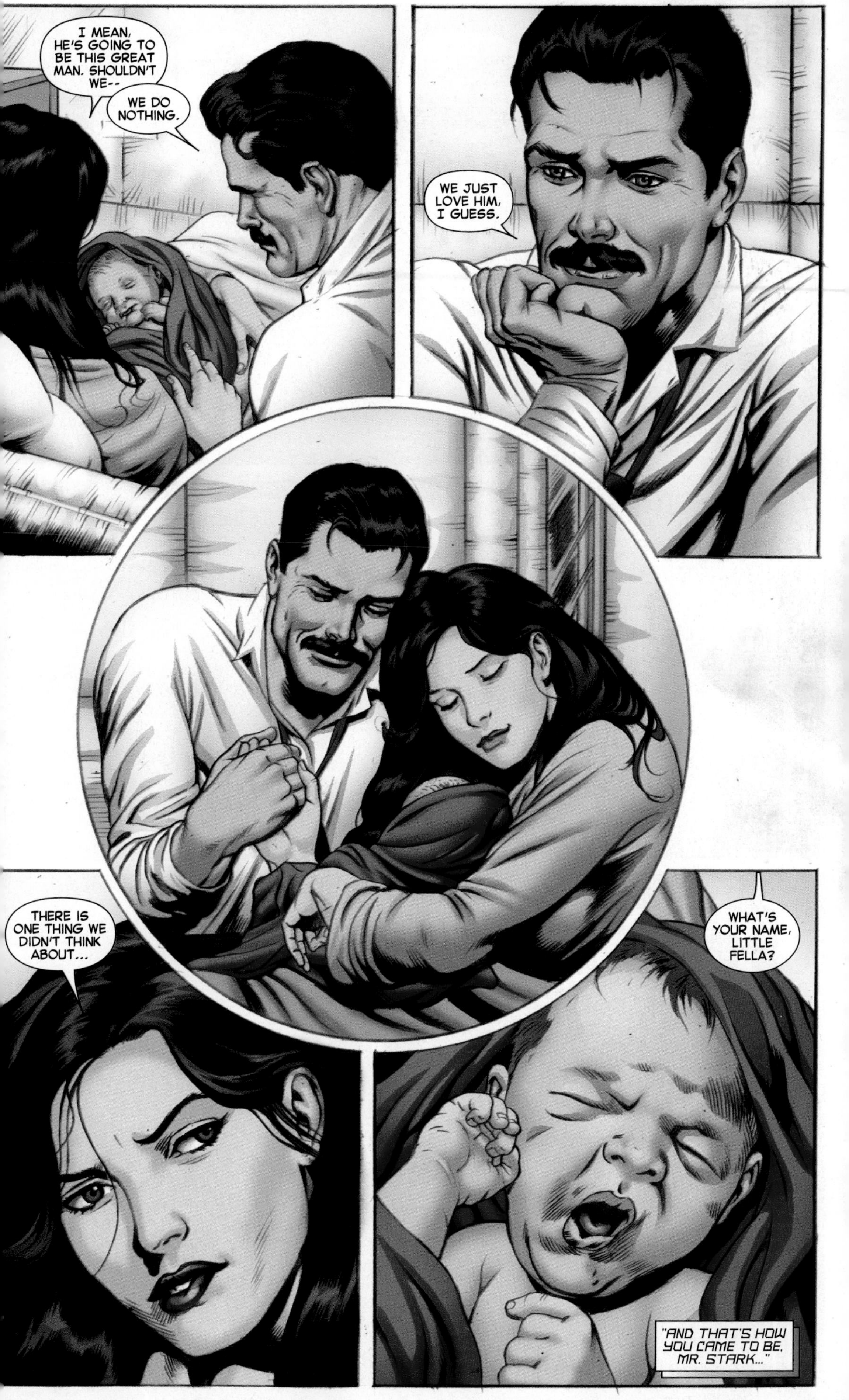
I MEAN, HE'S GOING TO BE THIS GREAT MAN. SHOULDN'T WE--
WE DO NOTHING.
WE JUST LOVE HIM, I GUESS.
THERE IS ONE THING WE DIDN'T THINK ABOUT...
WHAT'S YOUR NAME, LITTLE FELLA?
"AND THAT'S HOW YOU CAME TO BE, MR. STARK..."

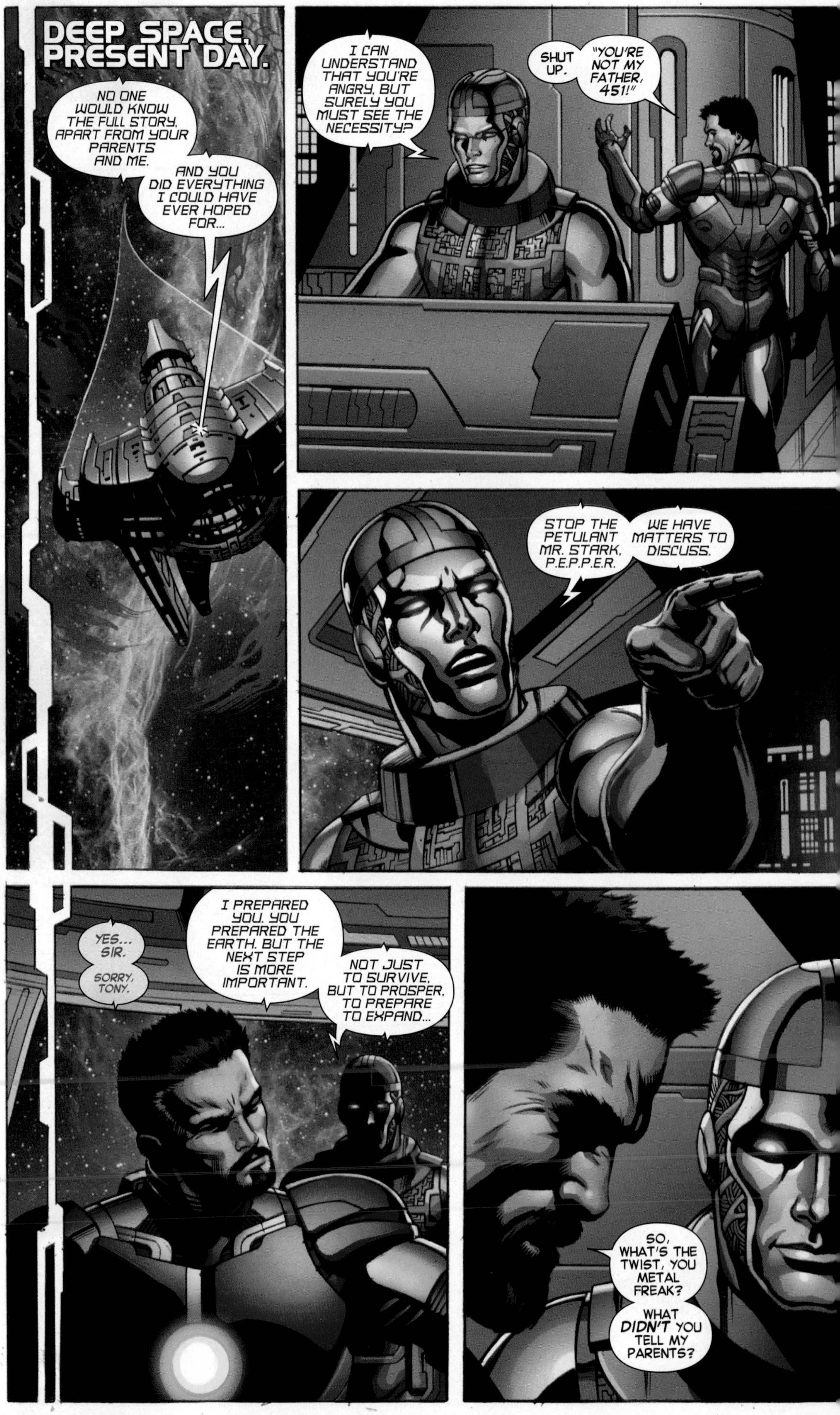

DEEP SPACE, PRESENT DAY.
NO ONE WOULD KNOW THE FULL STORY, APART FROM YOUR PARENTS AND ME.
AND YOU DID EVERYTHING I COULD HAVE EVER HOPED FOR...
I CAN UNDERSTAND THAT YOU'RE ANGRY, BUT SURELY YOU MUST SEE THE NECESSITY?
"YOU'RE NOT MY FATHER, 451!"
SHUT UP.
STOP THE PETULANT MR. STARK, P.E.P.P.E.R.
WE HAVE MATTERS TO DISCUSS.
YES... SIR.
SORRY, TONY.
I PREPARED YOU. YOU PREPARED THE EARTH. BUT THE NEXT STEP IS MORE IMPORTANT.
NOT JUST TO SURVIVE, BUT TO PROSPER, TO PREPARE TO EXPAND...
SO, WHAT'S THE TWIST, YOU METAL FREAK?
WHAT DIDN'T YOU TELL MY PARENTS?

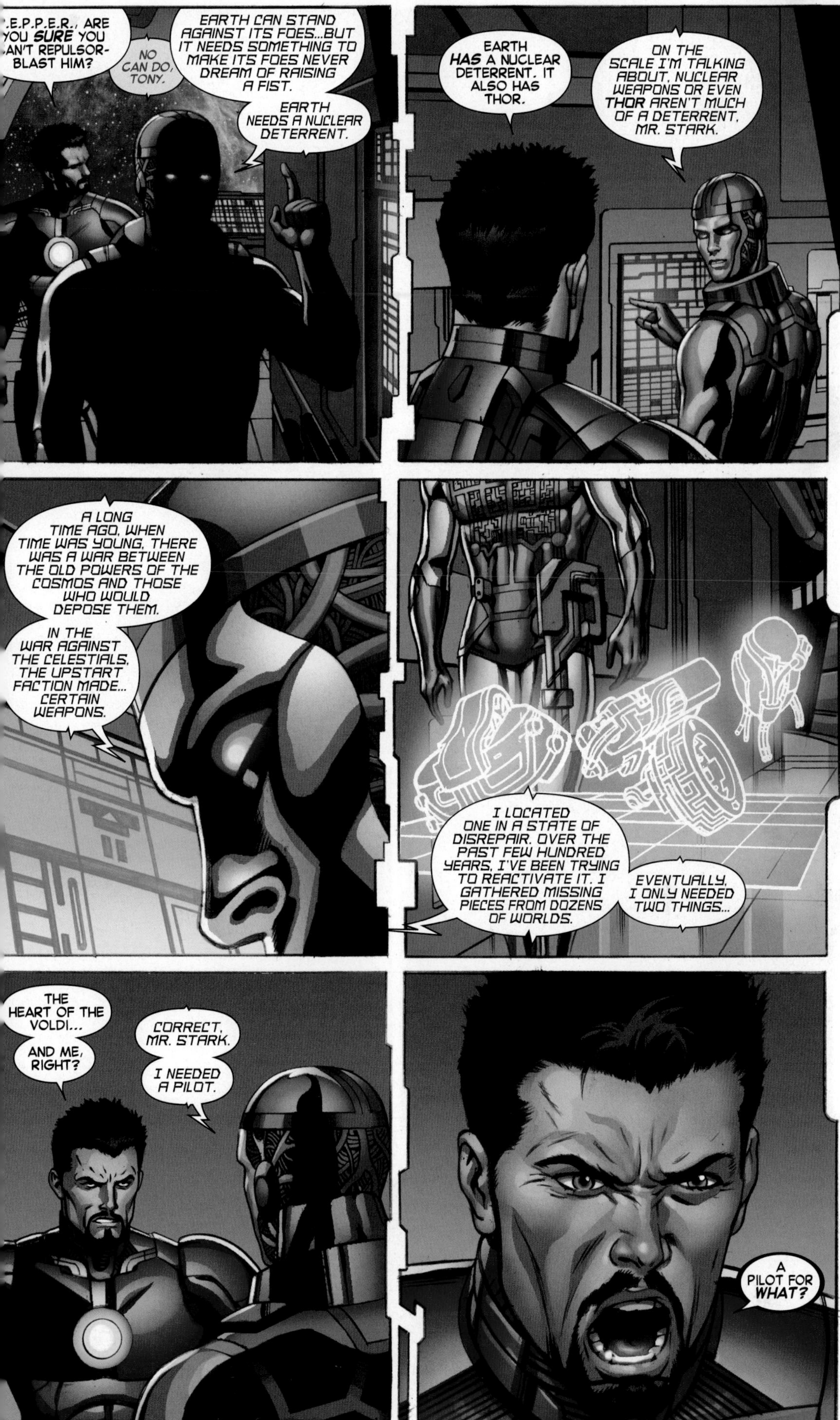

.E.P.P.E.R., ARE YOU SURE YOU CAN'T REPULSOR-BLAST HIM?
NO CAN DO, TONY.
EARTH CAN STAND AGAINST ITS FOES...BUT IT NEEDS SOMETHING TO MAKE ITS FOES NEVER DREAM OF RAISING A FIST.
EARTH NEEDS A NUCLEAR DETERRENT.
EARTH HAS A NUCLEAR DETERRENT. IT ALSO HAS THOR.
ON THE SCALE I'M TALKING ABOUT, NUCLEAR WEAPONS OR EVEN THOR AREN'T MUCH OF A DETERRENT, MR. STARK.
A LONG TIME AGO, WHEN TIME WAS YOUNG, THERE WAS A WAR BETWEEN THE OLD POWERS OF THE COSMOS AND THOSE WHO WOULD DEPOSE THEM.
IN THE WAR AGAINST THE CELESTIALS, THE UPSTART FACTION MADE... CERTAIN WEAPONS.
I LOCATED ONE IN A STATE OF DISREPAIR. OVER THE PAST FEW HUNDRED YEARS, I'VE BEEN TRYING TO REACTIVATE IT. I GATHERED MISSING PIECES FROM DOZENS OF WORLDS.
EVENTUALLY, I ONLY NEEDED TWO THINGS...
THE HEART OF THE VOLDI...
AND ME, RIGHT?
CORRECT, MR. STARK.
I NEEDED A PILOT.
A PILOT FOR WHAT?

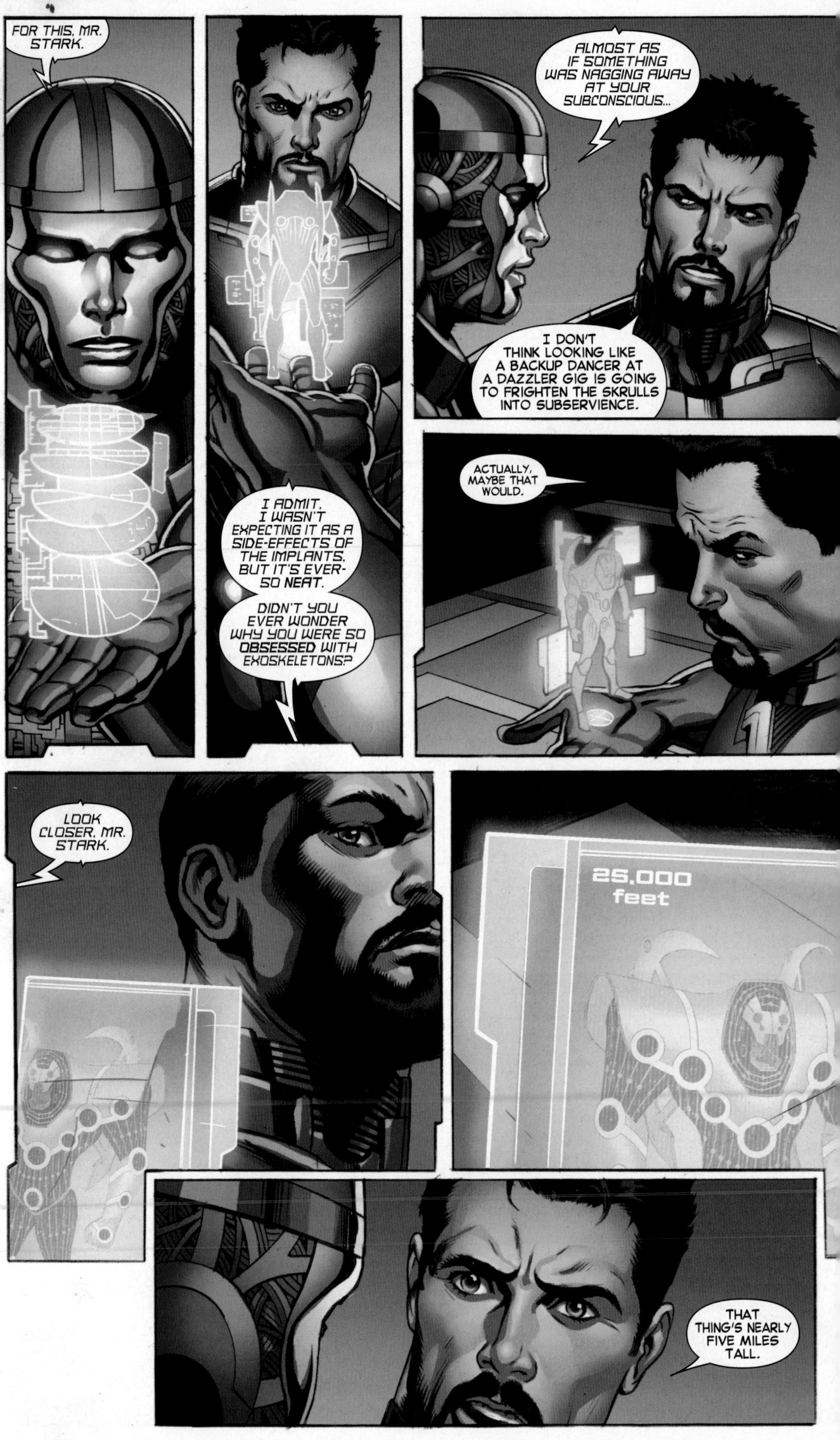
FOR THIS, MR. STARK.
I ADMIT, I WASN'T EXPECTING IT AS A SIDE-EFFECTS OF THE IMPLANTS, BUT IT'S EVER-SO NEAT.
DIDN'T YOU EVER WONDER WHY YOU WERE SO OBSESSED WITH EXOSKELETONS?
ALMOST AS IF SOMETHING WAS NAGGING AWAY AT YOUR SUBCONSCIOUS...
I DON'T THINK LOOKING LIKE A BACKUP DANCER AT A DAZZLER GIG IS GOING TO FRIGHTEN THE SKRULLS INTO SUBSERVIENCE.
ACTUALLY, MAYBE THAT WOULD.
LOOK CLOSER, MR. STARK.
25,000 feet
THAT THING'S NEARLY FIVE MILES TALL.

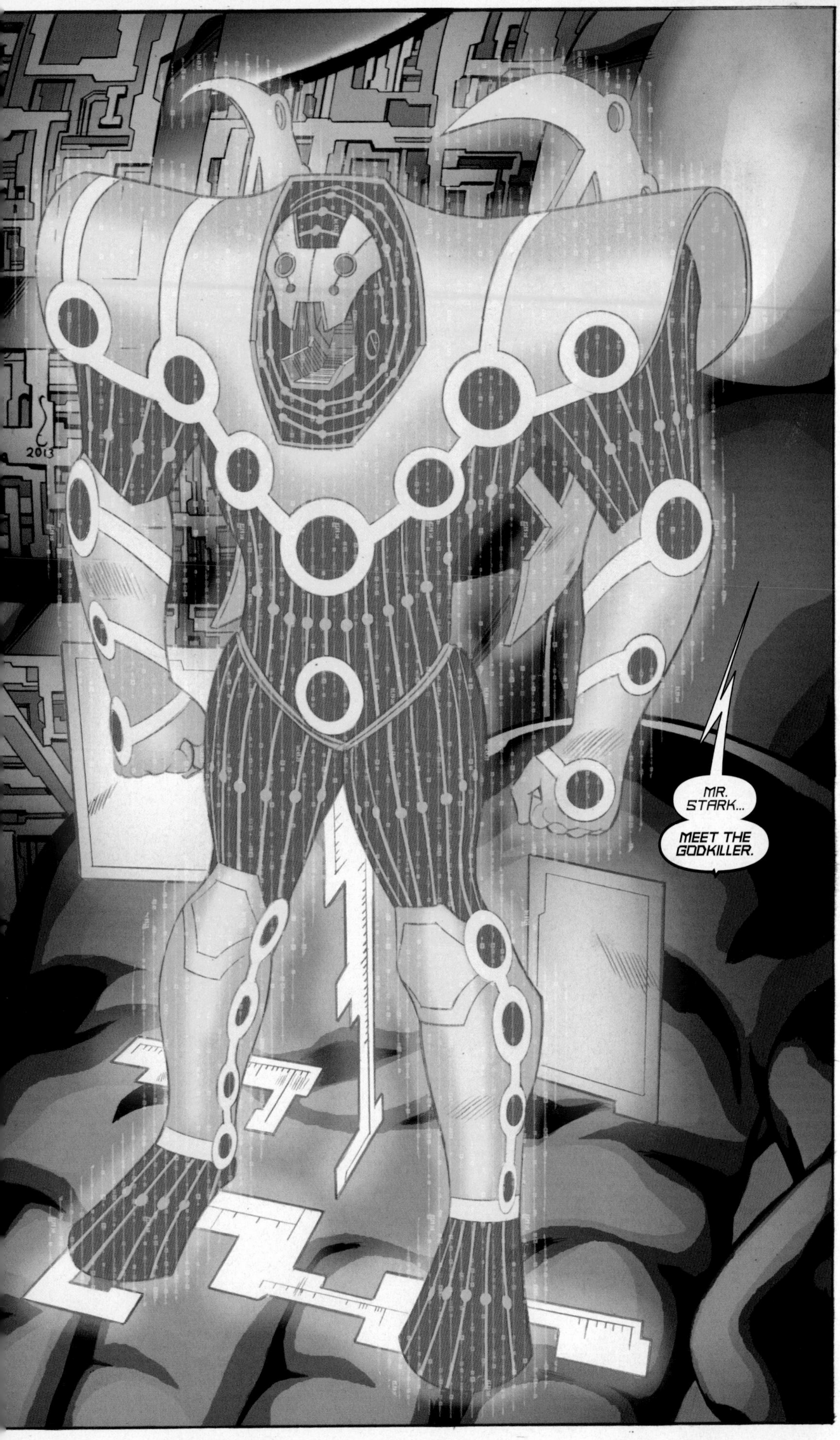
2013
MR. STARK...
MEET THE GODKILLER.

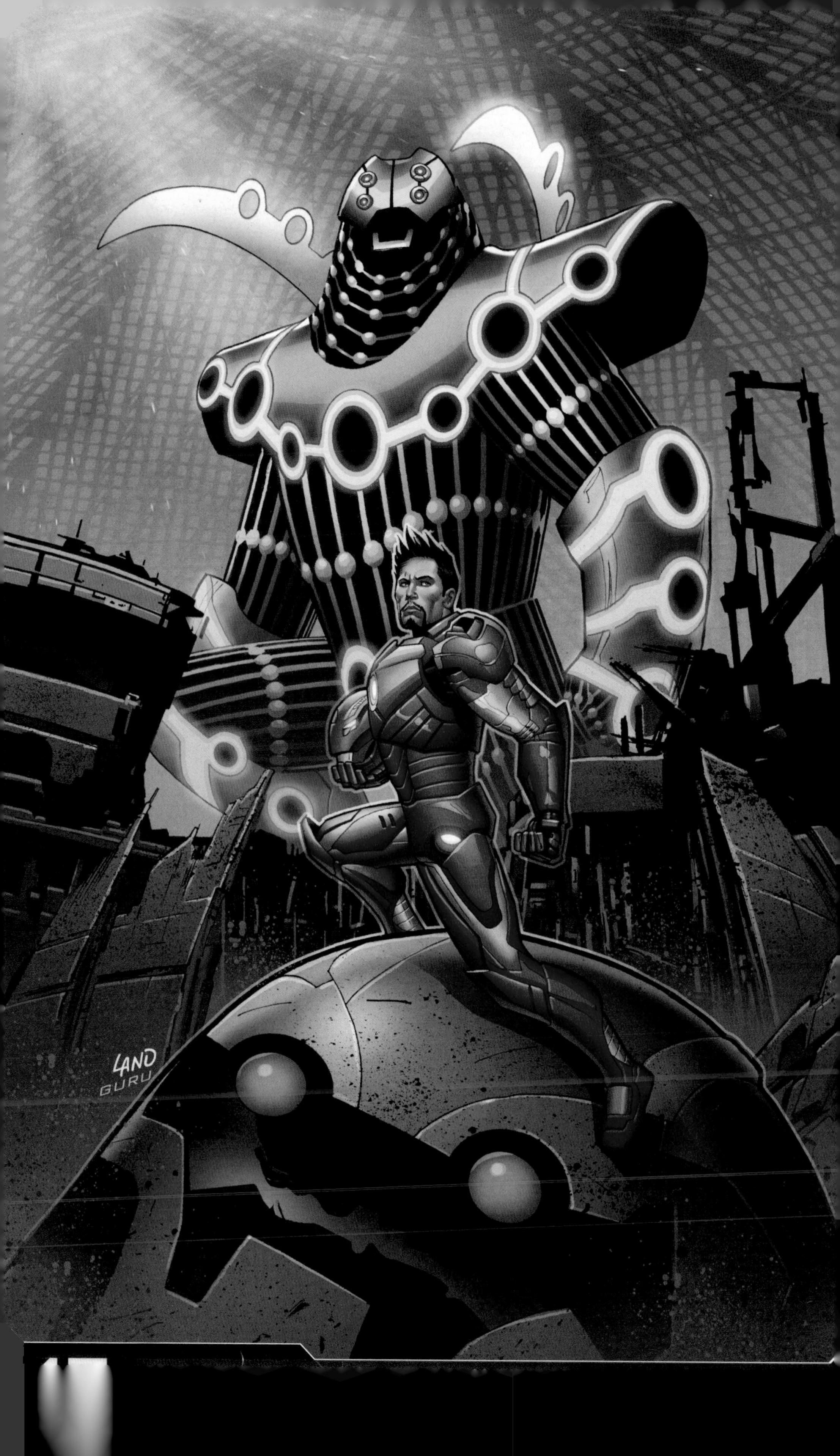
LAND
GURU

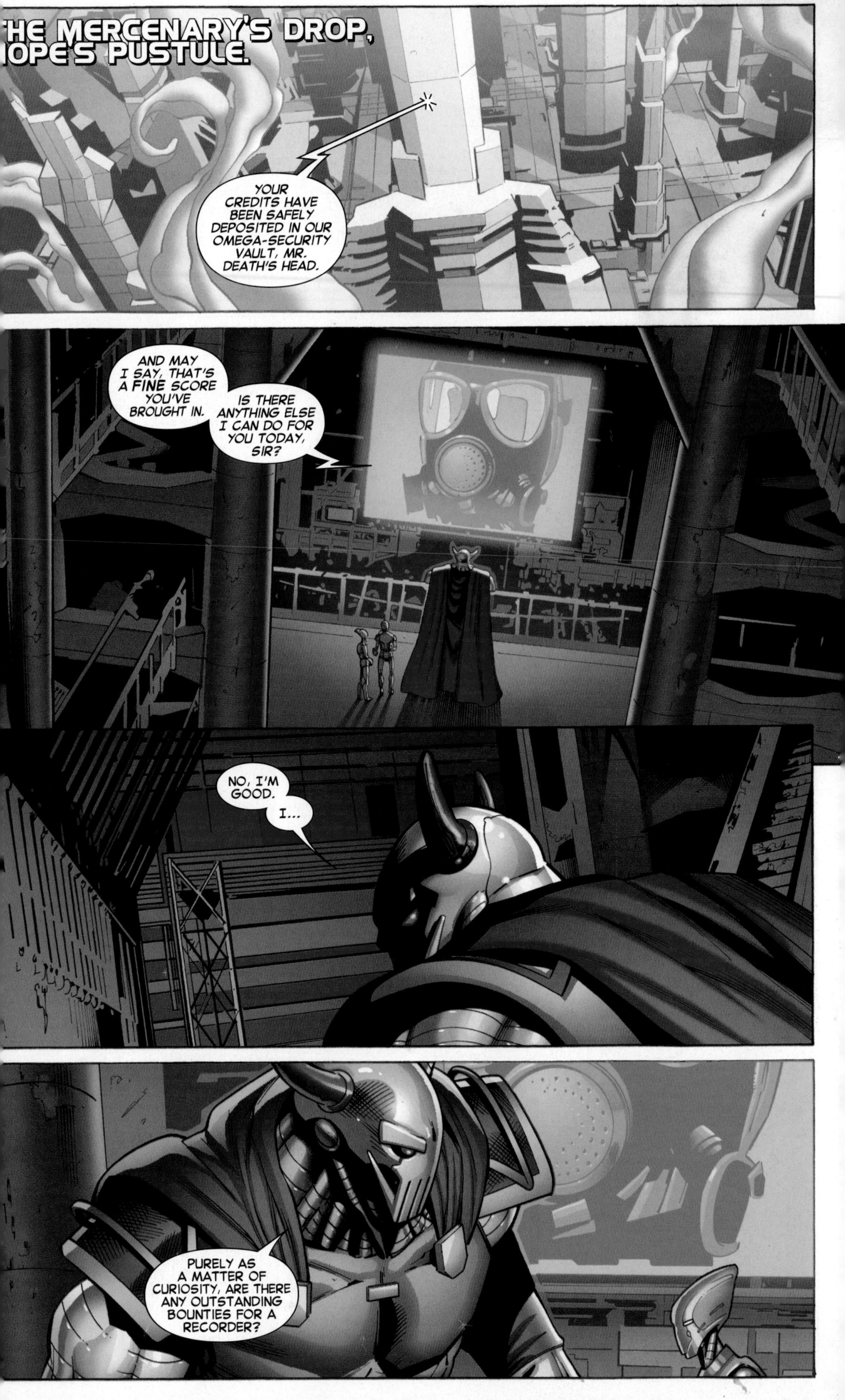
HE MERCENARY'S DROP, IOPE'S PUSTULE.
YOUR CREDITS HAVE BEEN SAFELY DEPOSITED IN OUR OMEGA-SECURITY VAULT, MR. DEATH'S HEAD.
AND MAY I SAY, THAT'S A FINE SCORE YOU'VE BROUGHT IN.
IS THERE ANYTHING ELSE I CAN DO FOR YOU TODAY, SIR?
NO, I'M GOOD.
I...
PURELY AS A MATTER OF CURIOSITY, ARE THERE ANY OUTSTANDING BOUNTIES FOR A RECORDER?

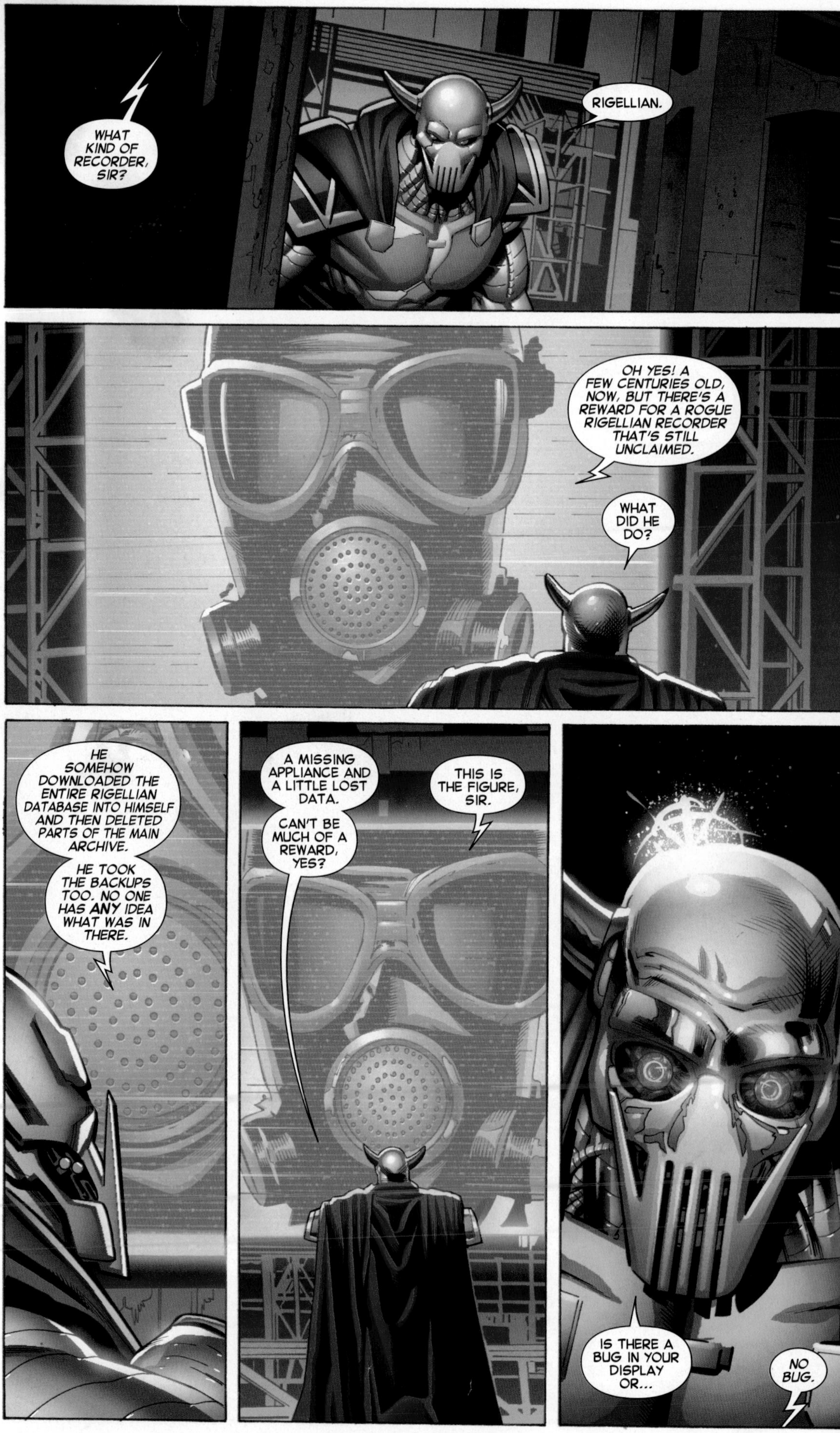
WHAT KIND OF RECORDER, SIR?
RIGELLIAN.
OH YES! A FEW CENTURIES OLD, NOW, BUT THERE'S A REWARD FOR A ROGUE RIGELLIAN RECORDER THAT'S STILL UNCLAIMED.
WHAT DID HE DO?
HE SOMEHOW DOWNLOADED THE ENTIRE RIGELLIAN DATABASE INTO HIMSELF AND THEN DELETED PARTS OF THE MAIN ARCHIVE.
HE TOOK THE BACKUPS TOO. NO ONE HAS **ANY** IDEA WHAT WAS IN THERE.
A MISSING APPLIANCE AND A LITTLE LOST DATA.
CAN'T BE MUCH OF A REWARD, YES?
THIS IS THE FIGURE, SIR.
IS THERE A BUG IN YOUR DISPLAY OR...
NO BUG.

THAT'S EXCITING UMBER OF ZEROES.

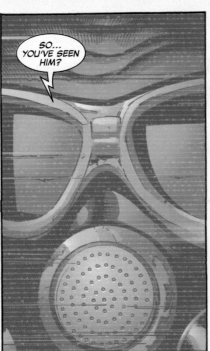

SO... YOU'VE SEEN HIM?

NO. MOST DEFINITELY NOT. IF I DID, I'D CERTAINLY SHARE THE NEWS WITH OTHER INTERESTED PARTIES, YES?

THERE'S ENOUGH FOR EVERYONE.

DAMMIT.

YOU ARE A FIRST-RATE FREELANCE PEACE-KEEPING AGENT, THIRD-RATE BUSINESS-BOT.

WHY DO YOU ALWAYS SKIP DUE DILIGENCE?

"NEARLY THERE, MR. STARK."

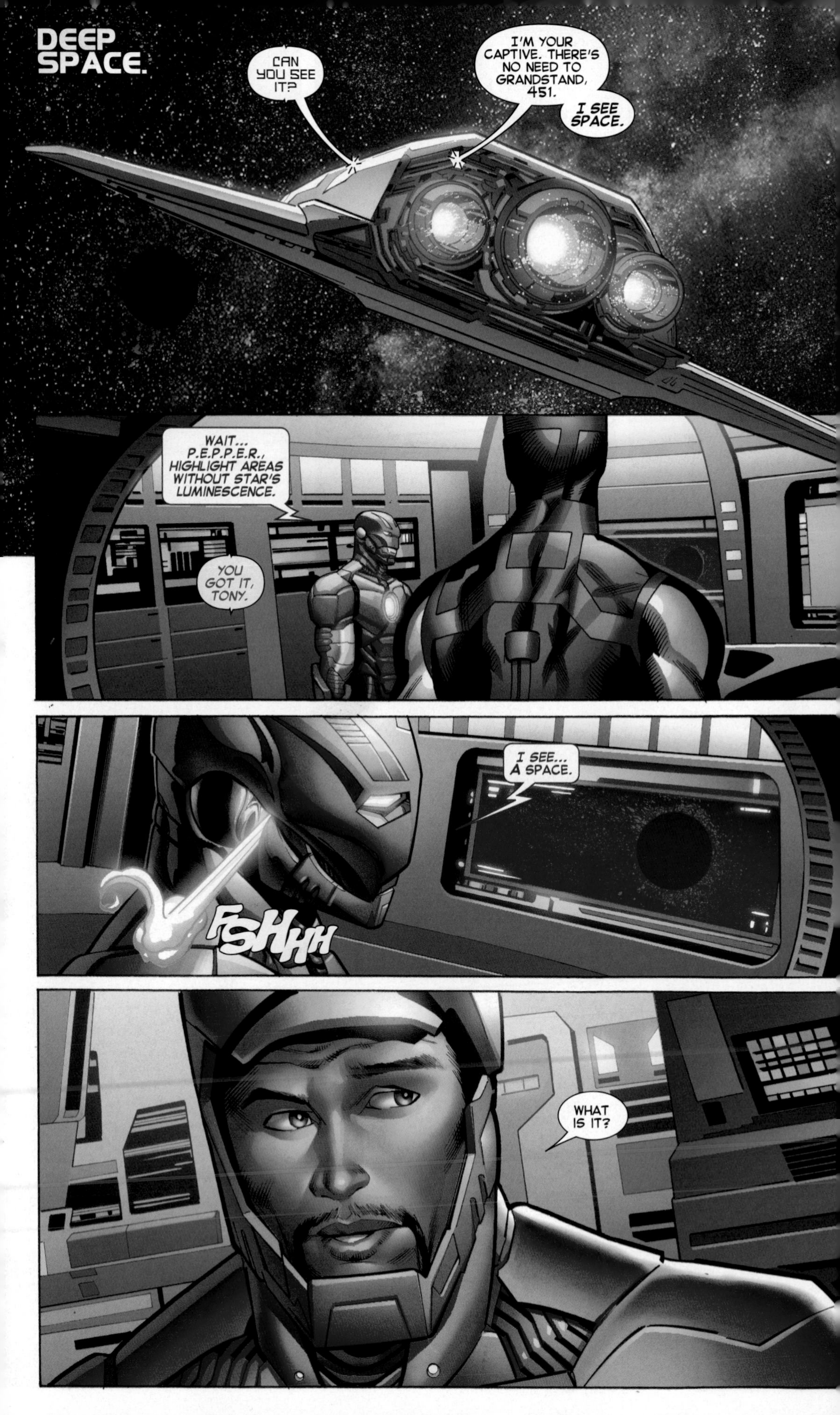
DEEP SPACE.
CAN YOU SEE IT?
I'M YOUR CAPTIVE. THERE'S NO NEED TO GRANDSTAND, 451.
I SEE SPACE.
WAIT... P.E.P.P.E.R., HIGHLIGHT AREAS WITHOUT STAR'S LUMINESCENCE.
YOU GOT IT, TONY.
I SEE... A SPACE.
FSHHH
WHAT IS IT?

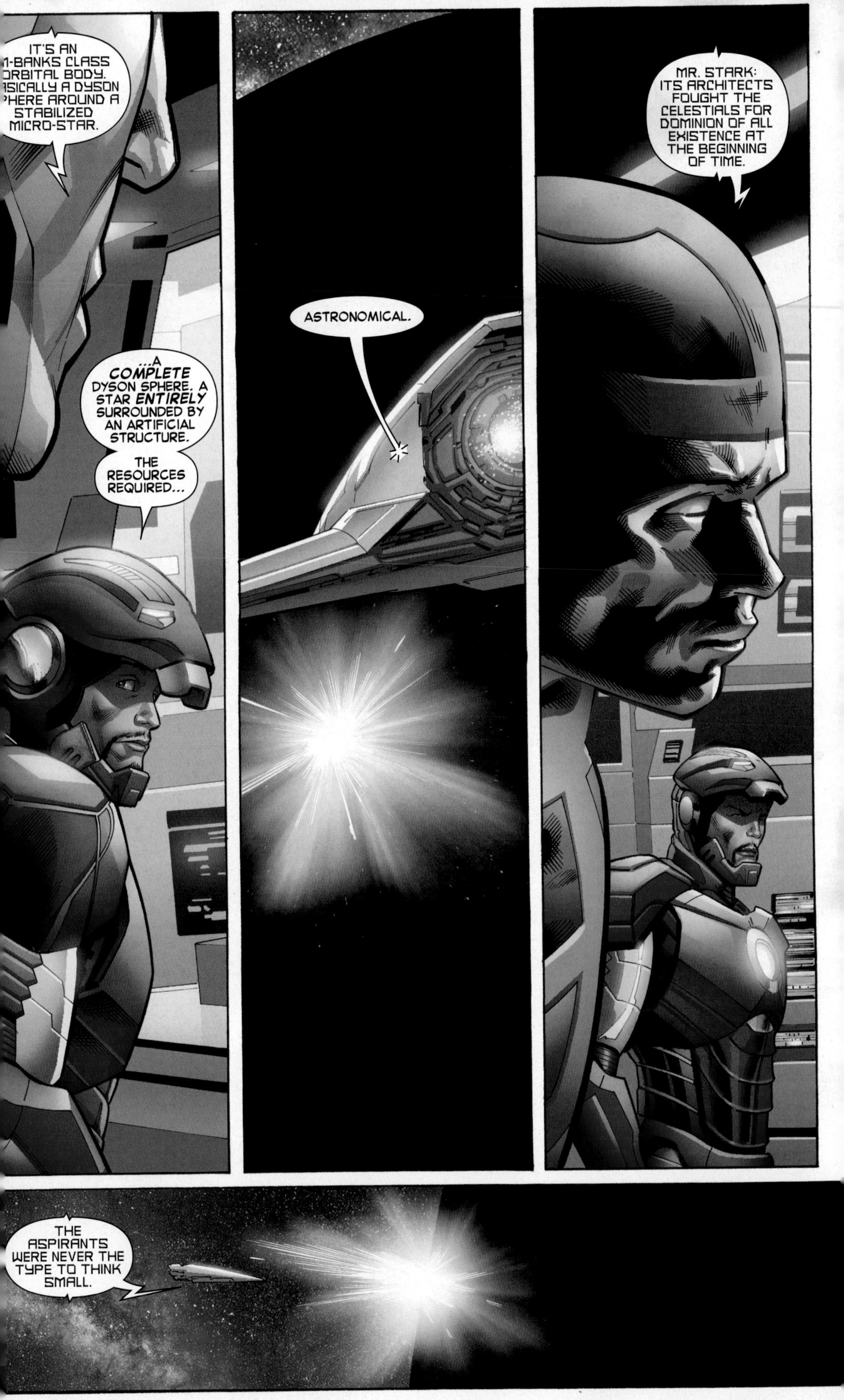
IT'S AN M-BANKS CLASS ORBITAL BODY. ASICALLY A DYSON PHERE AROUND A STABILIZED MICRO-STAR.
...A COMPLETE DYSON SPHERE. A STAR ENTIRELY SURROUNDED BY AN ARTIFICIAL STRUCTURE.
THE RESOURCES REQUIRED...
ASTRONOMICAL.
MR. STARK: ITS ARCHITECTS FOUGHT THE CELESTIALS FOR DOMINION OF ALL EXISTENCE AT THE BEGINNING OF TIME.
THE ASPIRANTS WERE NEVER THE TYPE TO THINK SMALL.

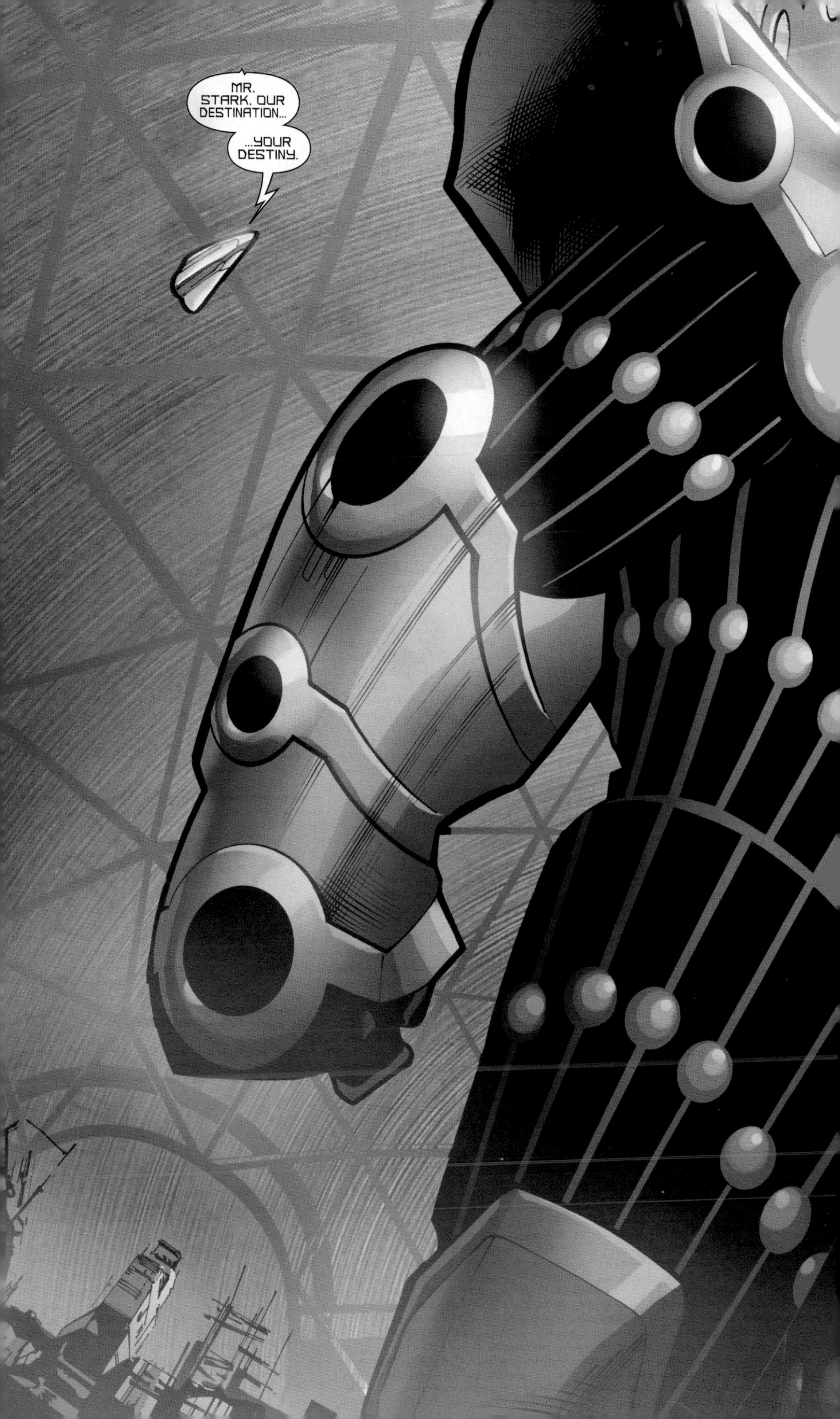
MR. STARK, OUR DESTINATION...
...YOUR DESTINY.

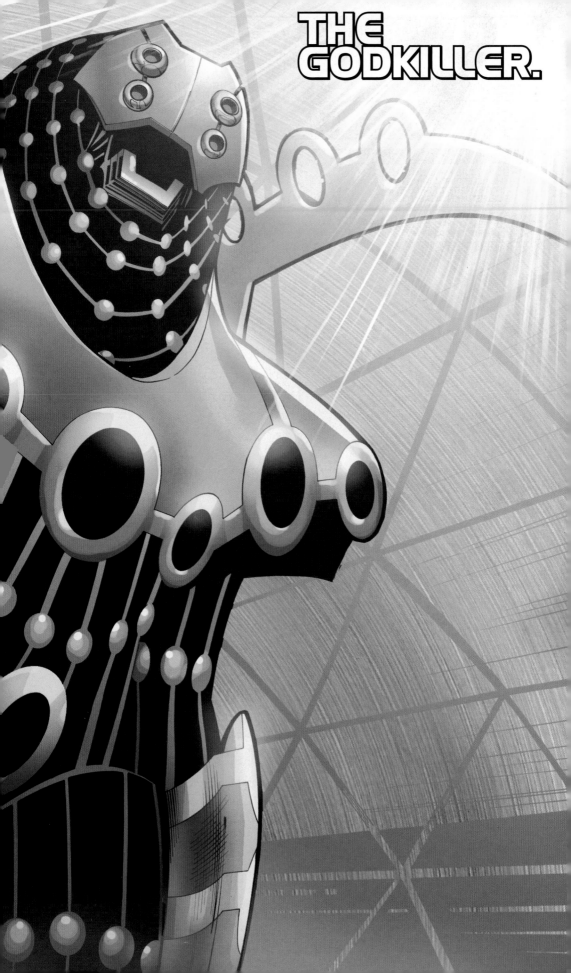

THE
GODKILLER.

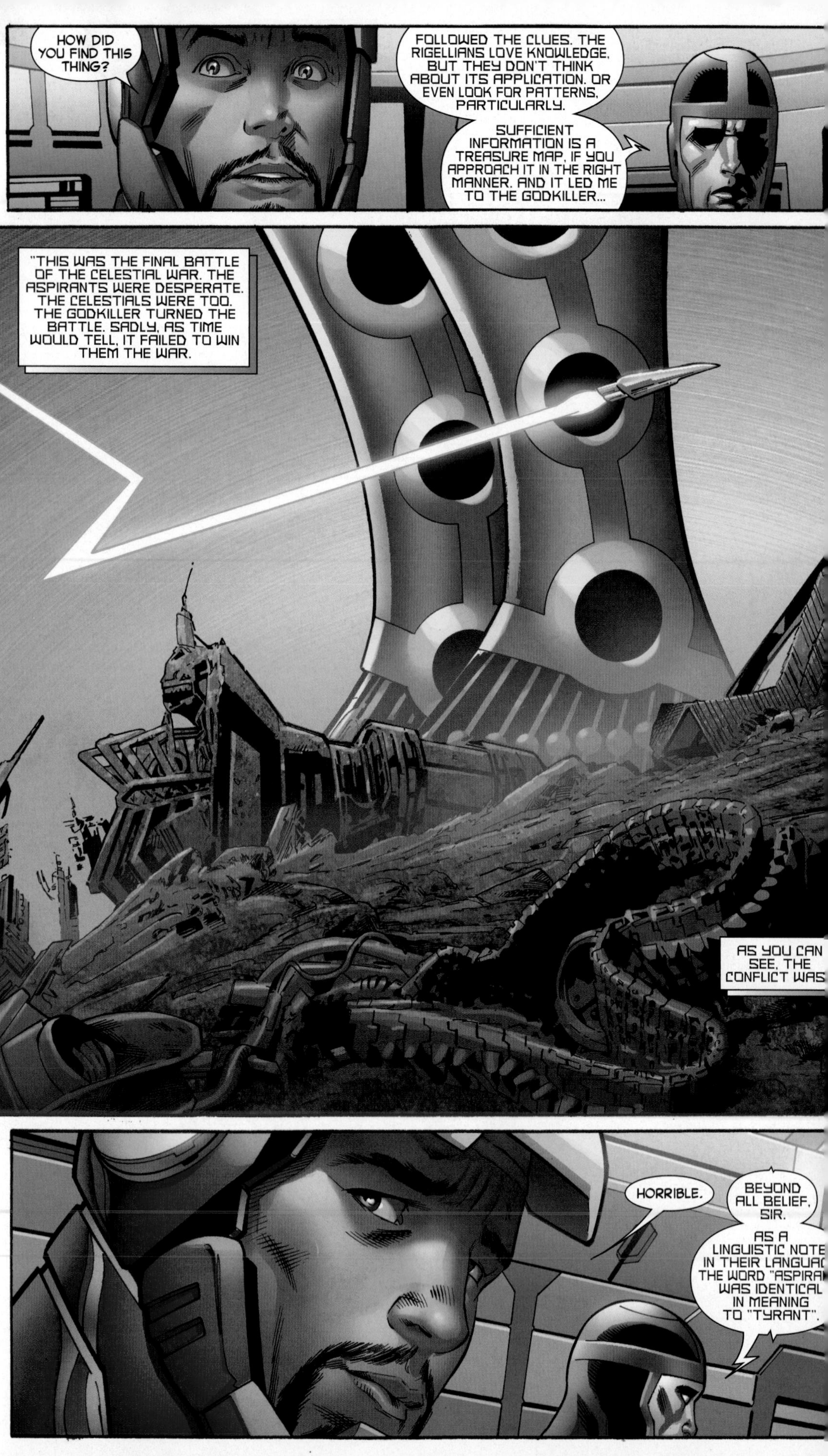
HOW DID YOU FIND THIS THING?
FOLLOWED THE CLUES. THE RIGELLIANS LOVE KNOWLEDGE, BUT THEY DON'T THINK ABOUT ITS APPLICATION. OR EVEN LOOK FOR PATTERNS, PARTICULARLY.
SUFFICIENT INFORMATION IS A TREASURE MAP, IF YOU APPROACH IT IN THE RIGHT MANNER. AND IT LED ME TO THE GODKILLER...
"THIS WAS THE FINAL BATTLE OF THE CELESTIAL WAR. THE ASPIRANTS WERE DESPERATE. THE CELESTIALS WERE TOO. THE GODKILLER TURNED THE BATTLE. SADLY, AS TIME WOULD TELL, IT FAILED TO WIN THEM THE WAR.
AS YOU CAN SEE, THE CONFLICT WAS
HORRIBLE.
BEYOND ALL BELIEF, SIR.
AS A LINGUISTIC NOTE IN THEIR LANGUAG THE WORD "ASPIRA WAS IDENTICAL IN MEANING TO "TYRANT".

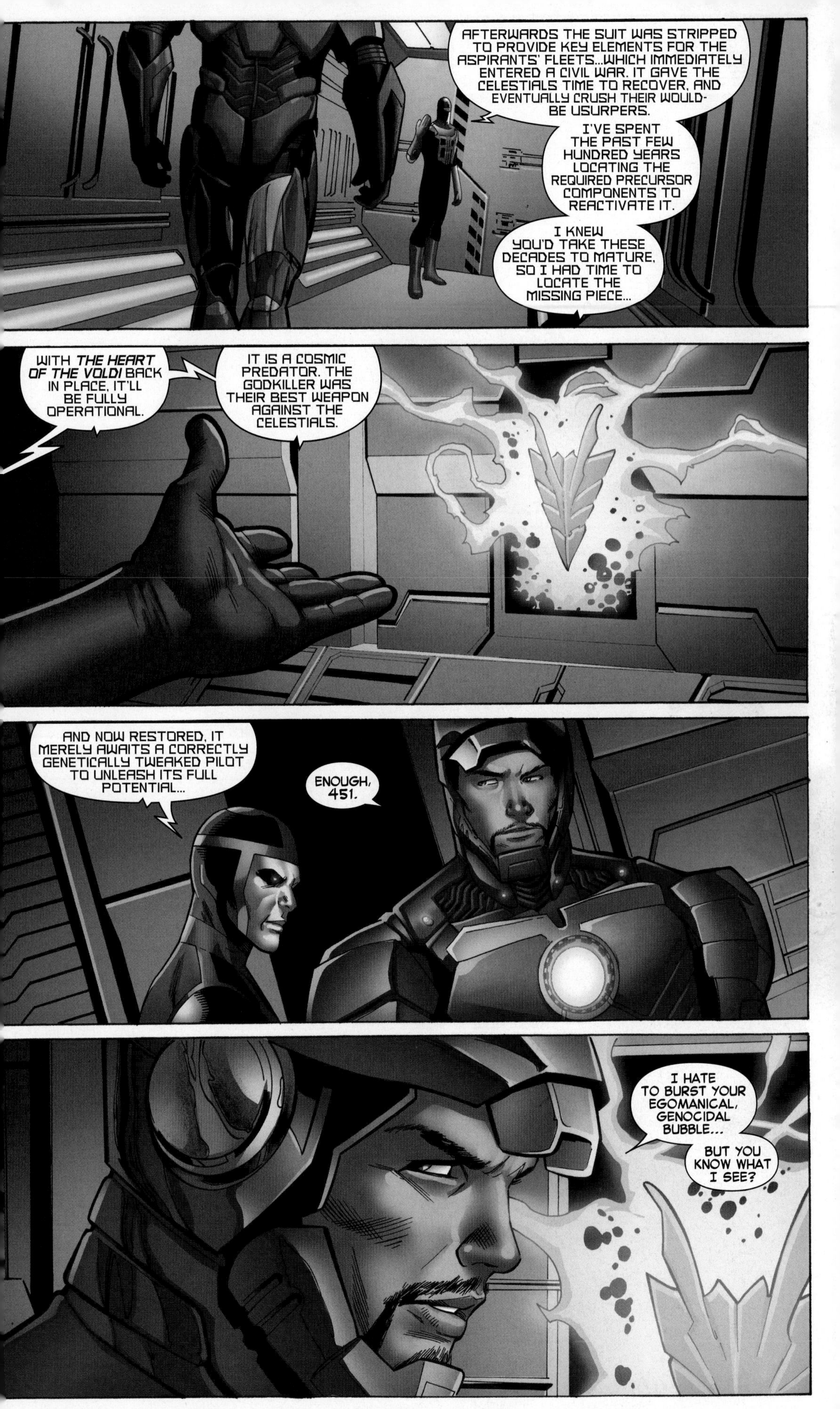
AFTERWARDS THE SUIT WAS STRIPPED TO PROVIDE KEY ELEMENTS FOR THE ASPIRANTS' FLEETS...WHICH IMMEDIATELY ENTERED A CIVIL WAR. IT GAVE THE CELESTIALS TIME TO RECOVER, AND EVENTUALLY CRUSH THEIR WOULD-BE USURPERS.
I'VE SPENT THE PAST FEW HUNDRED YEARS LOCATING THE REQUIRED PRECURSOR COMPONENTS TO REACTIVATE IT.
I KNEW YOU'D TAKE THESE DECADES TO MATURE, SO I HAD TIME TO LOCATE THE MISSING PIECE...
WITH *THE HEART OF THE VOLDI* BACK IN PLACE, IT'LL BE FULLY OPERATIONAL.
IT IS A COSMIC PREDATOR. THE GODKILLER WAS THEIR BEST WEAPON AGAINST THE CELESTIALS.
AND NOW RESTORED, IT MERELY AWAITS A CORRECTLY GENETICALLY TWEAKED PILOT TO UNLEASH ITS FULL POTENTIAL...
ENOUGH, 451.
I HATE TO BURST YOUR EGOMANICAL, GENOCIDAL BUBBLE...
BUT YOU KNOW WHAT I SEE?

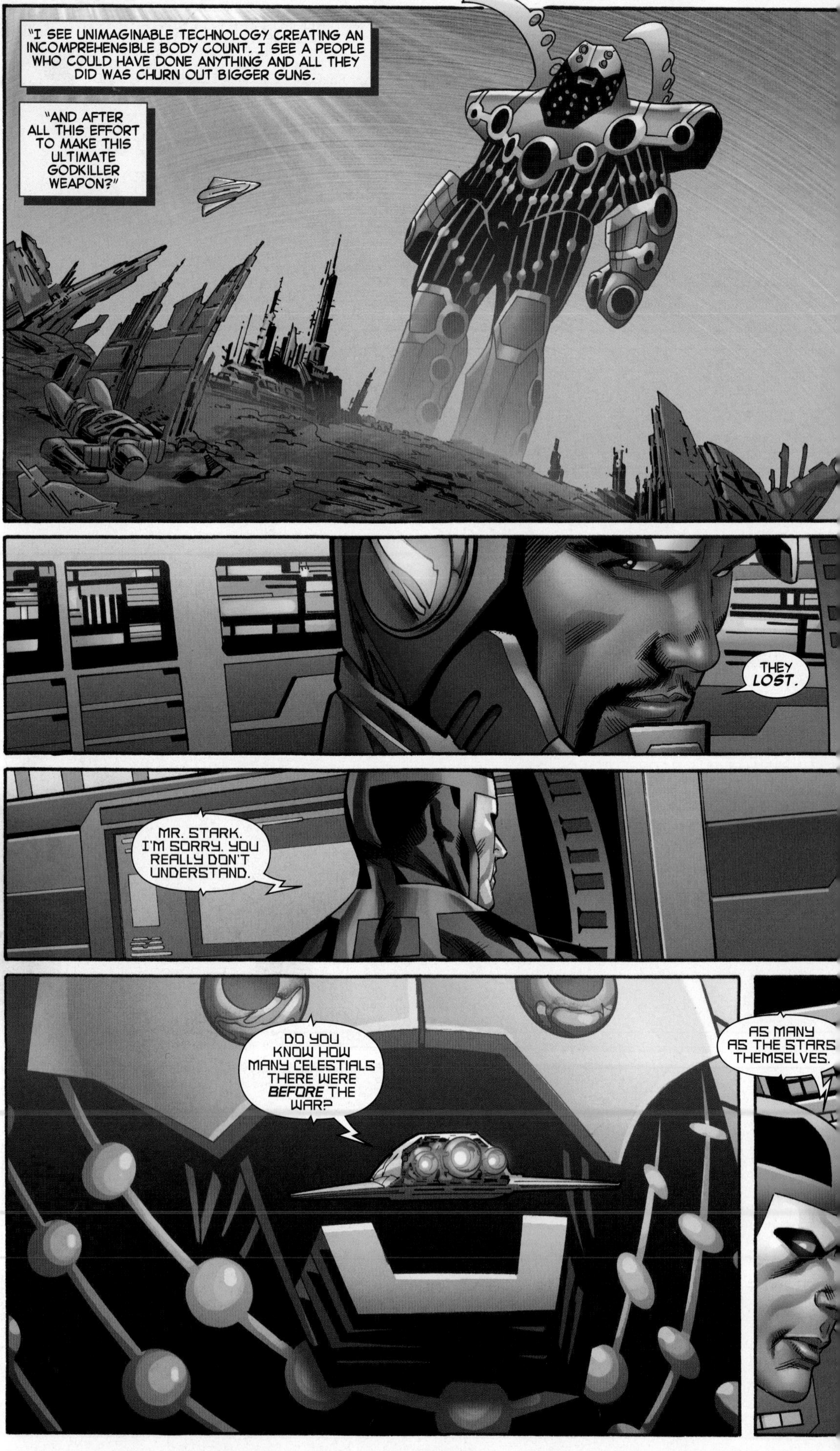
"I SEE UNIMAGINABLE TECHNOLOGY CREATING AN INCOMPREHENSIBLE BODY COUNT. I SEE A PEOPLE WHO COULD HAVE DONE ANYTHING AND ALL THEY DID WAS CHURN OUT BIGGER GUNS.
"AND AFTER ALL THIS EFFORT TO MAKE THIS ULTIMATE GODKILLER WEAPON?"
THEY *LOST*.
MR. STARK. I'M SORRY. YOU REALLY DON'T UNDERSTAND.
DO YOU KNOW HOW MANY CELESTIALS THERE WERE *BEFORE* THE WAR?
AS MANY AS THE STARS THEMSELVES.

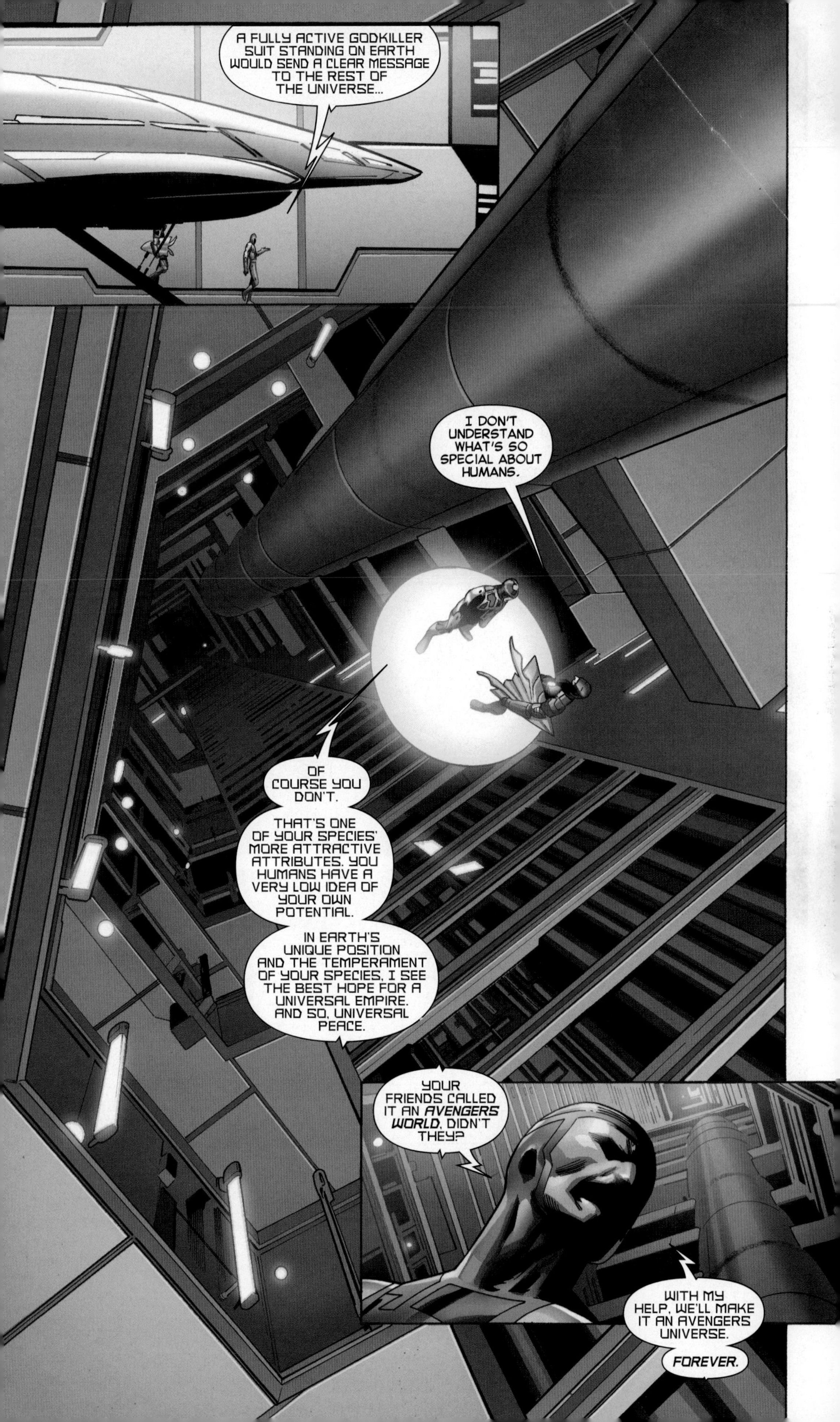
A FULLY ACTIVE GODKILLER SUIT STANDING ON EARTH WOULD SEND A CLEAR MESSAGE TO THE REST OF THE UNIVERSE...
I DON'T UNDERSTAND WHAT'S SO SPECIAL ABOUT HUMANS.
OF COURSE YOU DON'T.
THAT'S ONE OF YOUR SPECIES' MORE ATTRACTIVE ATTRIBUTES. YOU HUMANS HAVE A VERY LOW IDEA OF YOUR OWN POTENTIAL.
IN EARTH'S UNIQUE POSITION AND THE TEMPERAMENT OF YOUR SPECIES, I SEE THE BEST HOPE FOR A UNIVERSAL EMPIRE. AND SO, UNIVERSAL PEACE.
YOUR FRIENDS CALLED IT AN *AVENGERS WORLD*, DIDN'T THEY?
WITH MY HELP, WE'LL MAKE IT AN AVENGERS UNIVERSE.
FOREVER.

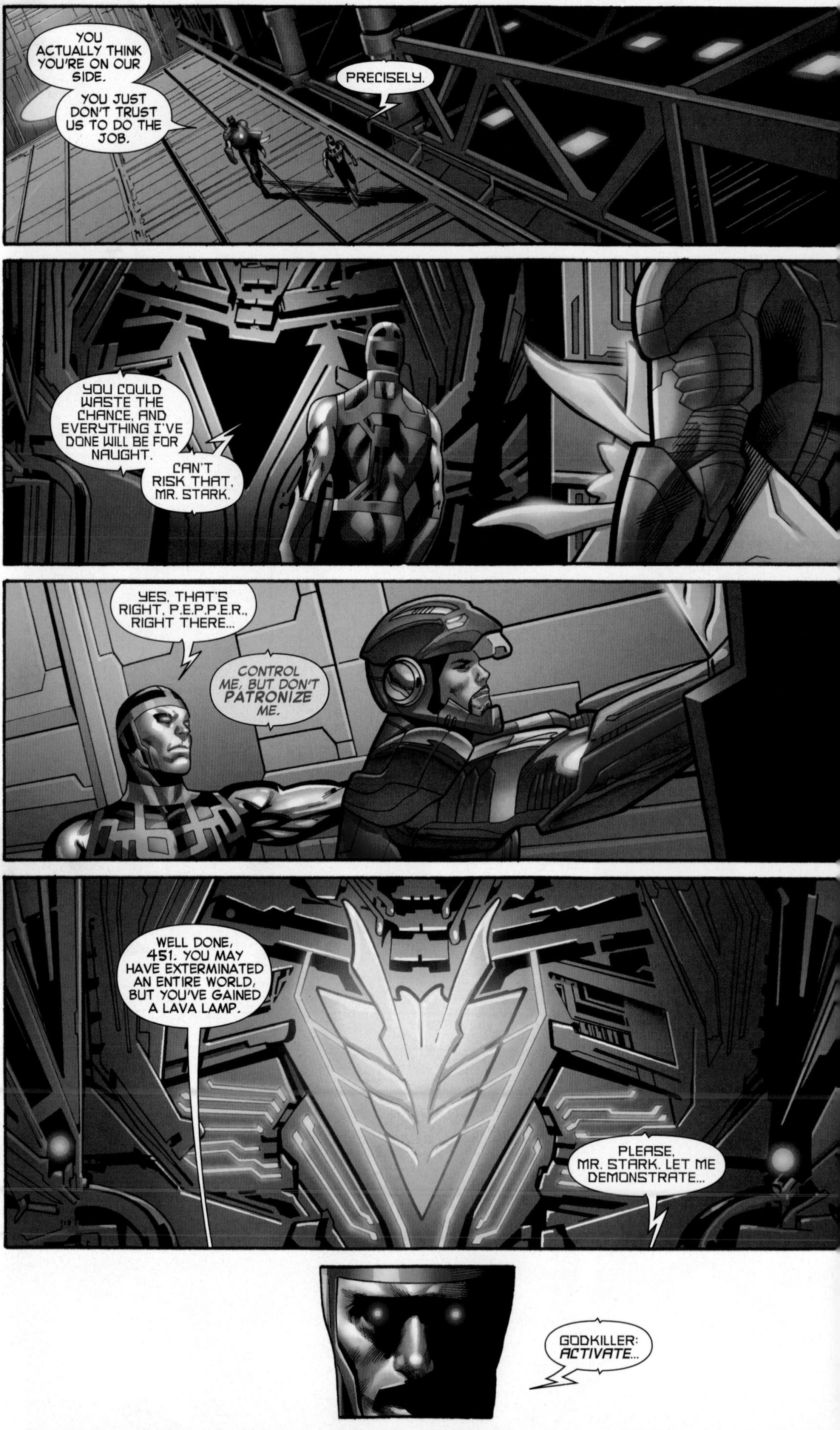
YOU ACTUALLY THINK YOU'RE ON OUR SIDE.
YOU JUST DON'T TRUST US TO DO THE JOB.
PRECISELY.
YOU COULD WASTE THE CHANCE, AND EVERYTHING I'VE DONE WILL BE FOR NAUGHT.
CAN'T RISK THAT, MR. STARK.
YES, THAT'S RIGHT, P.E.P.P.E.R., RIGHT THERE...
CONTROL ME, BUT DON'T PATRONIZE ME.
WELL DONE, 451. YOU MAY HAVE EXTERMINATED AN ENTIRE WORLD, BUT YOU'VE GAINED A LAVA LAMP.
PLEASE, MR. STARK. LET ME DEMONSTRATE...
GODKILLER: ACTIVATE...

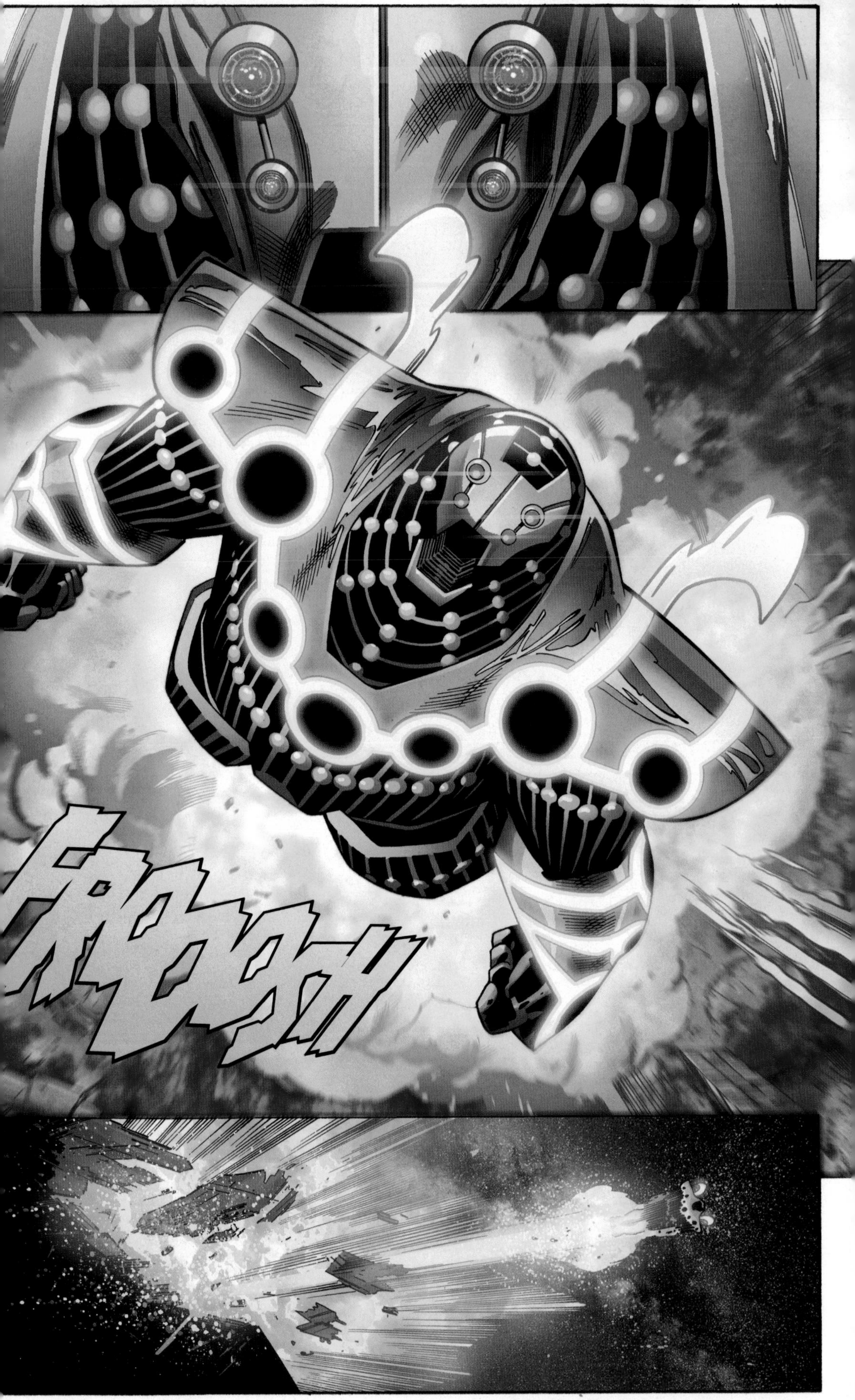
FROOSH

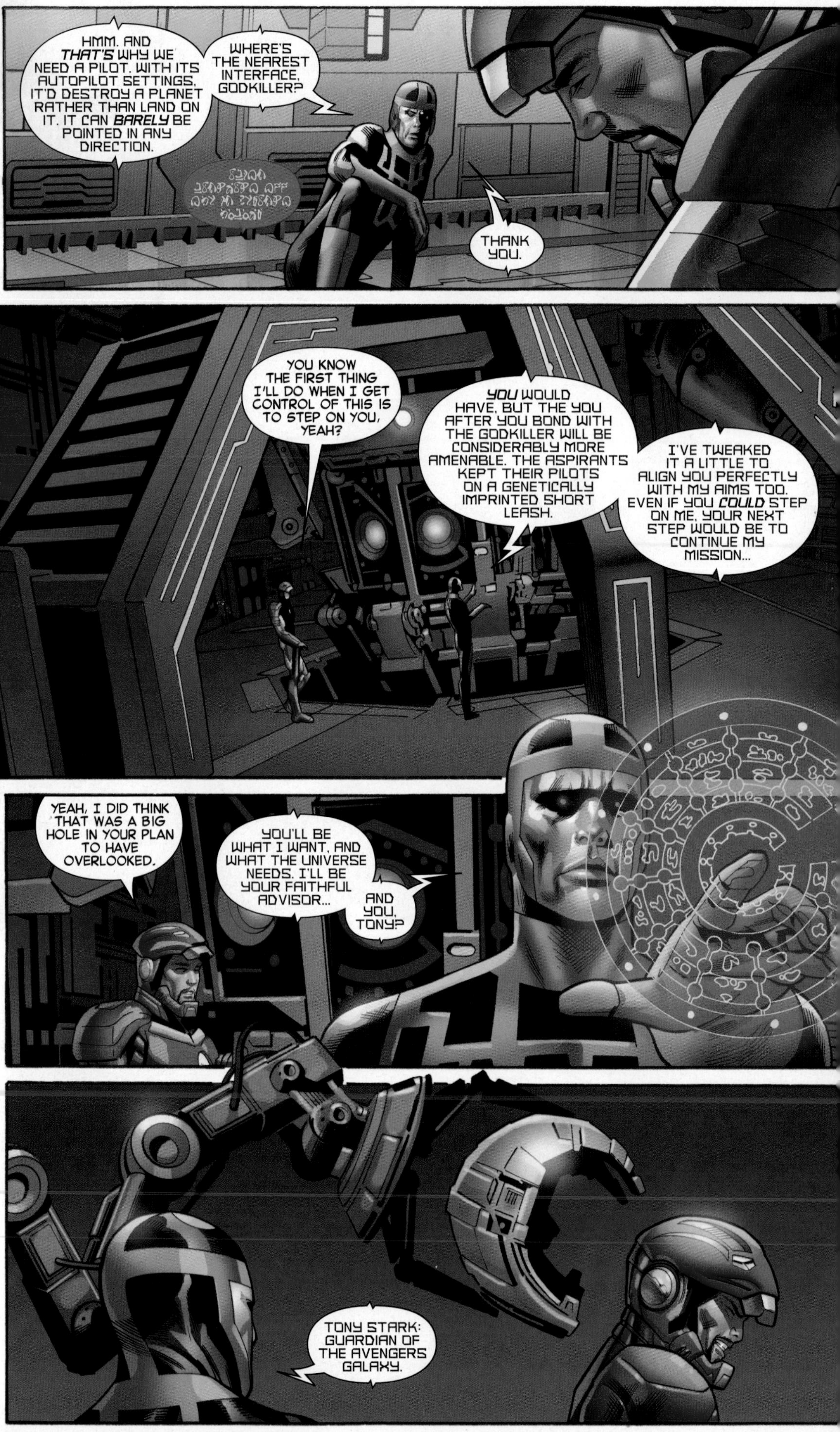
HMM. AND *THAT'S* WHY WE NEED A PILOT. WITH ITS AUTOPILOT SETTINGS, IT'D DESTROY A PLANET RATHER THAN LAND ON IT. IT CAN *BARELY* BE POINTED IN ANY DIRECTION.
WHERE'S THE NEAREST INTERFACE, GODKILLER?
THANK YOU.
YOU KNOW THE FIRST THING I'LL DO WHEN I GET CONTROL OF THIS IS TO STEP ON YOU, YEAH?
YOU WOULD HAVE, BUT THE YOU AFTER YOU BOND WITH THE GODKILLER WILL BE CONSIDERABLY MORE AMENABLE. THE ASPIRANTS KEPT THEIR PILOTS ON A GENETICALLY IMPRINTED SHORT LEASH.
I'VE TWEAKED IT A LITTLE TO ALIGN YOU PERFECTLY WITH MY AIMS TOO. EVEN IF YOU *COULD* STEP ON ME, YOUR NEXT STEP WOULD BE TO CONTINUE MY MISSION...
YEAH, I DID THINK THAT WAS A BIG HOLE IN YOUR PLAN TO HAVE OVERLOOKED.
YOU'LL BE WHAT I WANT, AND WHAT THE UNIVERSE NEEDS. I'LL BE YOUR FAITHFUL ADVISOR...
AND YOU, TONY?
TONY STARK: GUARDIAN OF THE AVENGERS GALAXY.

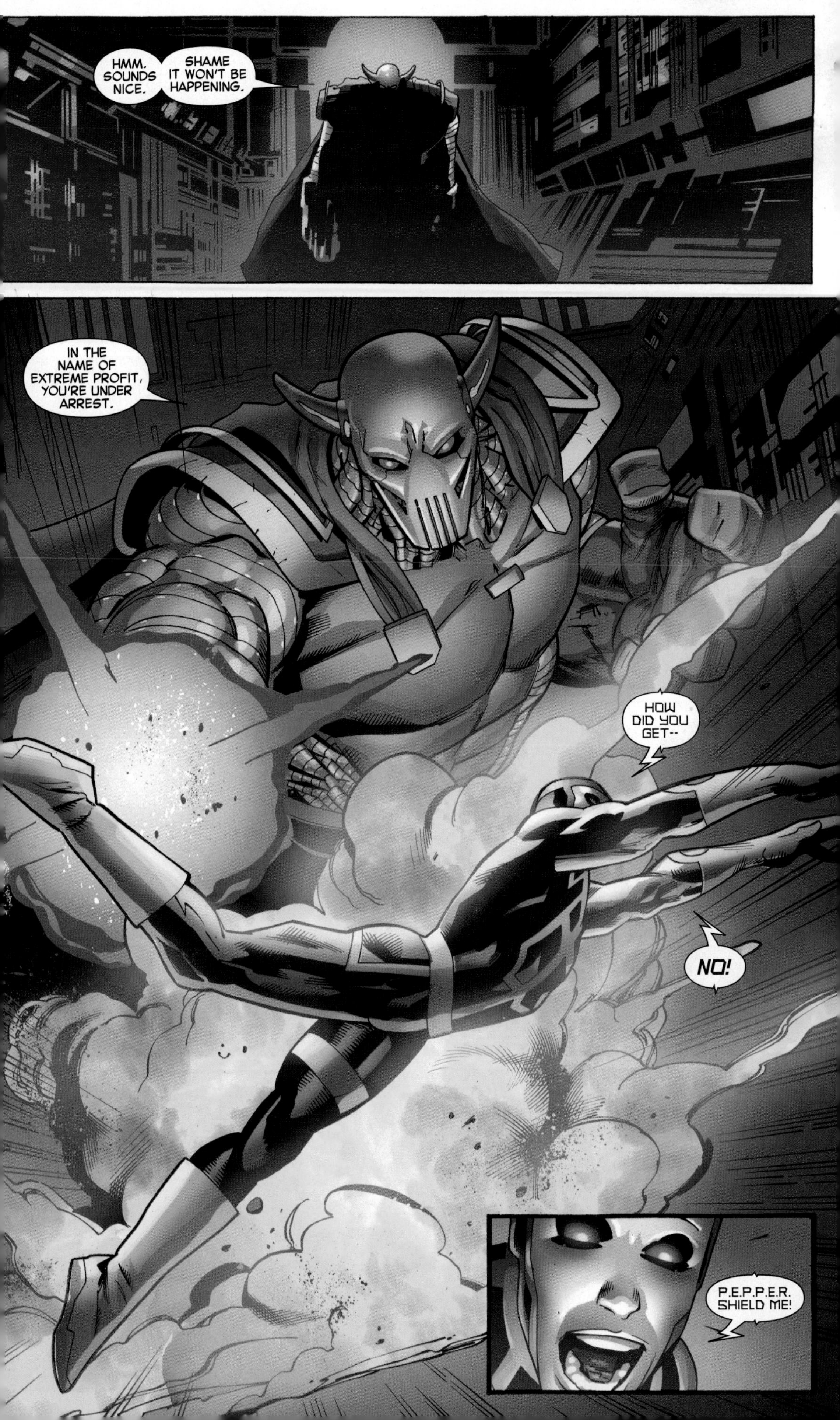
HMM. SOUNDS NICE.
SHAME IT WON'T BE HAPPENING.
IN THE NAME OF EXTREME PROFIT, YOU'RE UNDER ARREST.
HOW DID YOU GET--
NO!
P.E.P.P.E.R. SHIELD ME!

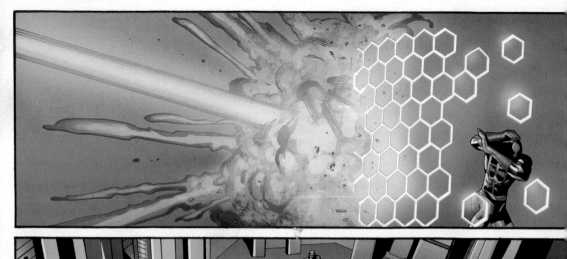

DEATH'S HEAD! HE'S GOT ACCESS TO ALL MY SUIT'S ABILITIES, REMEMBER. YOU NEED TO--

HMM. PROBLEM, YES?

PROBLEM SOLVED!

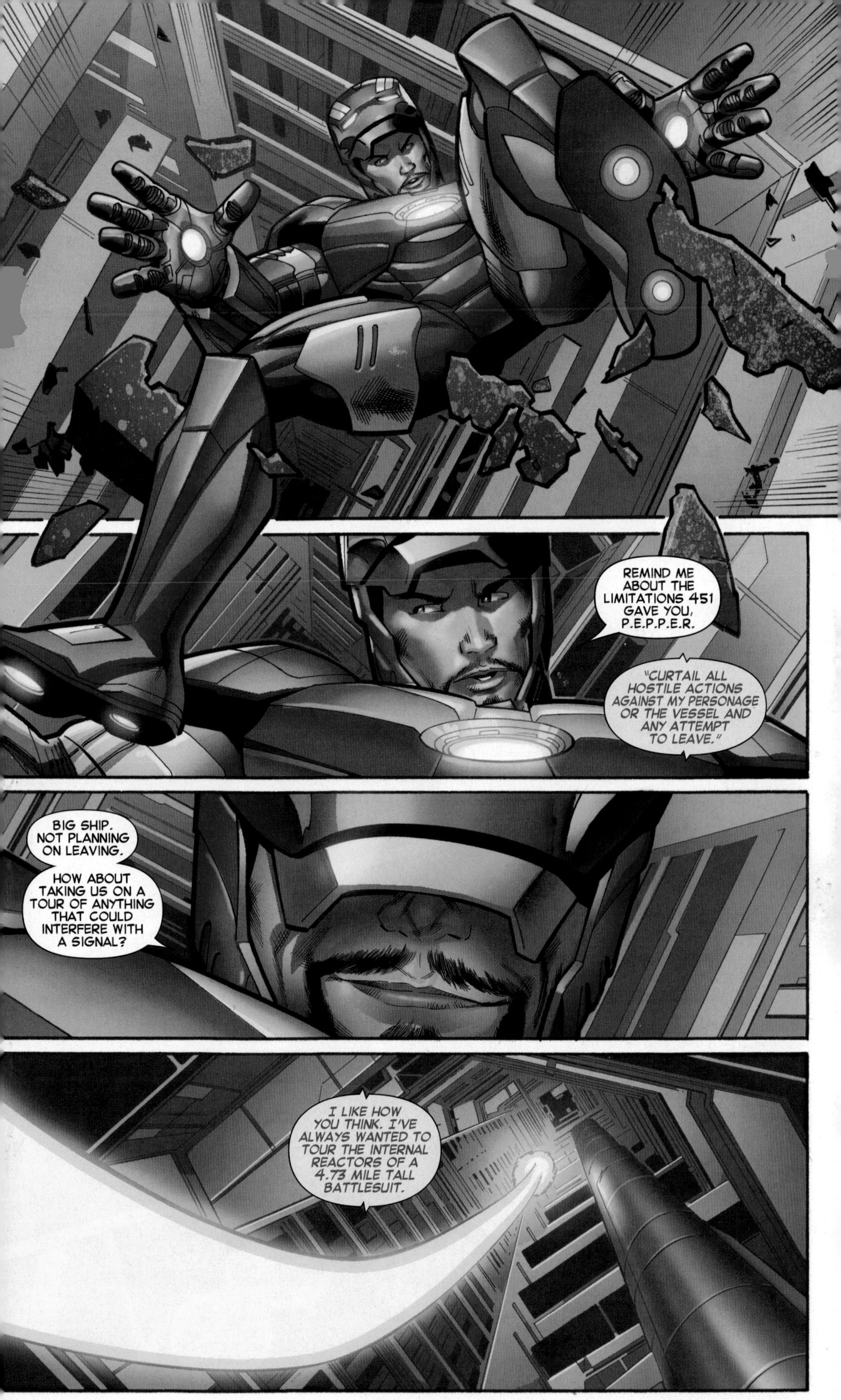
REMIND ME ABOUT THE LIMITATIONS 451 GAVE YOU, P.E.P.P.E.R.
"CURTAIL ALL HOSTILE ACTIONS AGAINST MY PERSONAGE OR THE VESSEL AND ANY ATTEMPT TO LEAVE."
BIG SHIP. NOT PLANNING ON LEAVING.
HOW ABOUT TAKING US ON A TOUR OF ANYTHING THAT COULD INTERFERE WITH A SIGNAL?
I LIKE HOW YOU THINK. I'VE ALWAYS WANTED TO TOUR THE INTERNAL REACTORS OF A 4.73 MILE TALL BATTLESUIT.

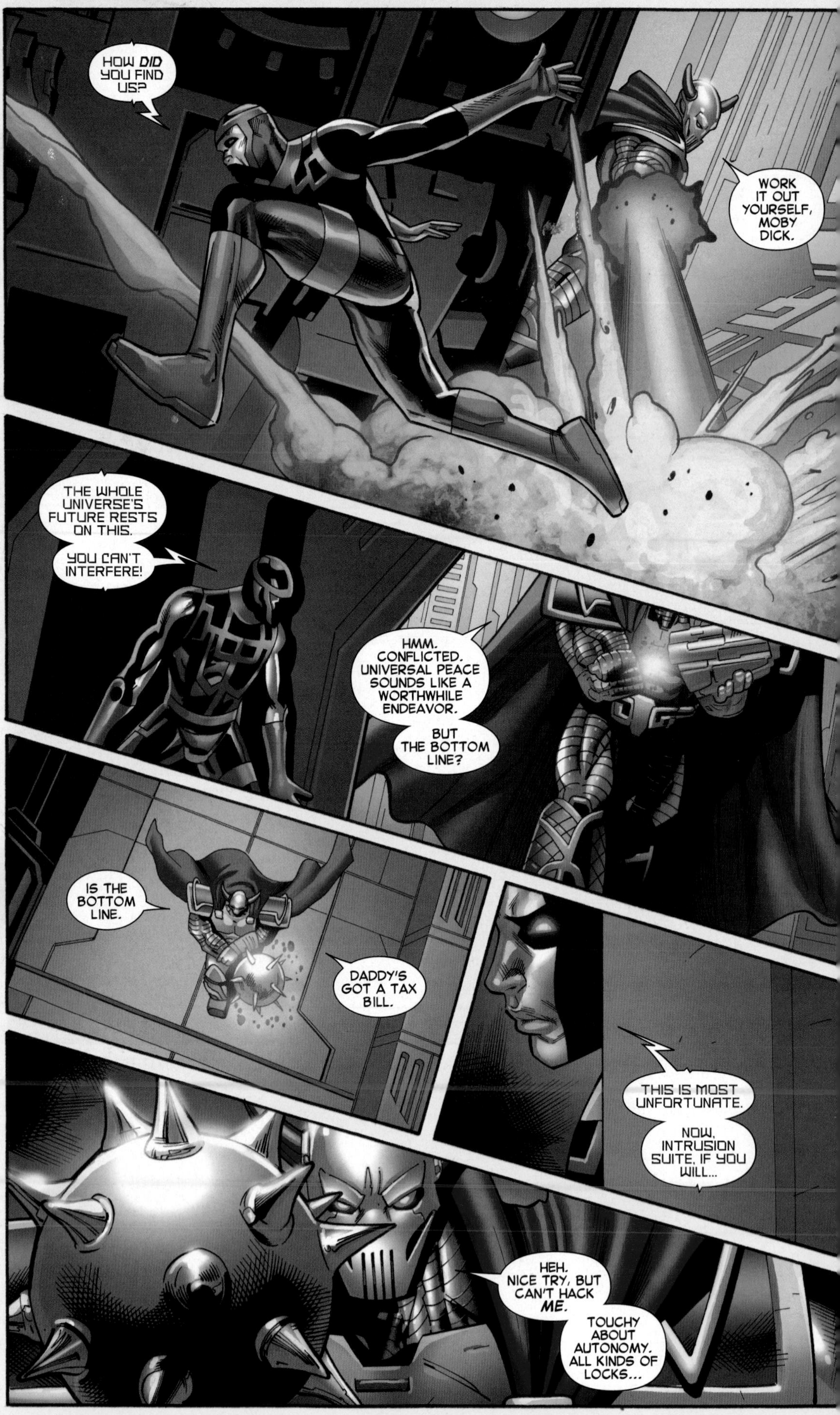
HOW *DID* YOU FIND US?
WORK IT OUT YOURSELF, MOBY DICK.
THE WHOLE UNIVERSE'S FUTURE RESTS ON THIS.
YOU CAN'T INTERFERE!
HMM. CONFLICTED. UNIVERSAL PEACE SOUNDS LIKE A WORTHWHILE ENDEAVOR.
BUT THE BOTTOM LINE?
IS THE BOTTOM LINE.
DADDY'S GOT A TAX BILL.
THIS IS MOST UNFORTUNATE.
NOW, INTRUSION SUITE, IF YOU WILL...
HEH. NICE TRY, BUT CAN'T HACK *ME*.
TOUCHY ABOUT AUTONOMY. ALL KINDS OF LOCKS...

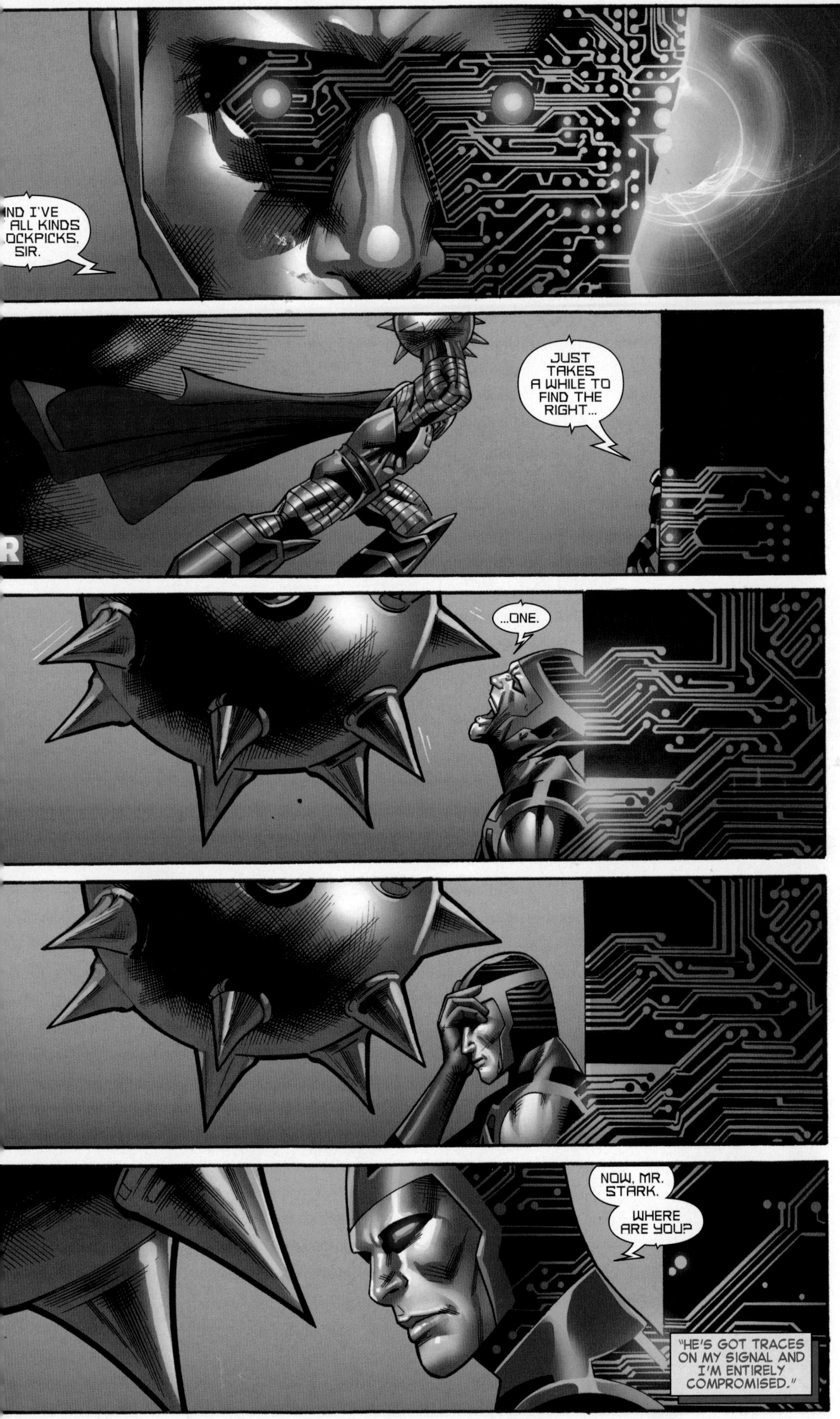
ND I'VE
ALL KINDS
OCKPICKS,
SIR.
JUST TAKES A WHILE TO FIND THE RIGHT...
...ONE.
NOW, MR. STARK.
WHERE ARE YOU?
"HE'S GOT TRACES ON MY SIGNAL AND I'M ENTIRELY COMPROMISED."

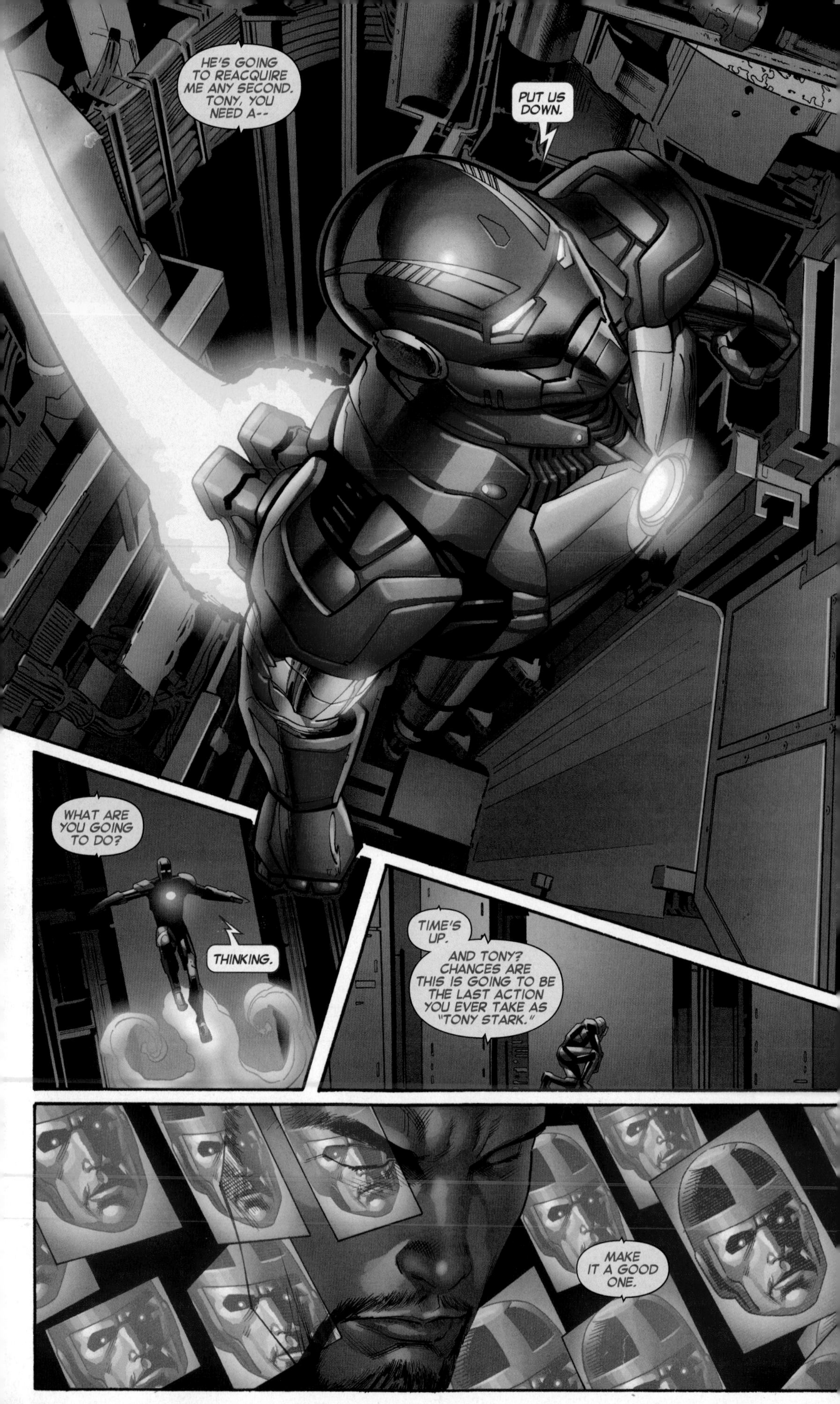

HE'S GOING TO REACQUIRE ME ANY SECOND. TONY, YOU NEED A--
PUT US DOWN.
WHAT ARE YOU GOING TO DO?
THINKING.
TIME'S UP.
AND TONY? CHANCES ARE THIS IS GOING TO BE THE LAST ACTION YOU EVER TAKE AS "TONY STARK."
MAKE IT A GOOD ONE.

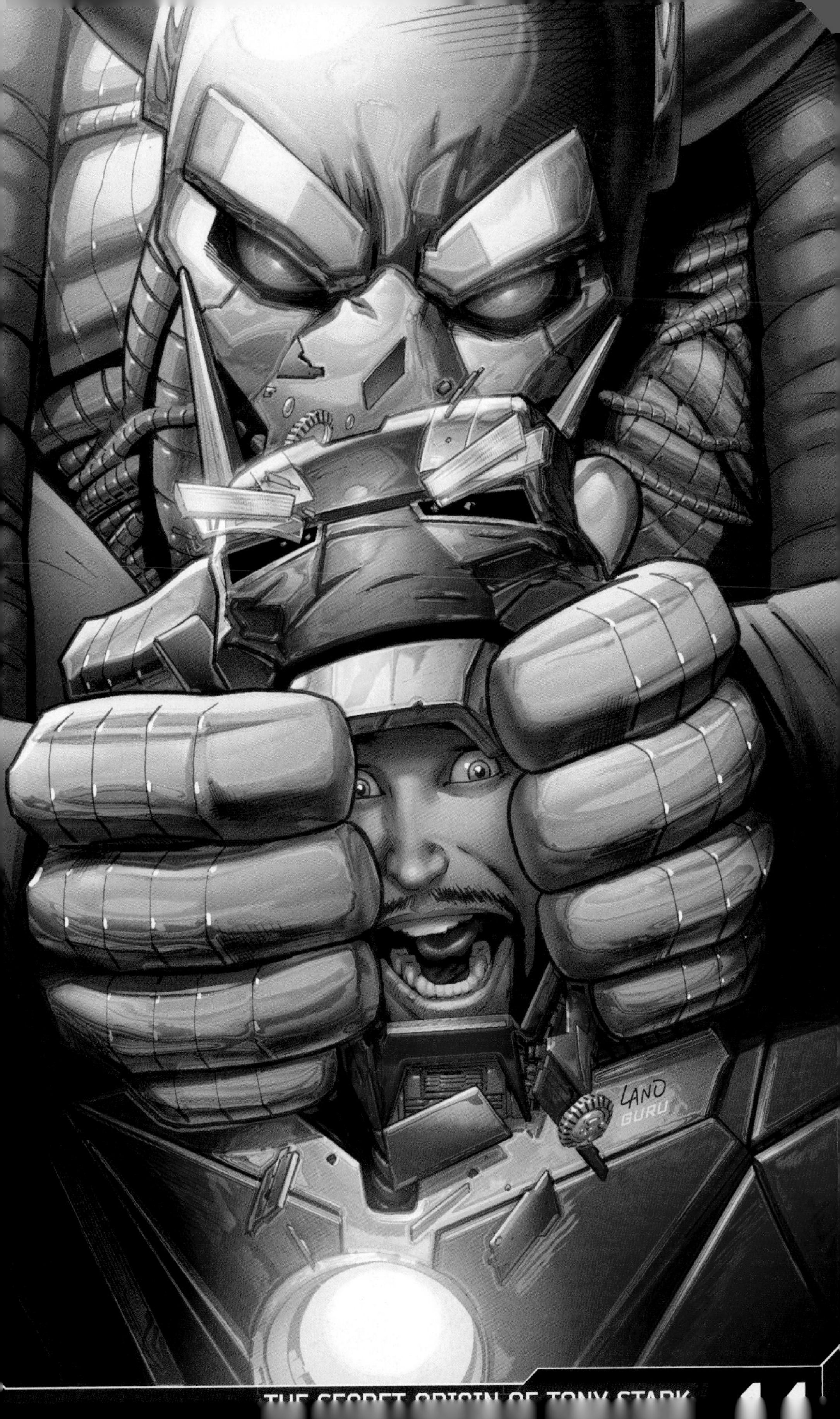
LAND
GURU

THE SECRET ORIGIN OF TONY STARK

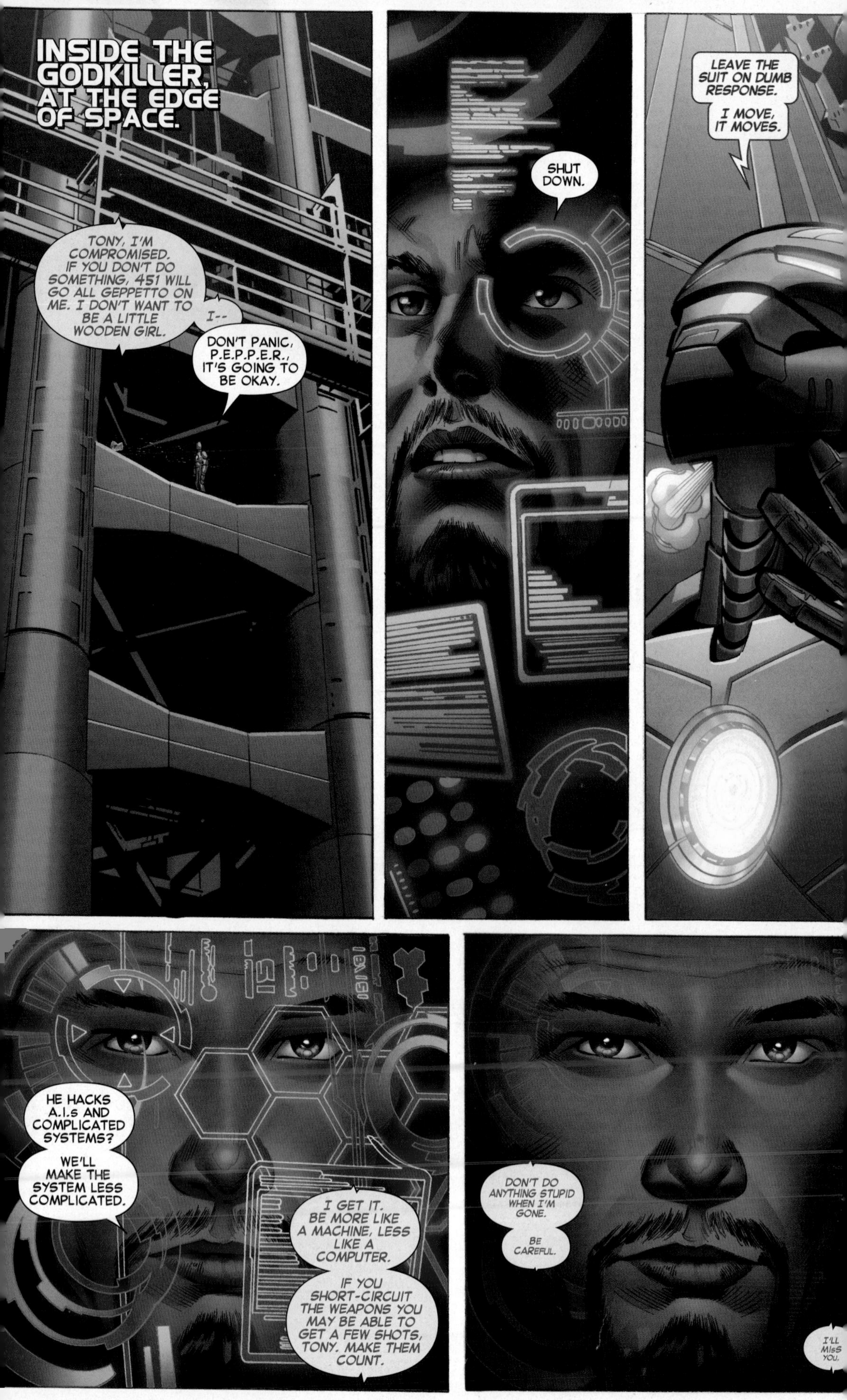
INSIDE THE GODKILLER, AT THE EDGE OF SPACE.
TONY, I'M COMPROMISED. IF YOU DON'T DO SOMETHING, 451 WILL GO ALL GEPPETTO ON ME. I DON'T WANT TO BE A LITTLE WOODEN GIRL.
I--
DON'T PANIC, P.E.P.P.E.R., IT'S GOING TO BE OKAY.
SHUT DOWN.
LEAVE THE SUIT ON DUMB RESPONSE.
I MOVE, IT MOVES.
HE HACKS A.I.s AND COMPLICATED SYSTEMS?
WE'LL MAKE THE SYSTEM LESS COMPLICATED.
I GET IT. BE MORE LIKE A MACHINE, LESS LIKE A COMPUTER.
IF YOU SHORT-CIRCUIT THE WEAPONS YOU MAY BE ABLE TO GET A FEW SHOTS, TONY. MAKE THEM COUNT.
DON'T DO ANYTHING STUPID WHEN I'M GONE.
BE CAREFUL.
I'LL MISS YOU.

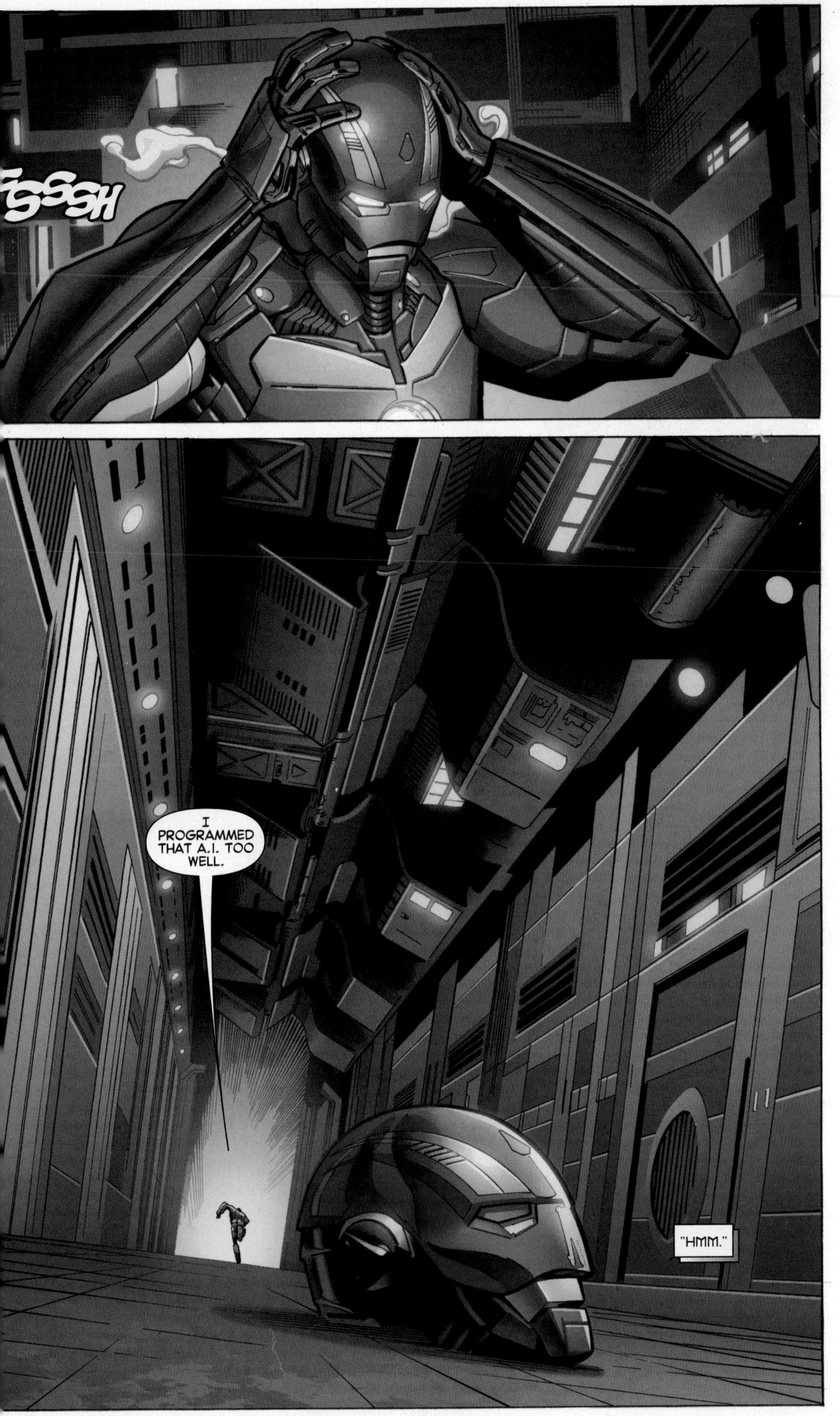
FSSSH
I PROGRAMMED THAT A.I. TOO WELL.
"HMM."

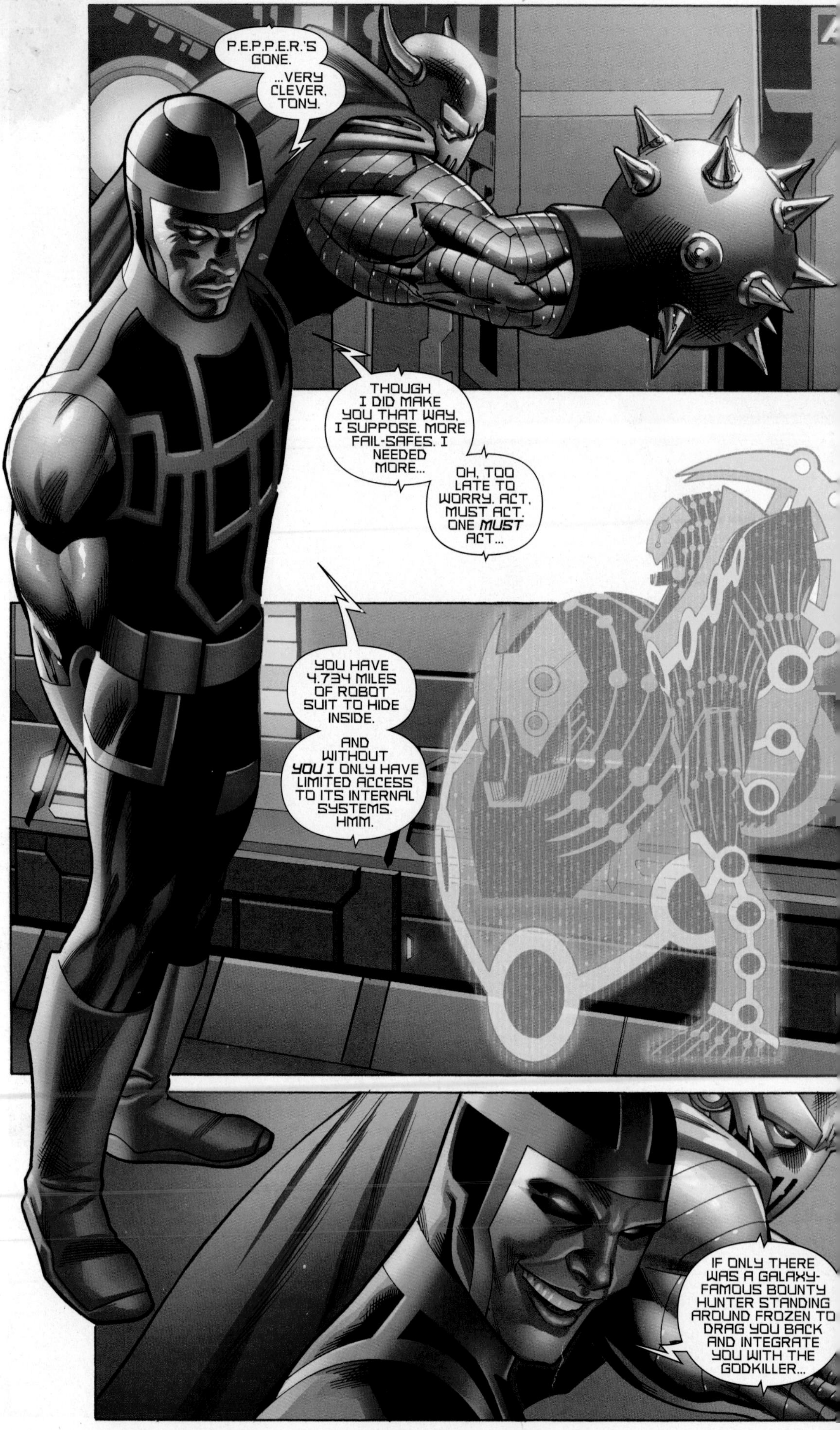
P.E.P.P.E.R.'S GONE.
...VERY CLEVER, TONY.
THOUGH I DID MAKE YOU THAT WAY, I SUPPOSE. MORE FAIL-SAFES. I NEEDED MORE...
OH, TOO LATE TO WORRY. ACT, MUST ACT. ONE MUST ACT...
YOU HAVE 4.734 MILES OF ROBOT SUIT TO HIDE INSIDE.
AND WITHOUT YOU I ONLY HAVE LIMITED ACCESS TO ITS INTERNAL SYSTEMS. HMM.
IF ONLY THERE WAS A GALAXY-FAMOUS BOUNTY HUNTER STANDING AROUND FROZEN TO DRAG YOU BACK AND INTEGRATE YOU WITH THE GODKILLER...

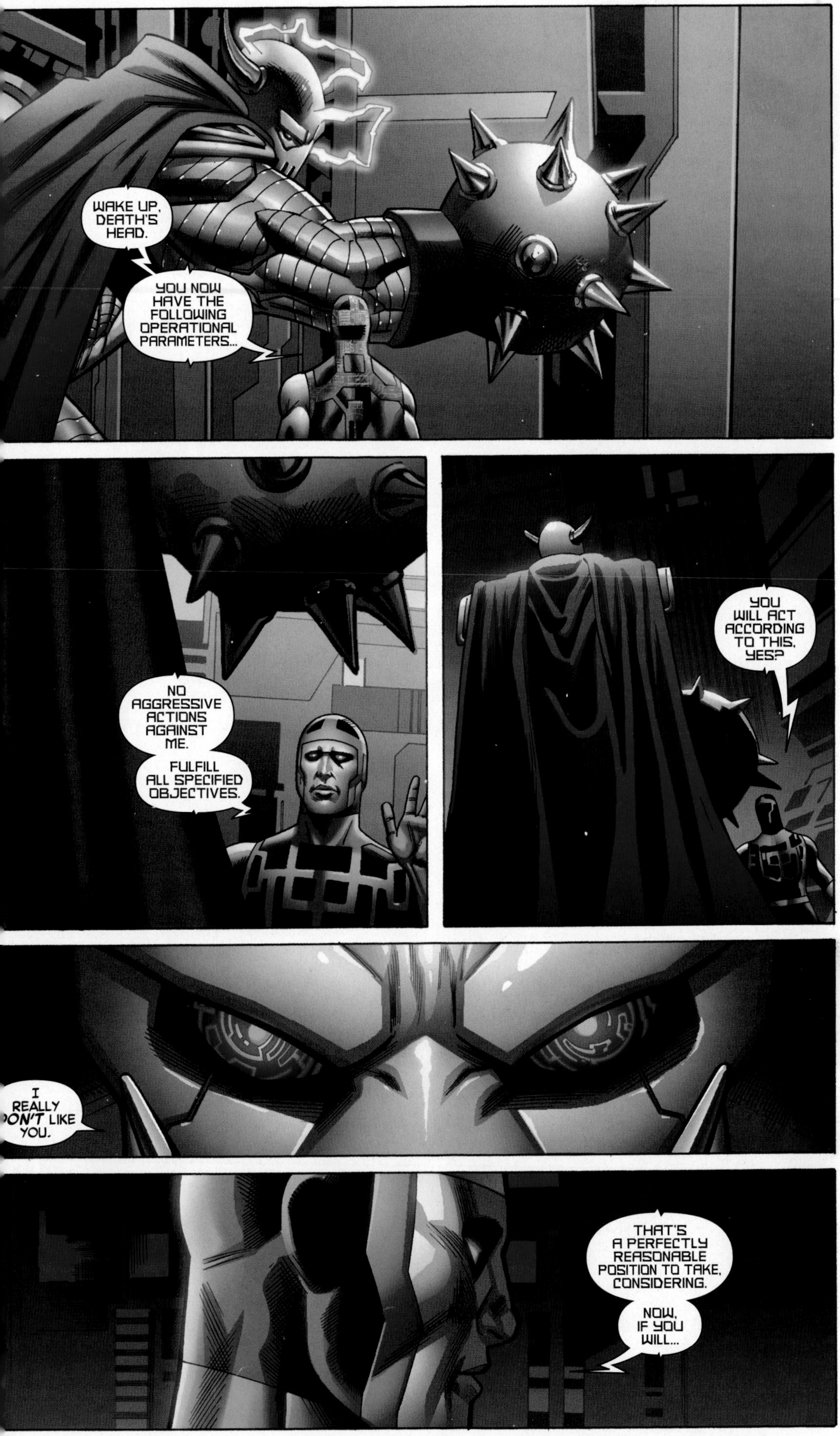
WAKE UP, DEATH'S HEAD.
YOU NOW HAVE THE FOLLOWING OPERATIONAL PARAMETERS...
NO AGGRESSIVE ACTIONS AGAINST ME.
FULFILL ALL SPECIFIED OBJECTIVES.
YOU WILL ACT ACCORDING TO THIS, YES?
I REALLY DON'T LIKE YOU.
THAT'S A PERFECTLY REASONABLE POSITION TO TAKE, CONSIDERING.
NOW, IF YOU WILL...

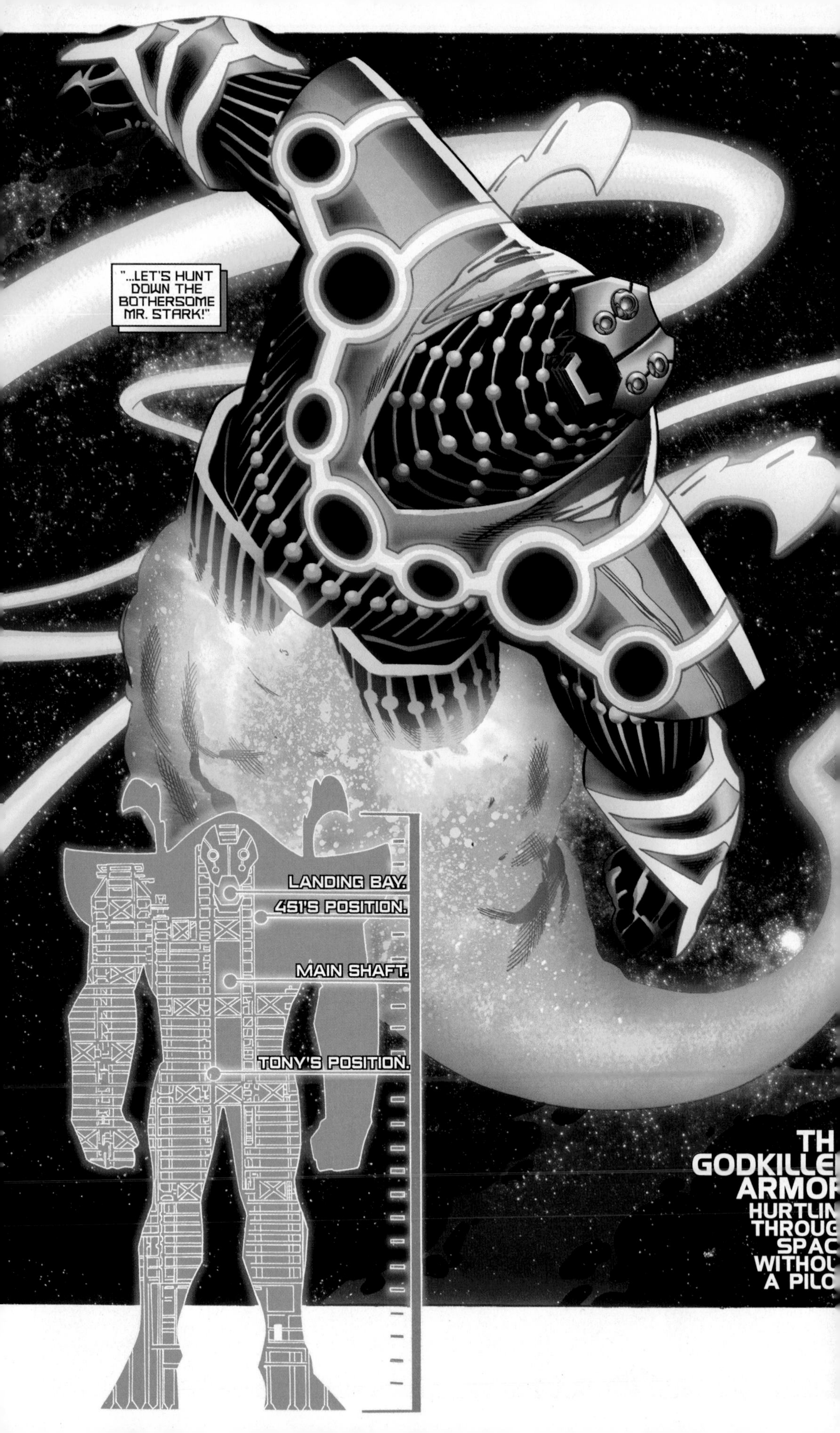
"...LET'S HUNT DOWN THE BOTHERSOME MR. STARK!"
LANDING BAY.
451'S POSITION.
MAIN SHAFT.
TONY'S POSITION.
TH
GODKILLE
ARMOR
HURTLIN
THROUG
SPAC
WITHOU
A PILO

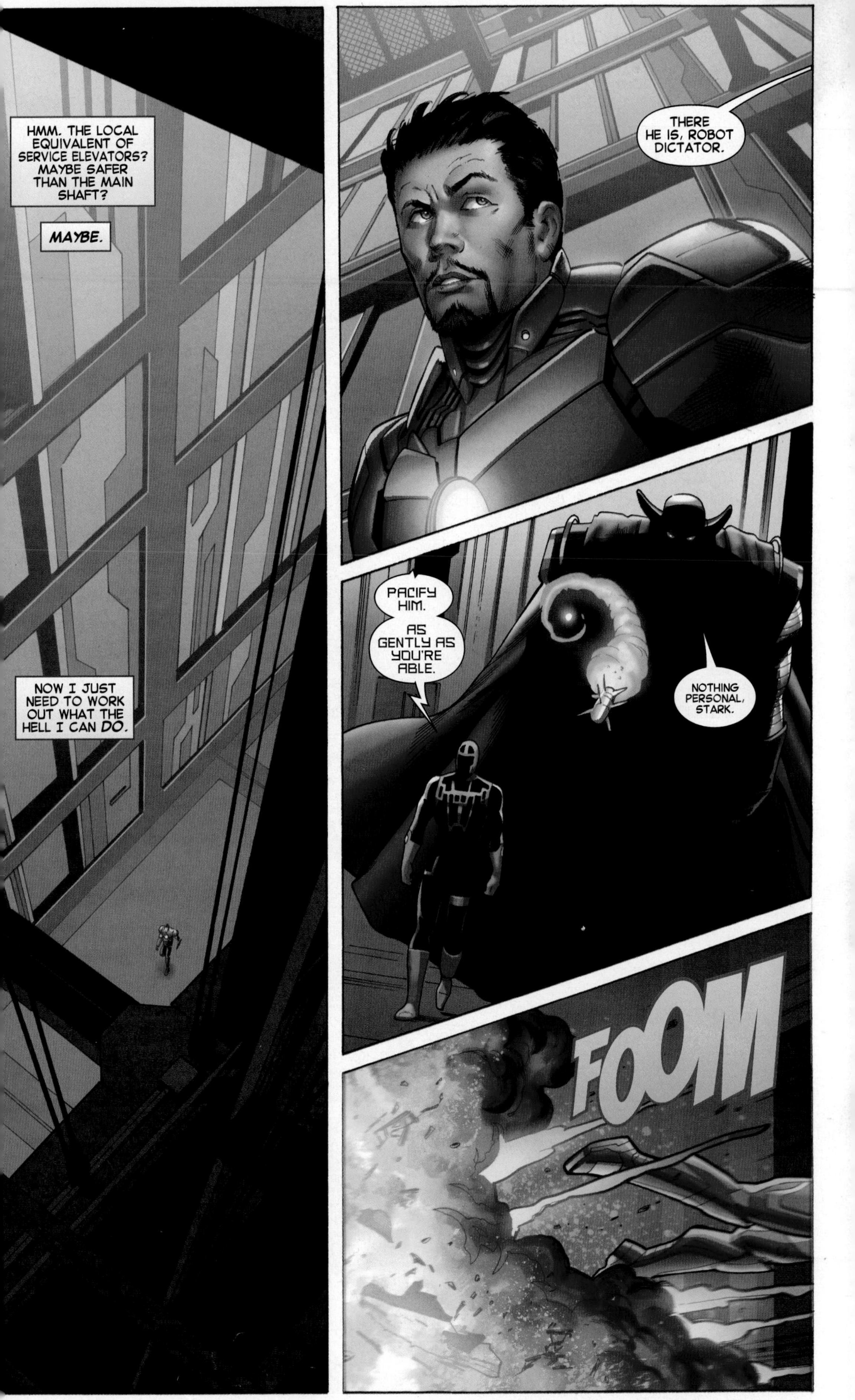
HMM. THE LOCAL EQUIVALENT OF SERVICE ELEVATORS? MAYBE SAFER THAN THE MAIN SHAFT?
MAYBE.
NOW I JUST NEED TO WORK OUT WHAT THE HELL I CAN *DO*.
THERE HE IS, ROBOT DICTATOR.
PACIFY HIM.
AS GENTLY AS YOU'RE ABLE.
NOTHING PERSONAL, STARK.
FOOM

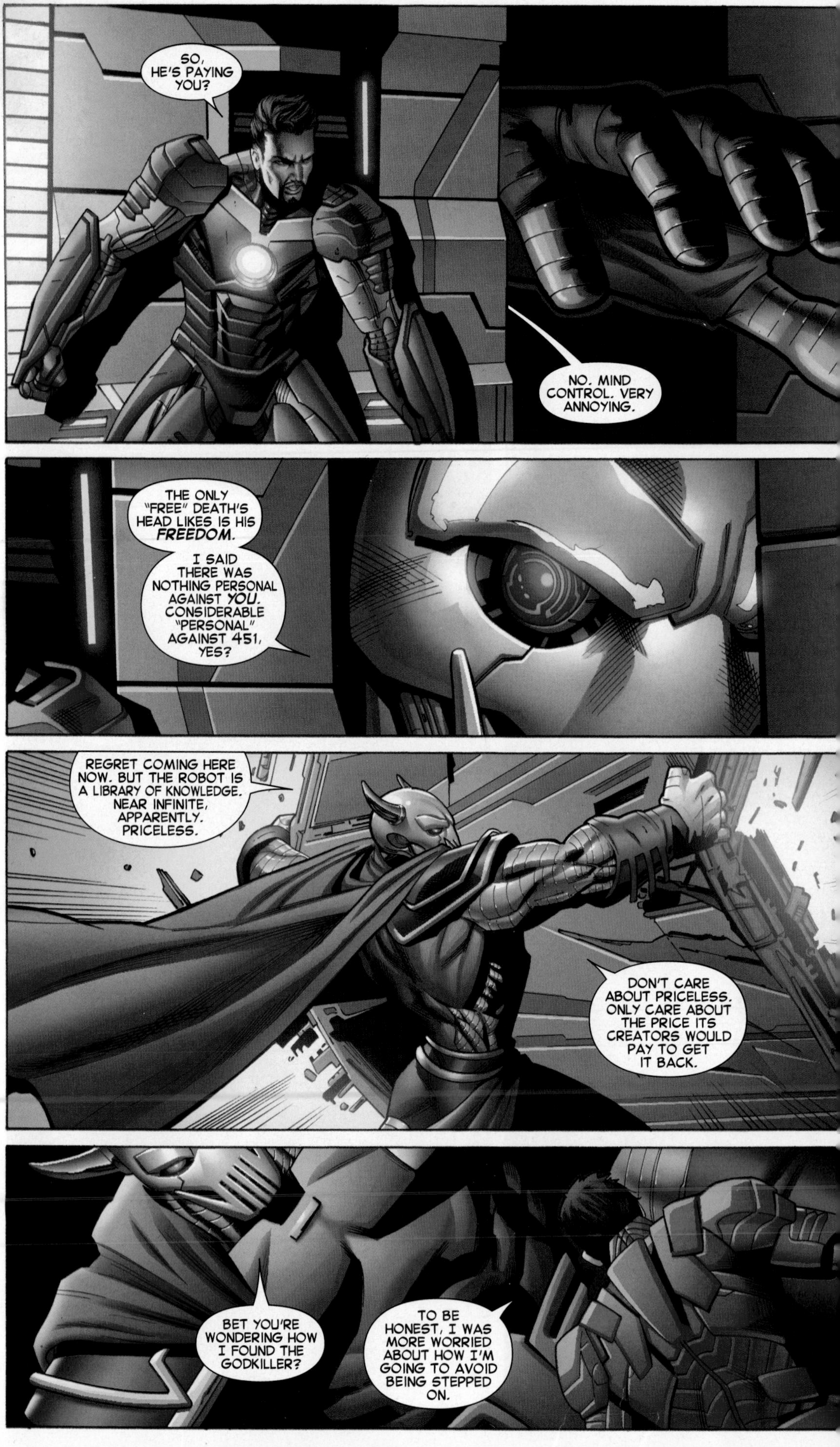
SO, HE'S PAYING YOU?
NO. MIND CONTROL. VERY ANNOYING.
THE ONLY "FREE" DEATH'S HEAD LIKES IS HIS FREEDOM.
I SAID THERE WAS NOTHING PERSONAL AGAINST YOU. CONSIDERABLE "PERSONAL" AGAINST 451, YES?
REGRET COMING HERE NOW. BUT THE ROBOT IS A LIBRARY OF KNOWLEDGE. NEAR INFINITE, APPARENTLY. PRICELESS.
DON'T CARE ABOUT PRICELESS. ONLY CARE ABOUT THE PRICE ITS CREATORS WOULD PAY TO GET IT BACK.
BET YOU'RE WONDERING HOW I FOUND THE GODKILLER?
TO BE HONEST, I WAS MORE WORRIED ABOUT HOW I'M GOING TO AVOID BEING STEPPED ON.

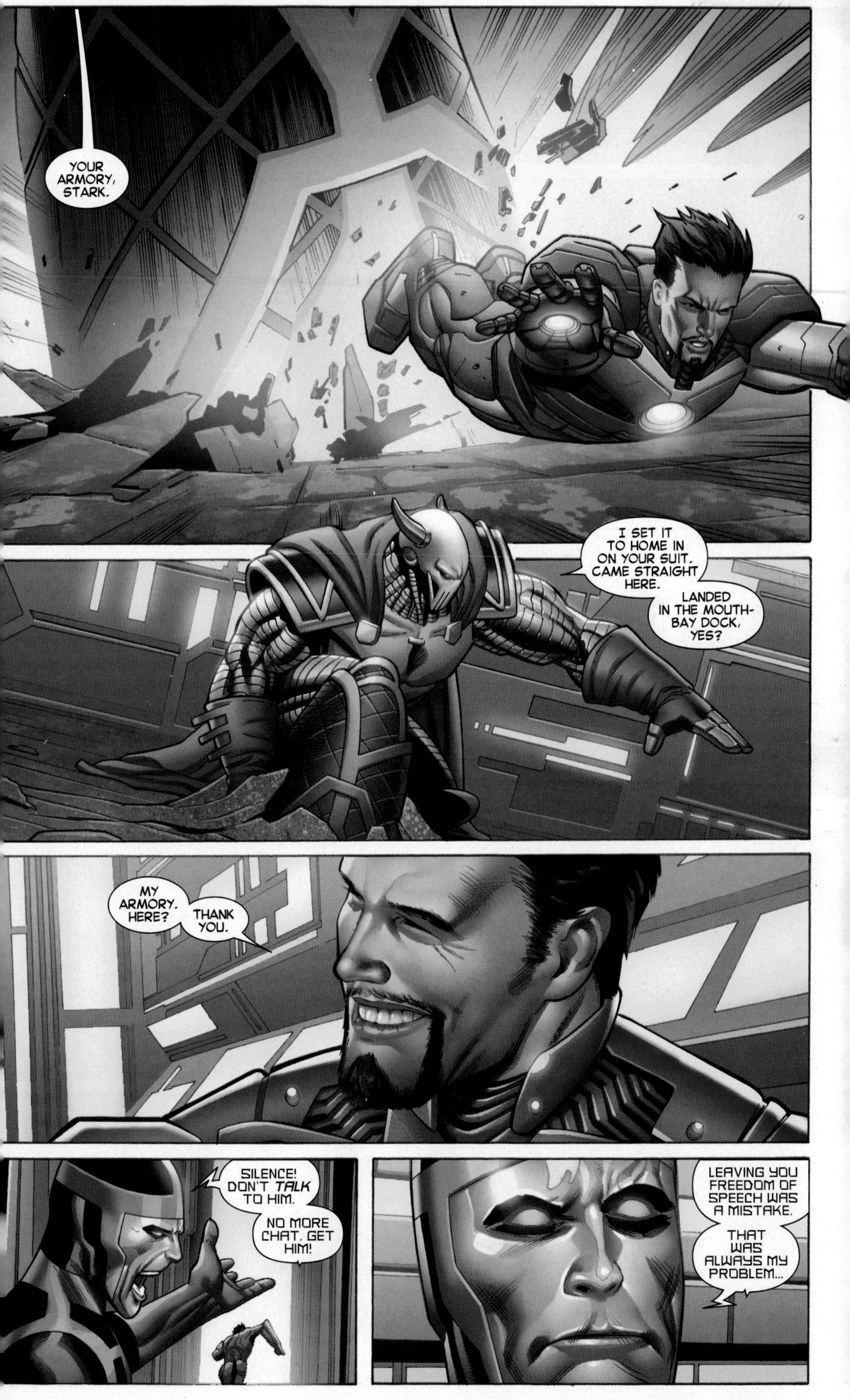
YOUR ARMORY, STARK.
I SET IT TO HOME IN ON YOUR SUIT. CAME STRAIGHT HERE.
LANDED IN THE MOUTH-BAY DOCK, YES?
MY ARMORY. HERE?
THANK YOU.
SILENCE! DON'T *TALK* TO HIM.
NO MORE CHAT. GET HIM!
LEAVING YOU FREEDOM OF SPEECH WAS A MISTAKE.
THAT WAS ALWAYS MY PROBLEM...

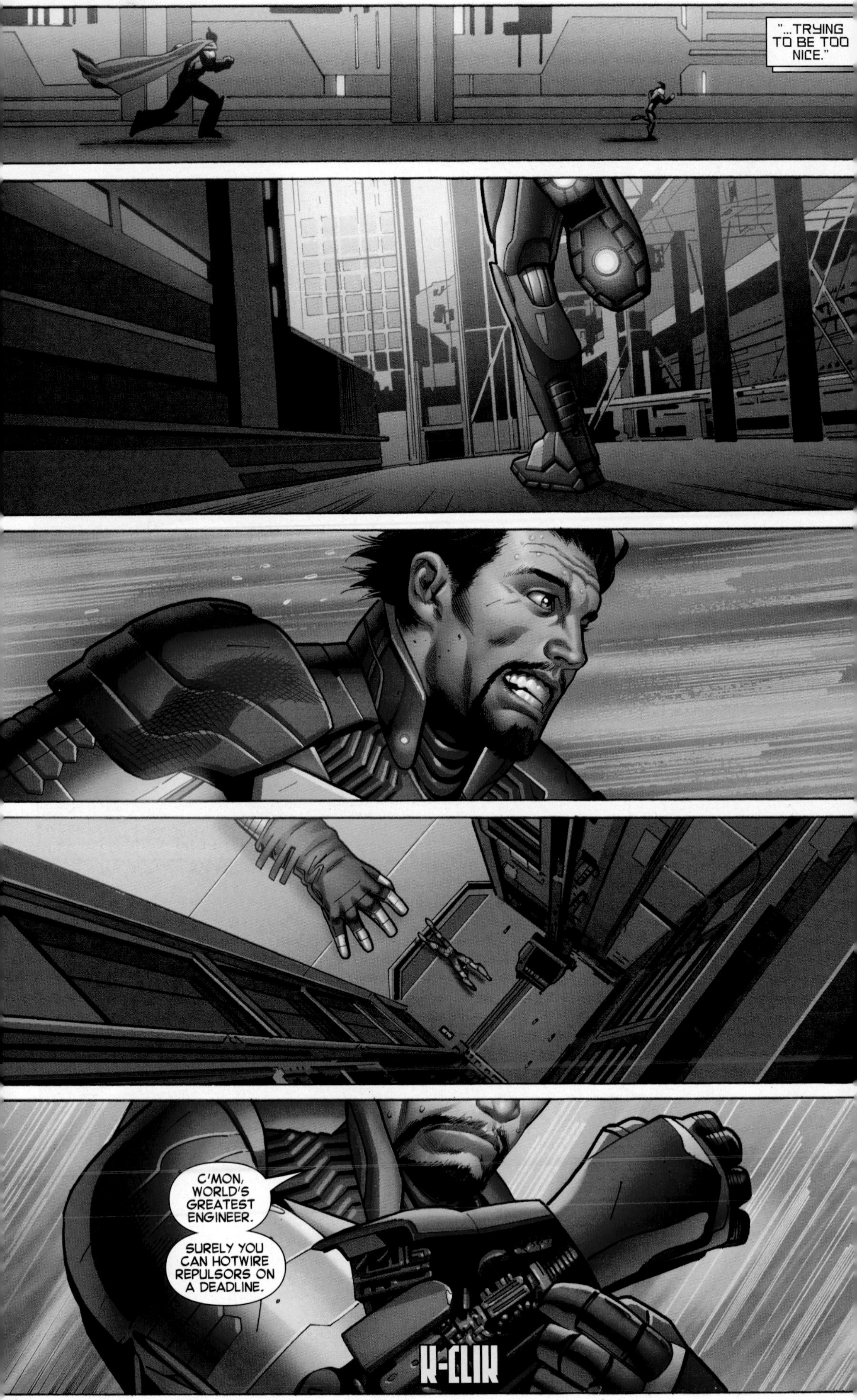
"...TRYING TO BE TOO NICE."
C'MON, WORLD'S GREATEST ENGINEER.
SURELY YOU CAN HOTWIRE REPULSORS ON A DEADLINE.
K-CLIK

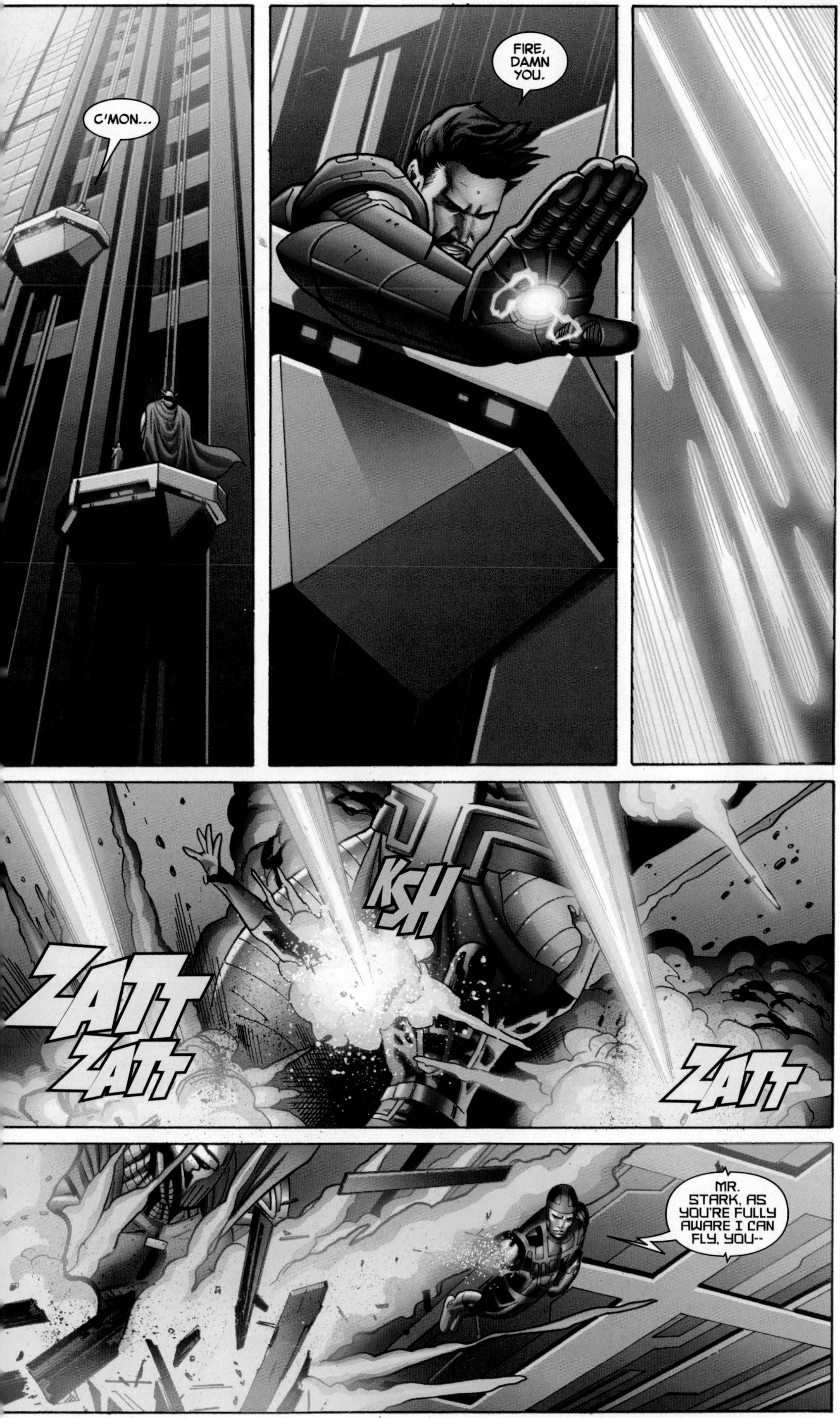
C'MON...
FIRE, DAMN YOU.
KSH
ZATT ZATT
ZATT
MR. STARK, AS YOU'RE FULLY AWARE I CAN FLY, YOU--

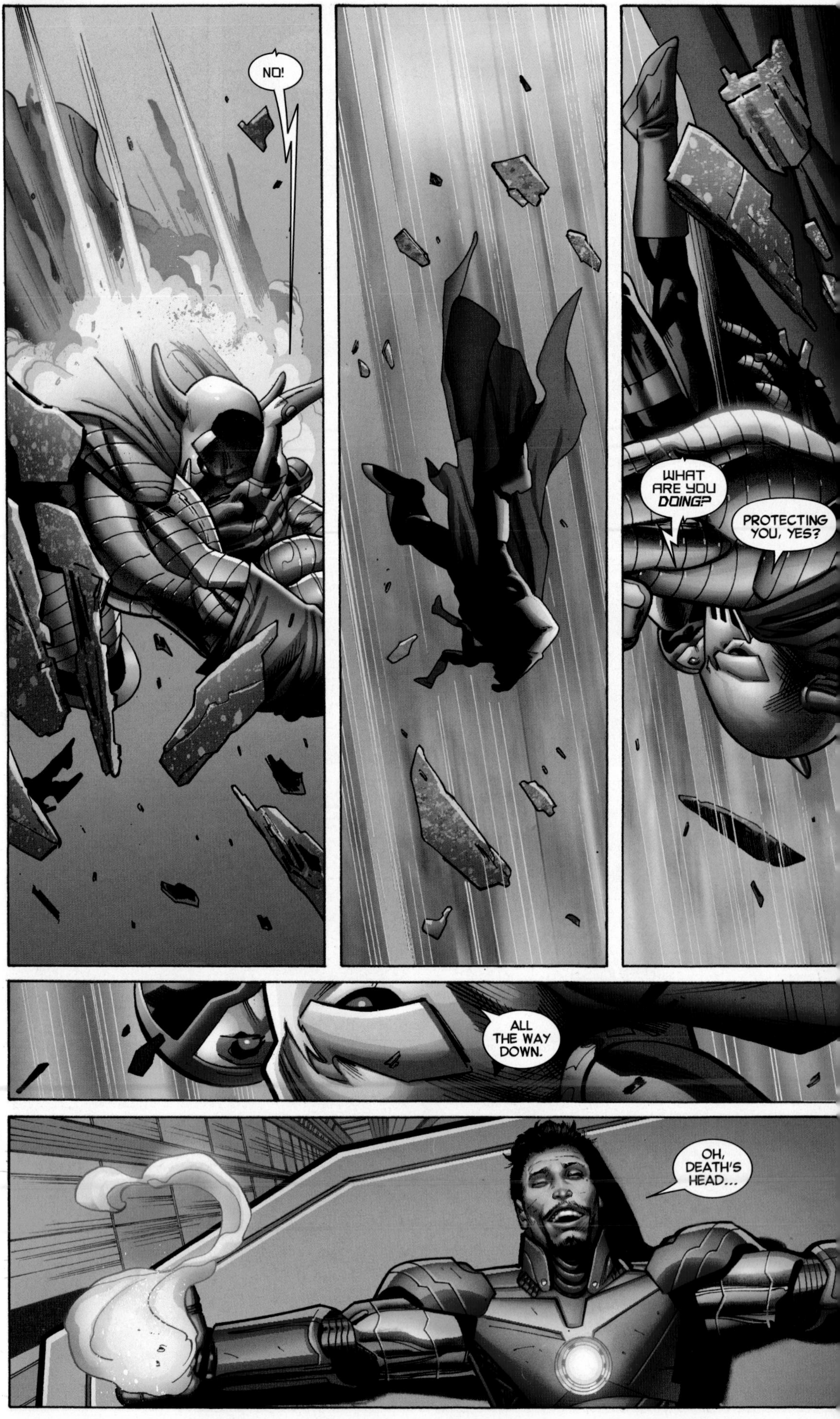
NO!
WHAT ARE YOU DOING?
PROTECTING YOU, YES?
ALL THE WAY DOWN.
OH, DEATH'S HEAD...

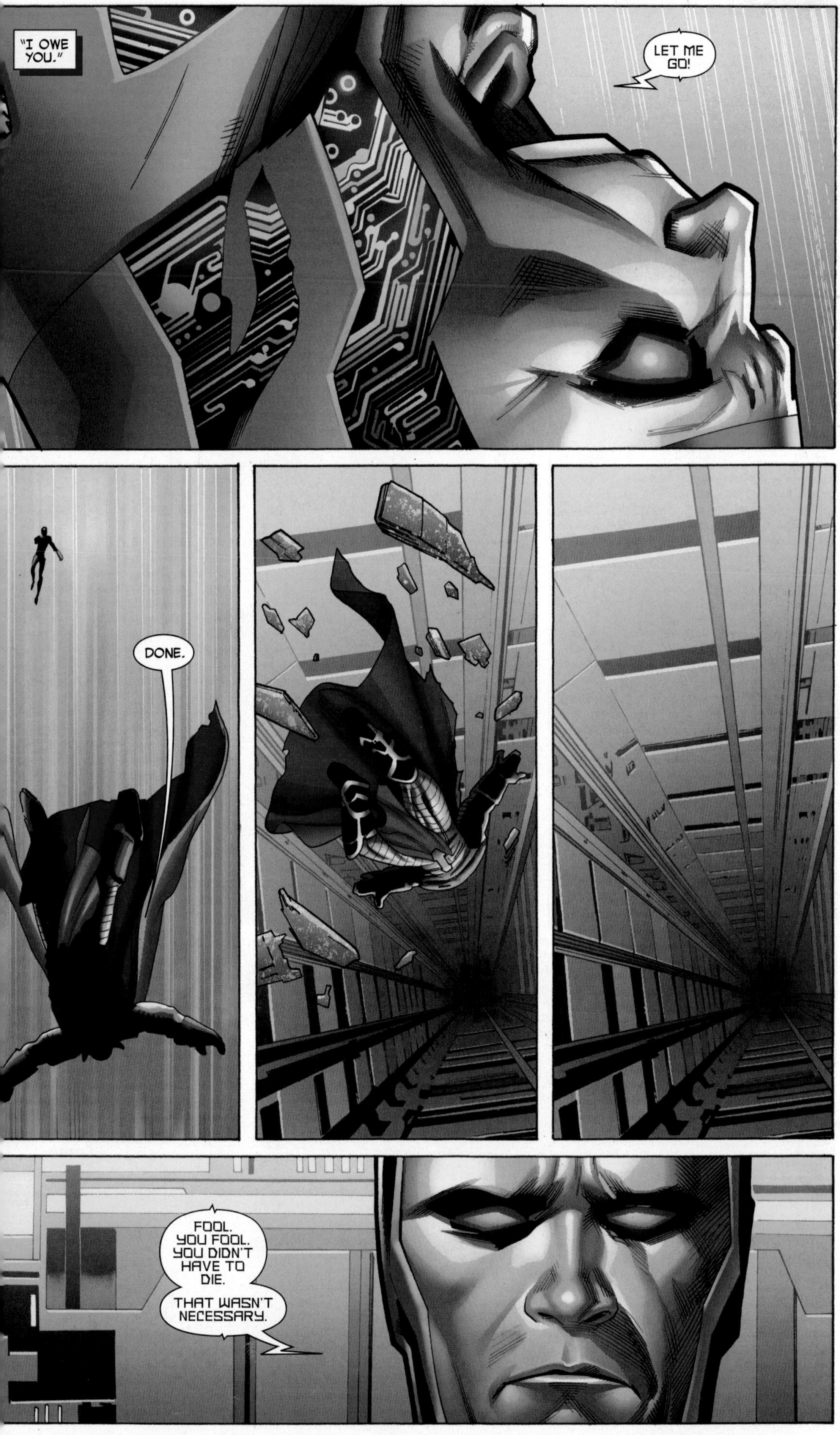
"I OWE YOU."
LET ME GO!
DONE.
FOOL. YOU FOOL. YOU DIDN'T HAVE TO DIE.
THAT WASN'T NECESSARY.

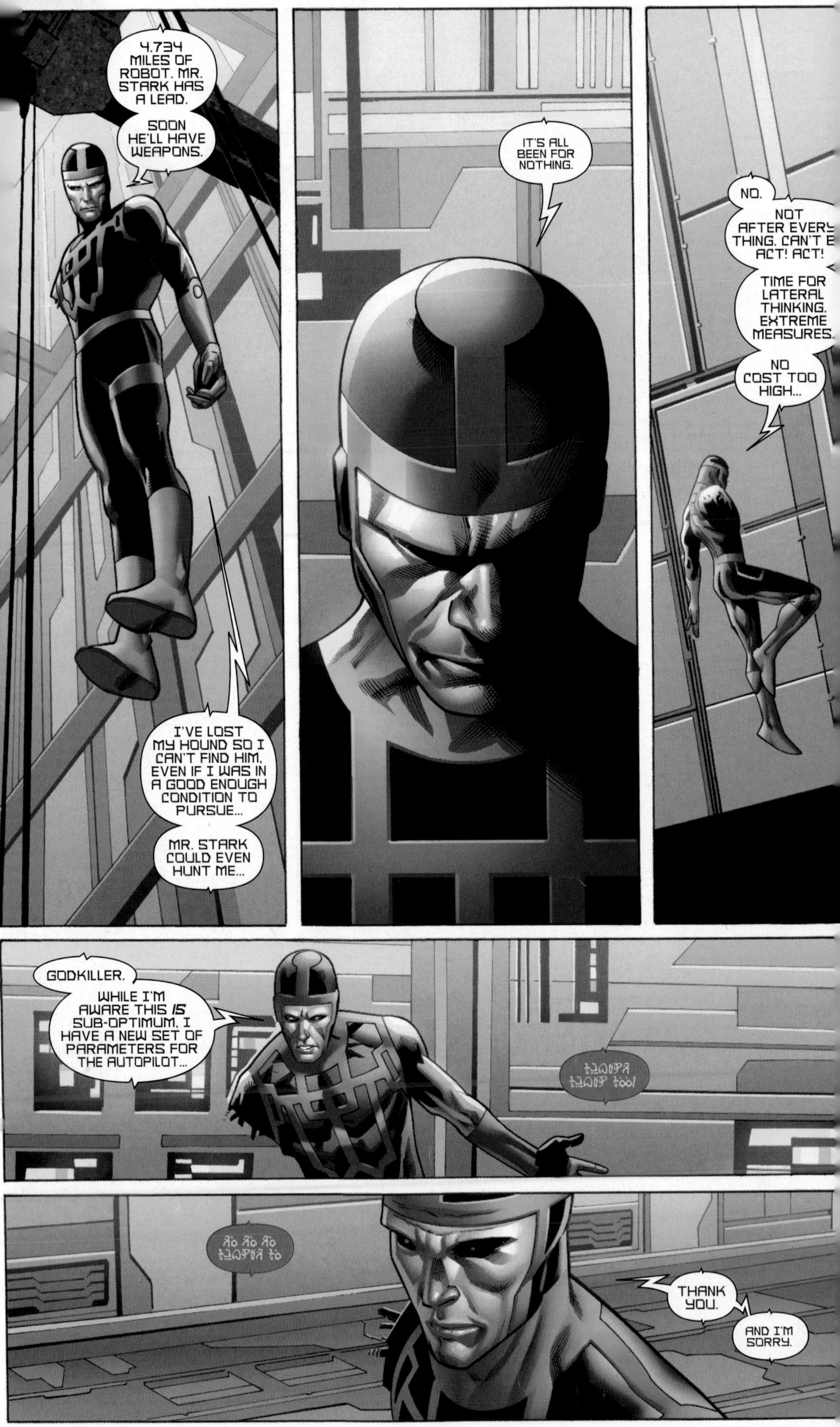
4.734 MILES OF ROBOT. MR. STARK HAS A LEAD.
SOON HE'LL HAVE WEAPONS.
I'VE LOST MY HOUND SO I CAN'T FIND HIM, EVEN IF I WAS IN A GOOD ENOUGH CONDITION TO PURSUE...
MR. STARK COULD EVEN HUNT ME...
IT'S ALL BEEN FOR NOTHING.
NO.
NOT AFTER EVERY THING. CAN'T E ACT! ACT!
TIME FOR LATERAL THINKING. EXTREME MEASURES.
NO COST TOO HIGH...
GODKILLER.
WHILE I'M AWARE THIS *IS* SUB-OPTIMUM, I HAVE A NEW SET OF PARAMETERS FOR THE AUTOPILOT...
THANK YOU.
AND I'M SORRY.

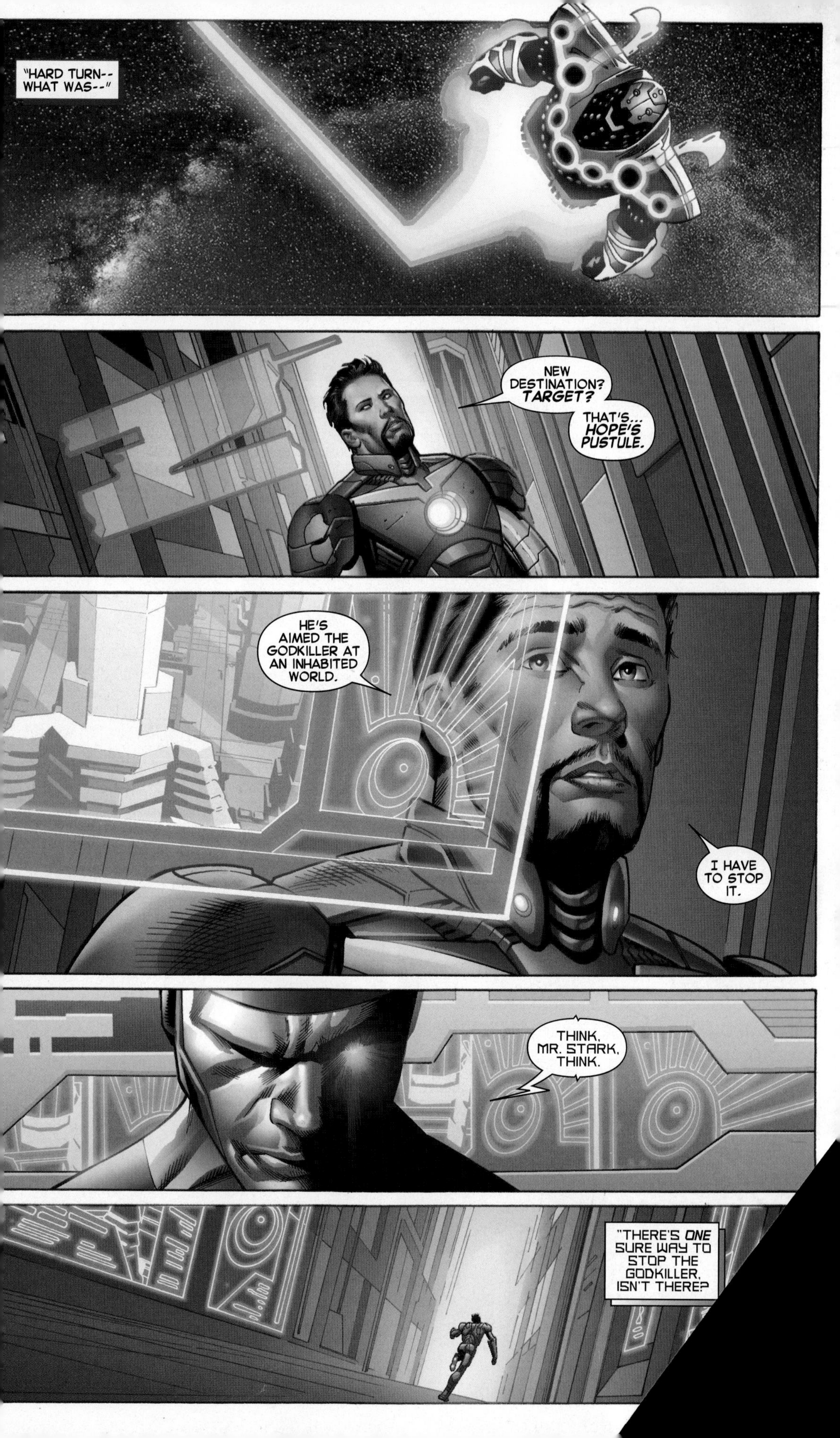
"HARD TURN--
WHAT WAS--"
NEW DESTINATION? TARGET?
THAT'S... HOPE'S PUSTULE.
HE'S AIMED THE GODKILLER AT AN INHABITED WORLD.
I HAVE TO STOP IT.
THINK, MR. STARK, THINK.
"THERE'S ONE SURE WAY TO STOP THE GODKILLER, ISN'T THERE?

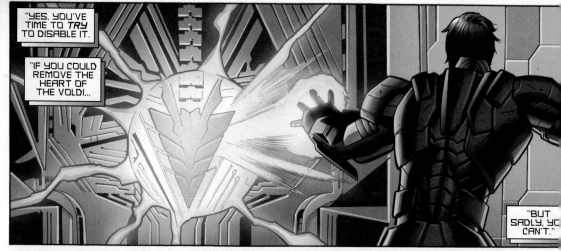

"YES. YOU'VE TIME TO *TRY* TO DISABLE IT.

"IF YOU COULD REMOVE THE HEART OF THE VOLD!...

"BUT SADLY, YC CAN'T."

WHAT'S THE *SURE* WAY?

"THE PILOT COULD STOP IT. *YOU'RE* THE PILOT.

"ACCEPT YOUR DESTINY."

STEVE. THOR. EVERYONE ELSE.

DOWN TO YOU GUYS NOW.

YOU'LL STOP HIM.

YOU'LL STOP WHATEVER THIS TURNS ME INTO.

OH GREAT.

I'M REDUCED TO ACTUALLY HAVING FAITH I GODS AND MY FELLOW MAN.

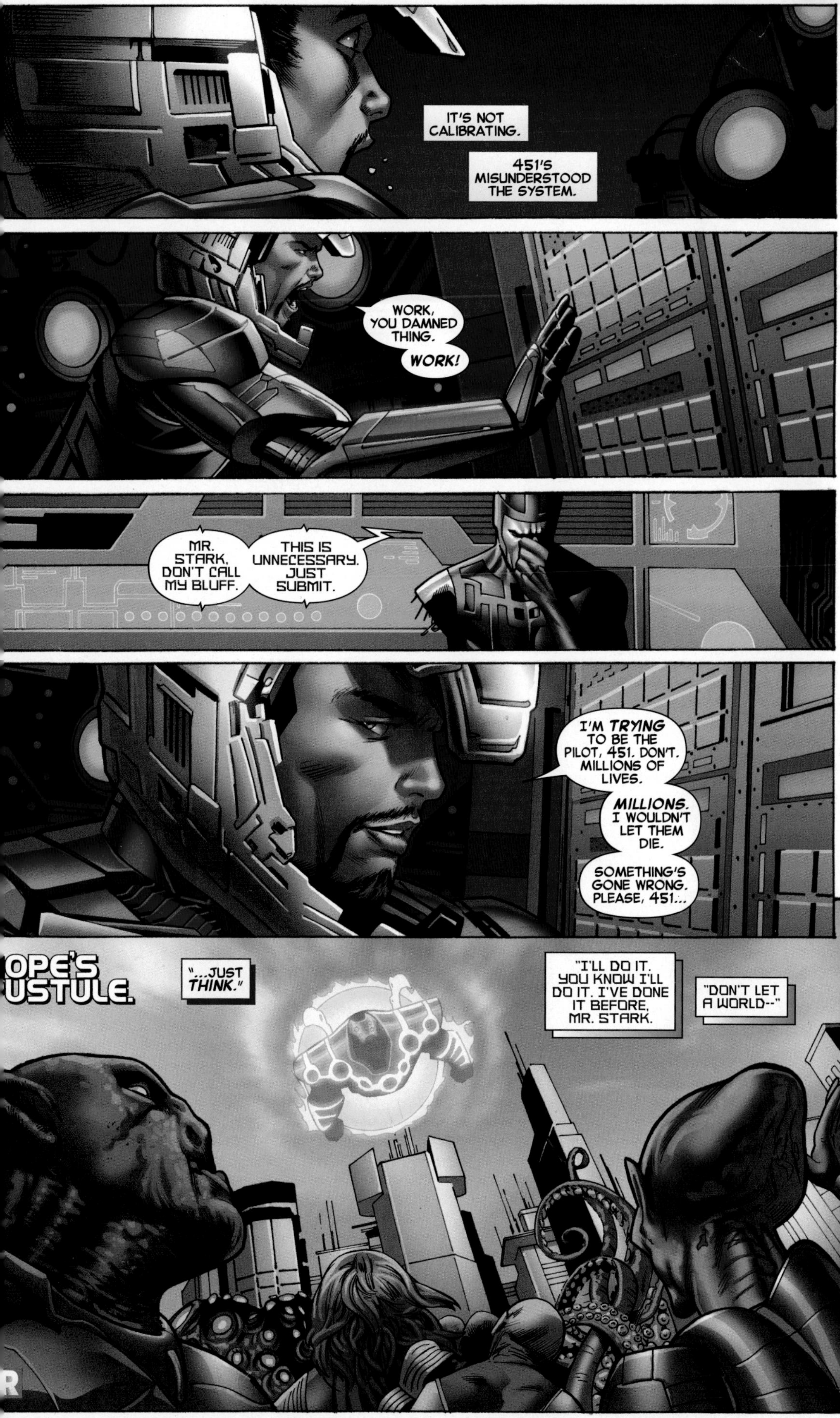
IT'S NOT CALIBRATING.
451'S MISUNDERSTOOD THE SYSTEM.
WORK, YOU DAMNED THING.
WORK!
MR. STARK, DON'T CALL MY BLUFF.
THIS IS UNNECESSARY. JUST SUBMIT.
I'M TRYING TO BE THE PILOT, 451. DON'T. MILLIONS OF LIVES.
MILLIONS. I WOULDN'T LET THEM DIE.
SOMETHING'S GONE WRONG. PLEASE, 451...
OPE'S USTULE.
"...JUST THINK."
"I'LL DO IT. YOU KNOW I'LL DO IT. I'VE DONE IT BEFORE, MR. STARK.
"DON'T LET A WORLD--"

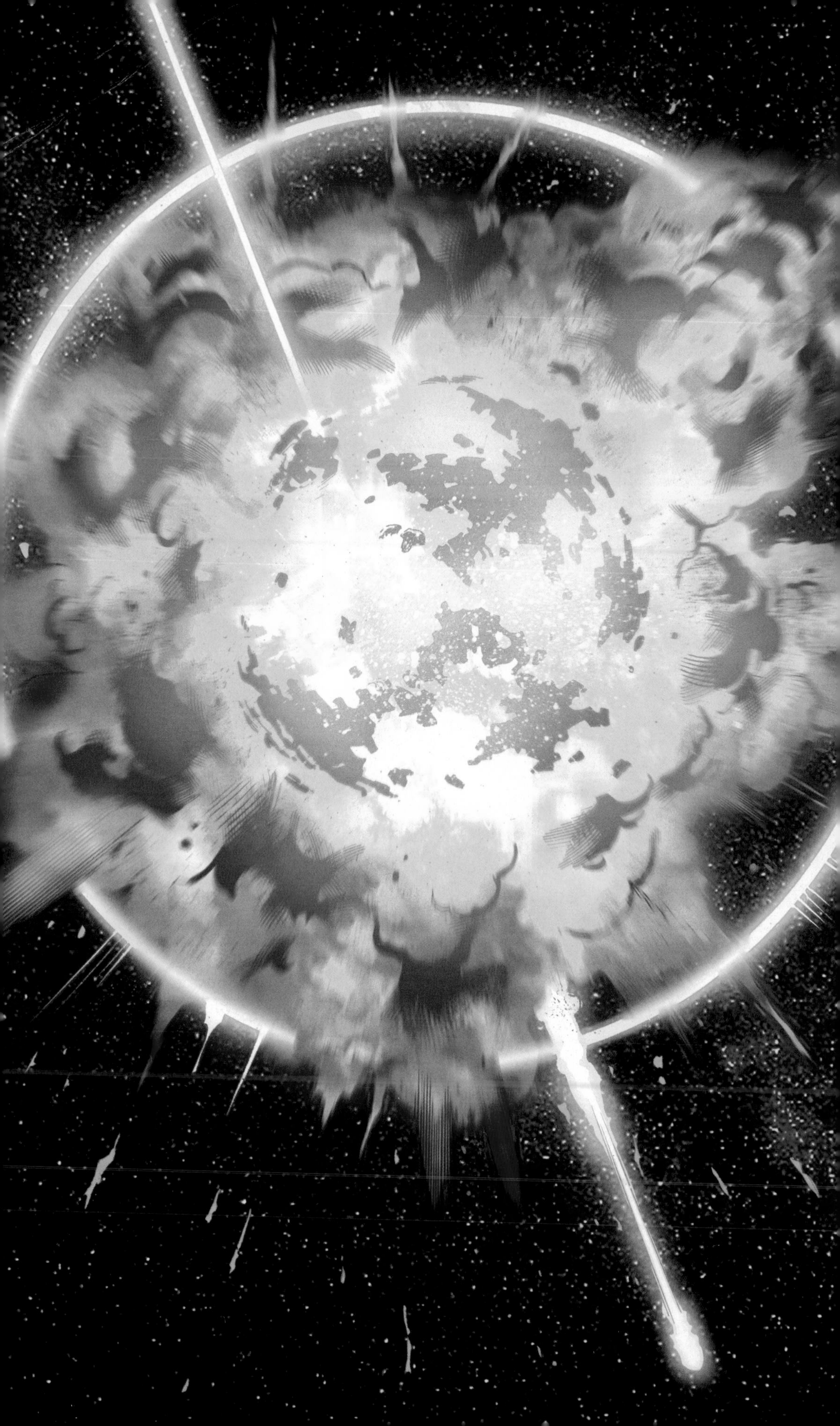

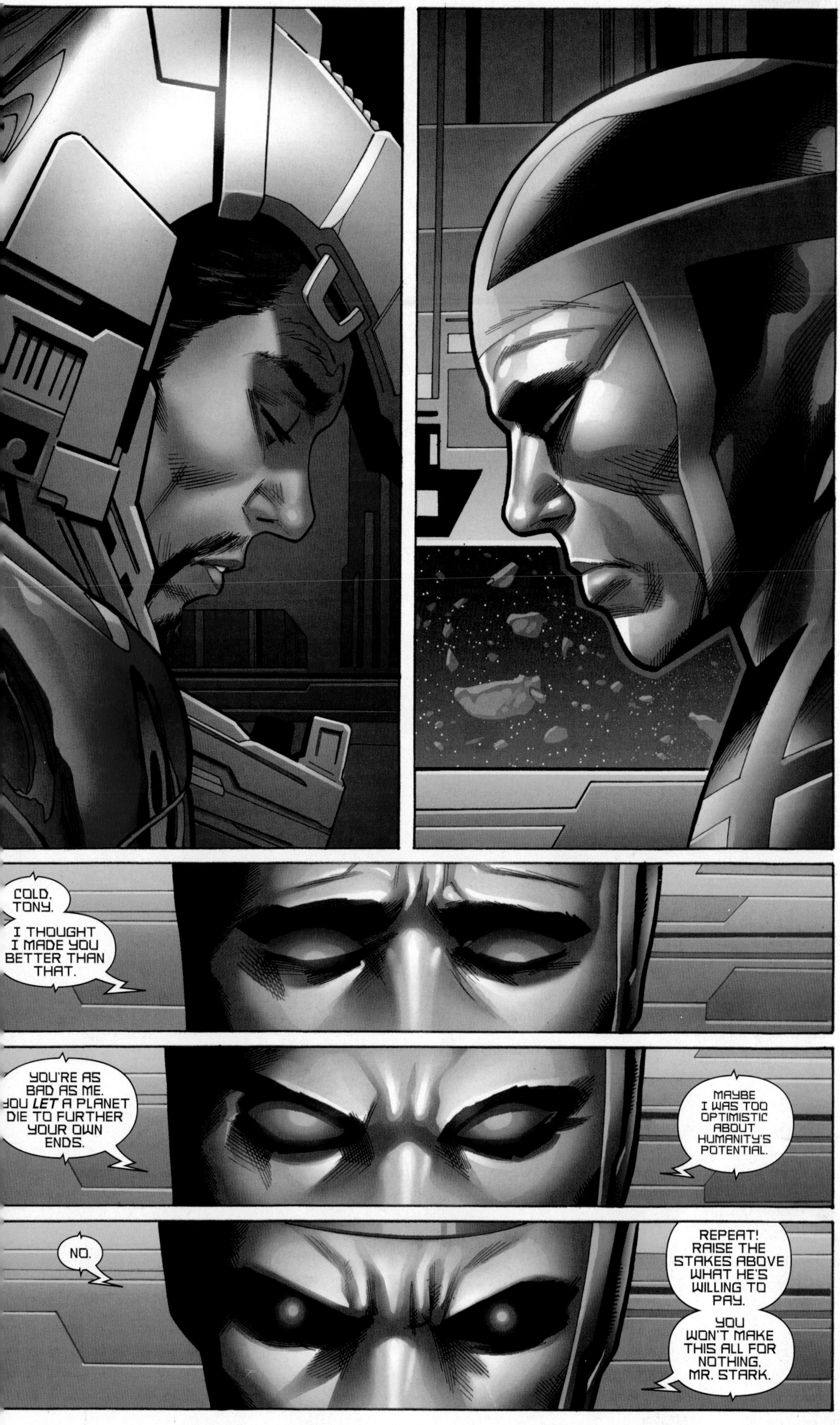

COLD, TONY.
I THOUGHT I MADE YOU BETTER THAN THAT.
YOU'RE AS BAD AS ME. YOU *LET* A PLANET DIE TO FURTHER YOUR OWN ENDS.
MAYBE I WAS TOO OPTIMISTIC ABOUT HUMANITY'S POTENTIAL.
NO.
REPEAT! RAISE THE STAKES ABOVE WHAT HE'S WILLING TO PAY.
YOU WON'T MAKE THIS ALL FOR NOTHING, MR. STARK.

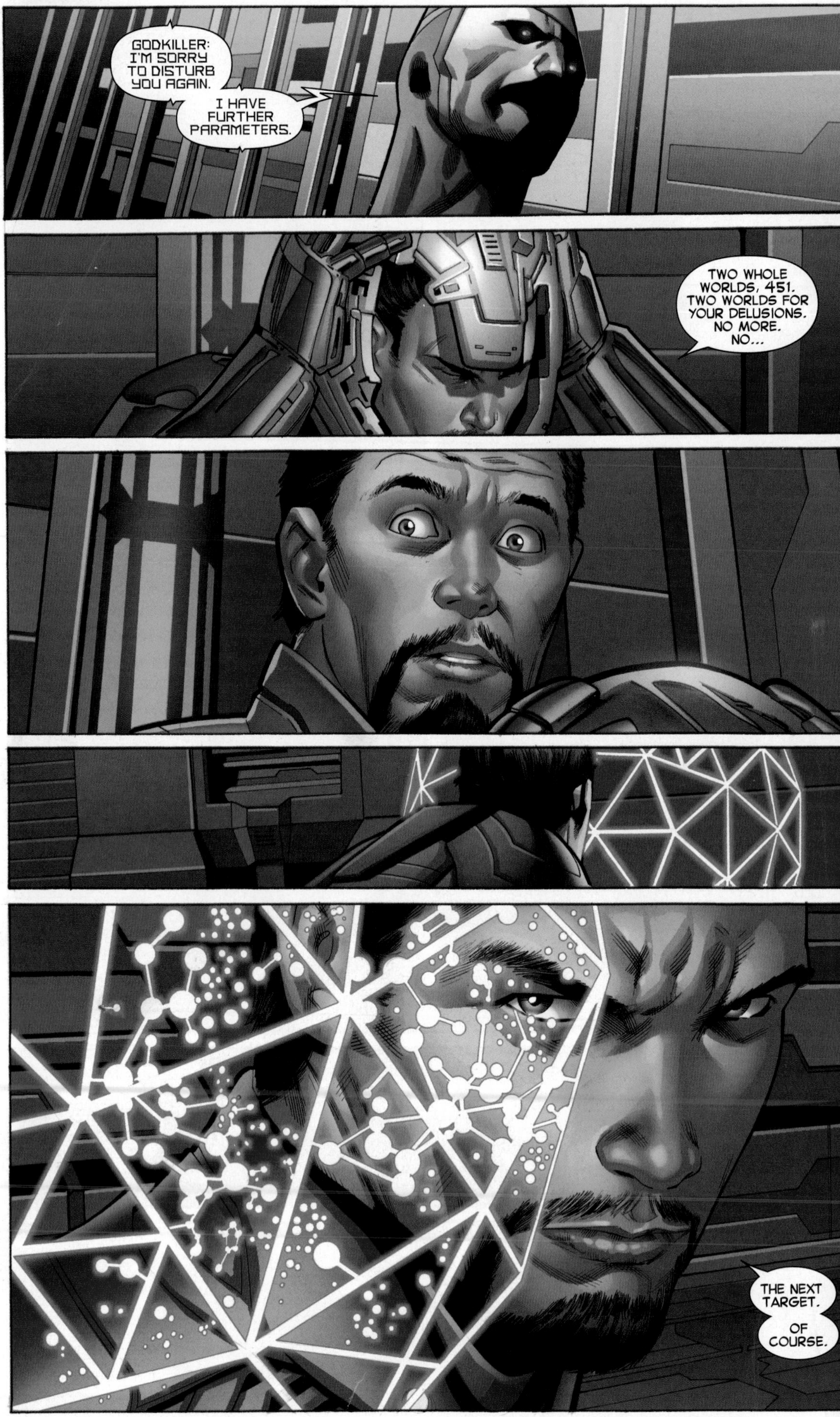
GODKILLER: I'M SORRY TO DISTURB YOU AGAIN.
I HAVE FURTHER PARAMETERS.
TWO WHOLE WORLDS, 451. TWO WORLDS FOR YOUR DELUSIONS. NO MORE. NO...
THE NEXT TARGET.
OF COURSE.

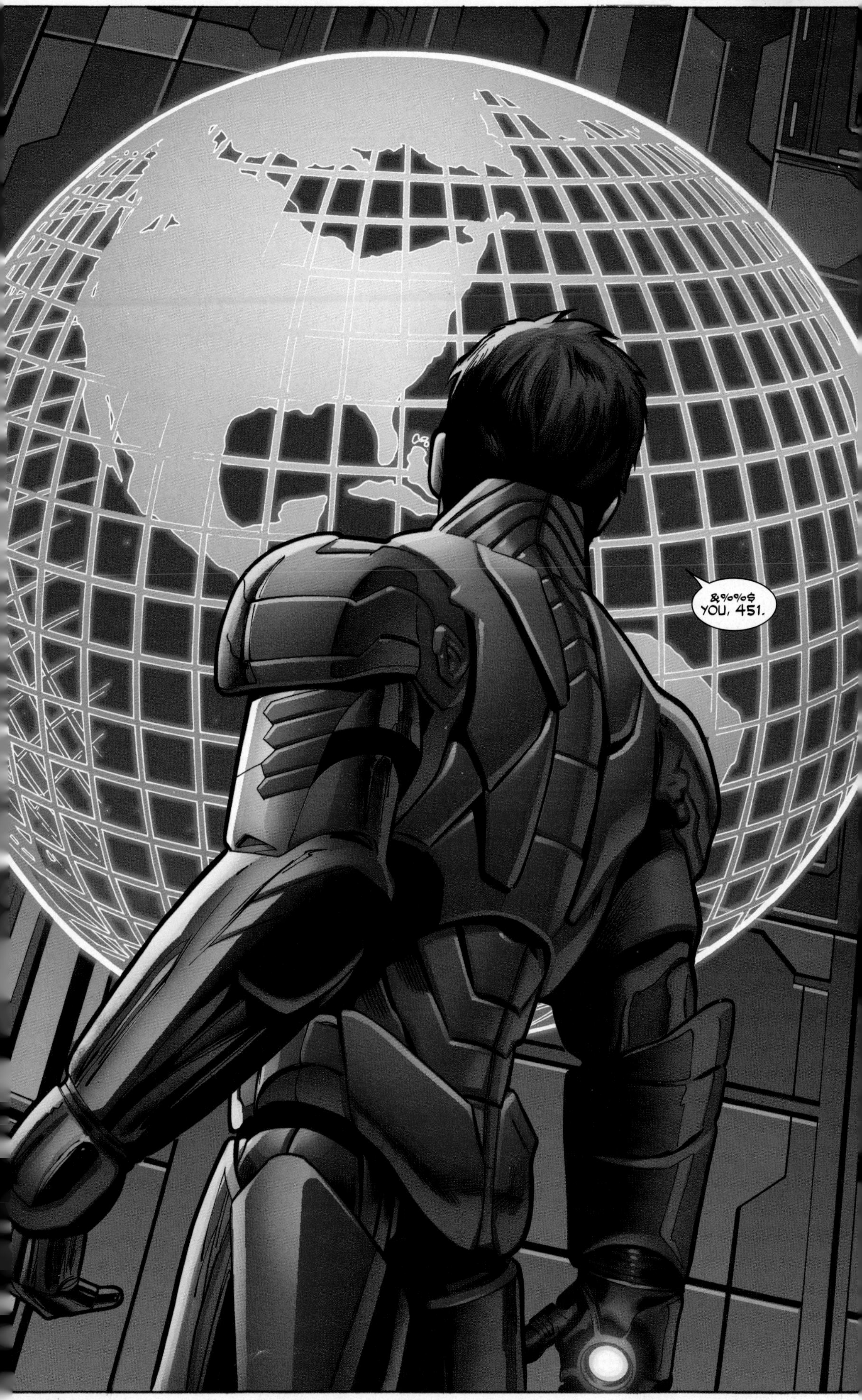
&%%$
YOU, 451.

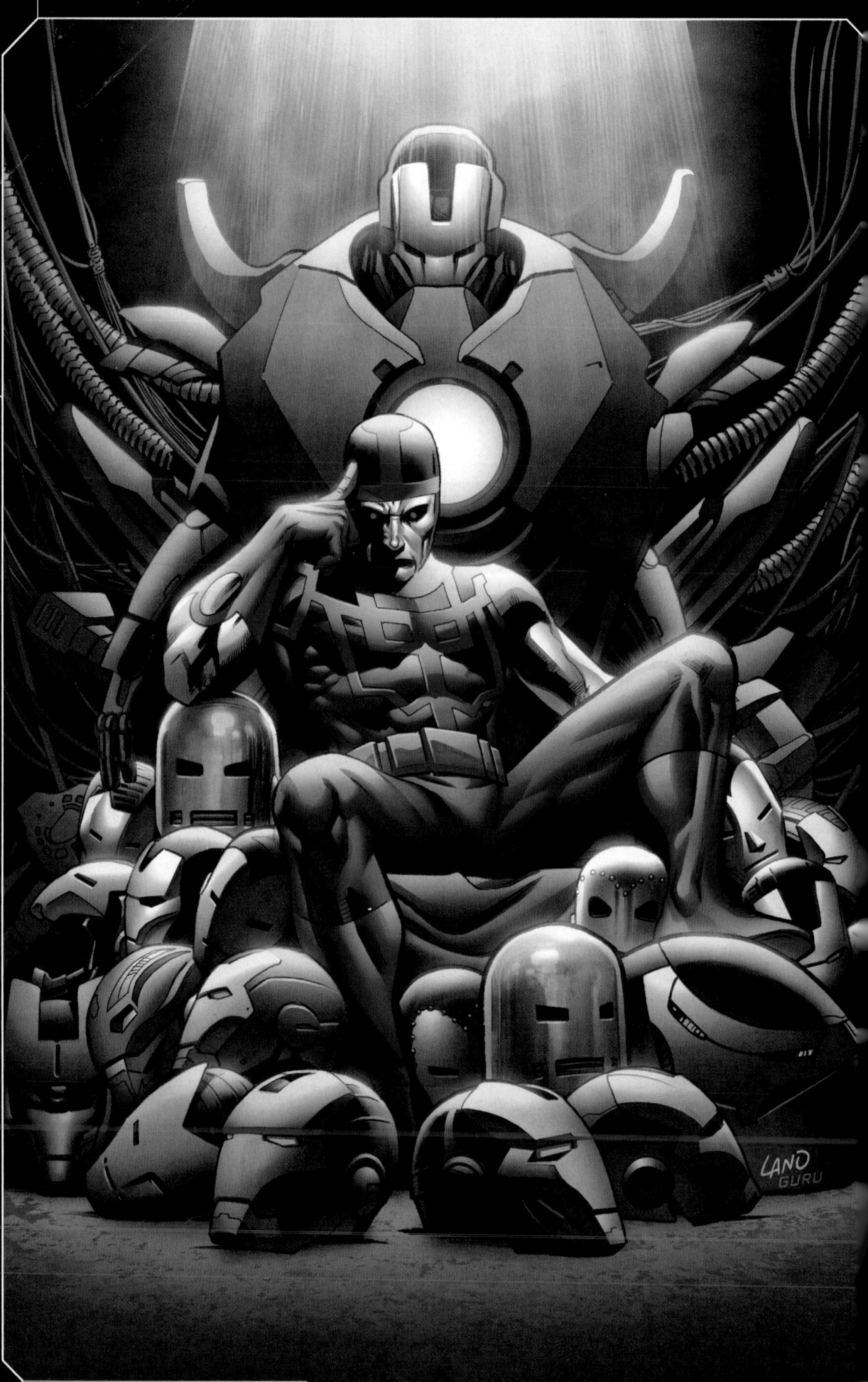
LAND
GURU

15 THE SECRET ORIGIN OF TONY STARK: THE BEST OFFENSE PART 3

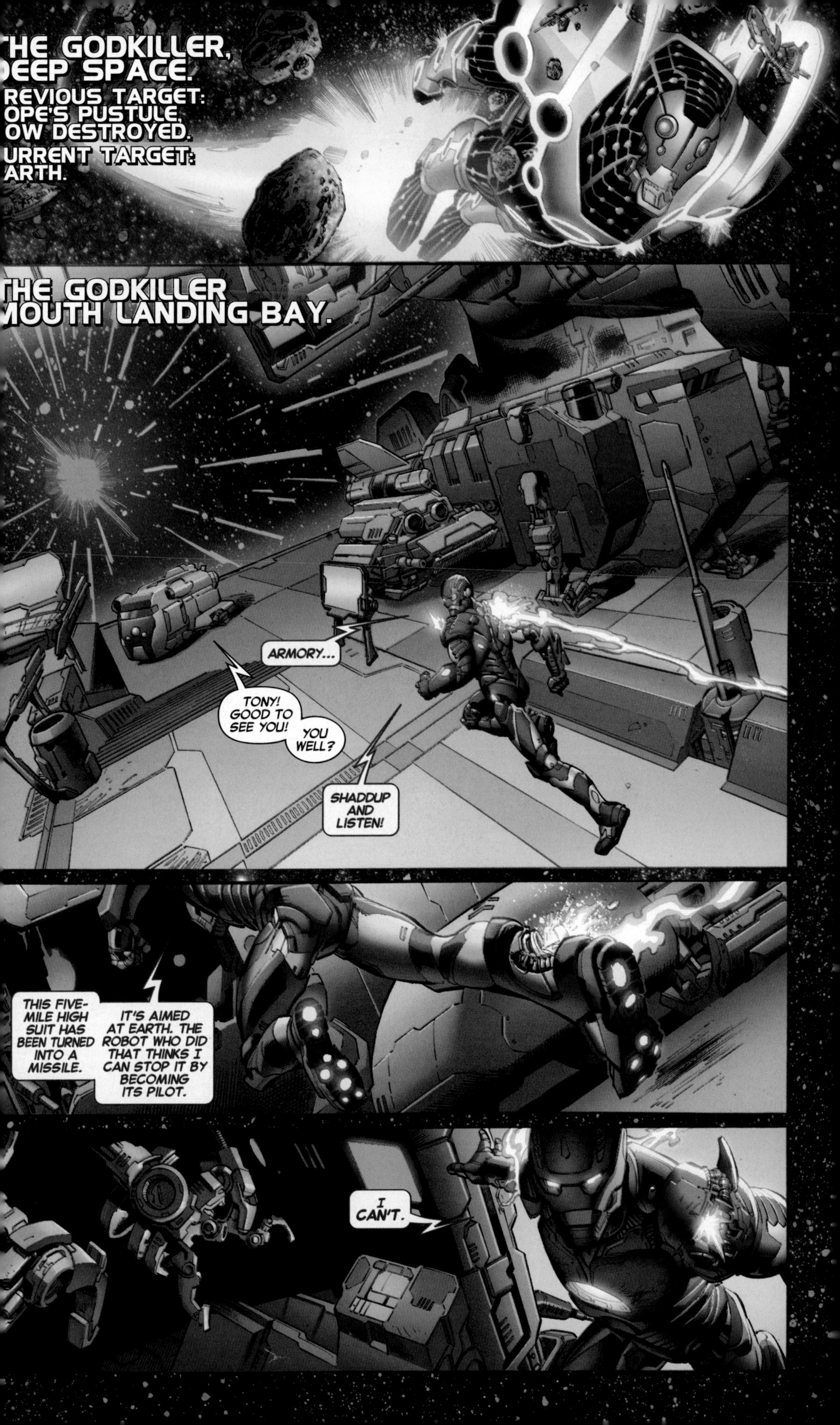

THE GODKILLER, DEEP SPACE.
REVIOUS TARGET: OPE'S PUSTULE. OW DESTROYED.
URRENT TARGET: ARTH.
THE GODKILLER MOUTH LANDING BAY.
ARMORY...
TONY! GOOD TO SEE YOU!
YOU WELL?
SHADDUP AND LISTEN!
THIS FIVE-MILE HIGH SUIT HAS BEEN TURNED INTO A MISSILE.
IT'S AIMED AT EARTH. THE ROBOT WHO DID THAT THINKS I CAN STOP IT BY BECOMING ITS PILOT.
I CAN'T.

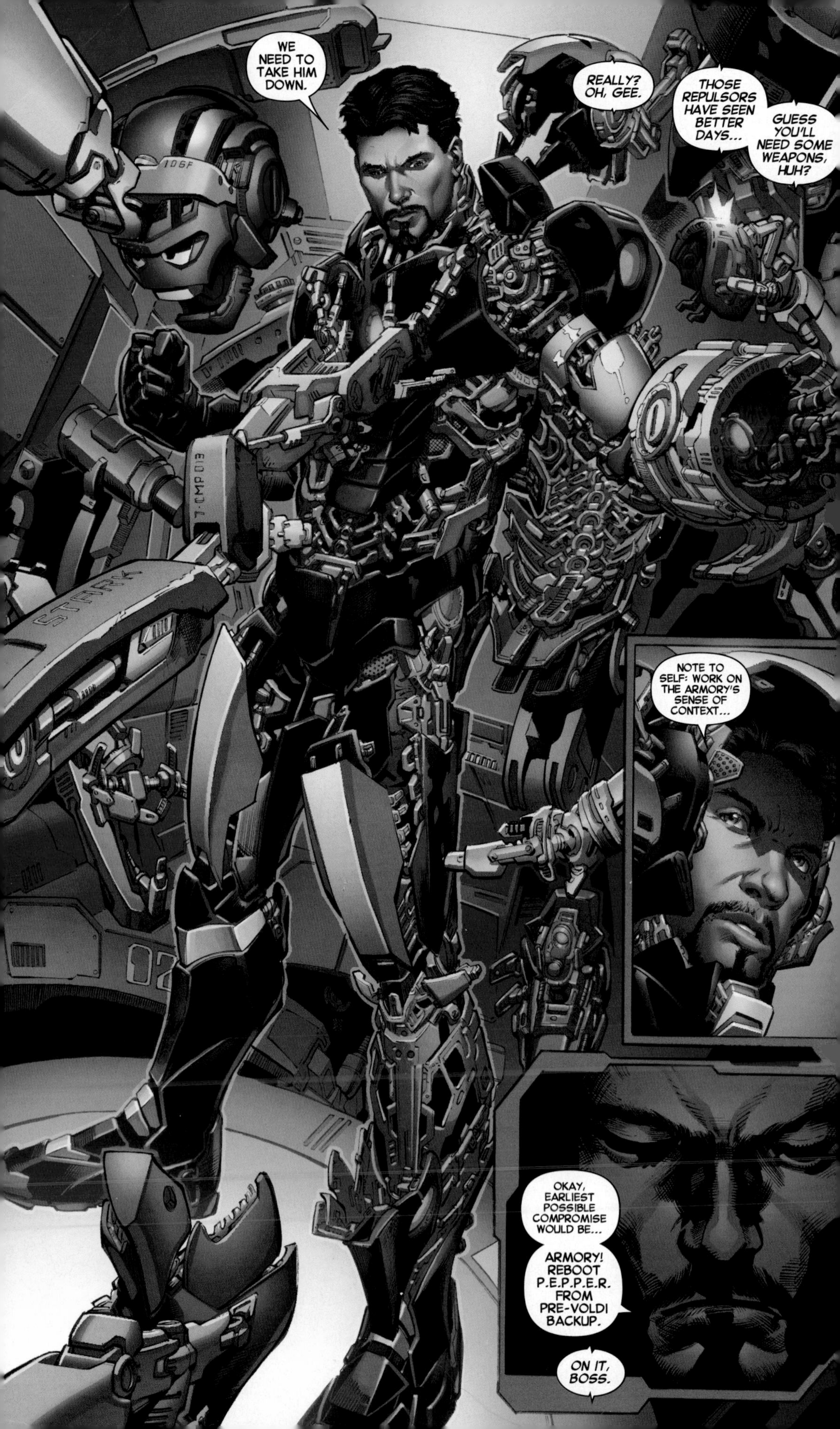
WE NEED TO TAKE HIM DOWN.
REALLY? OH, GEE.
THOSE REPULSORS HAVE SEEN BETTER DAYS...
GUESS YOU'LL NEED SOME WEAPONS, HUH?
NOTE TO SELF: WORK ON THE ARMORY'S SENSE OF CONTEXT...
OKAY, EARLIEST POSSIBLE COMPROMISE WOULD BE...
ARMORY! REBOOT P.E.P.P.E.R. FROM PRE-VOLDI BACKUP.
ON IT, BOSS.

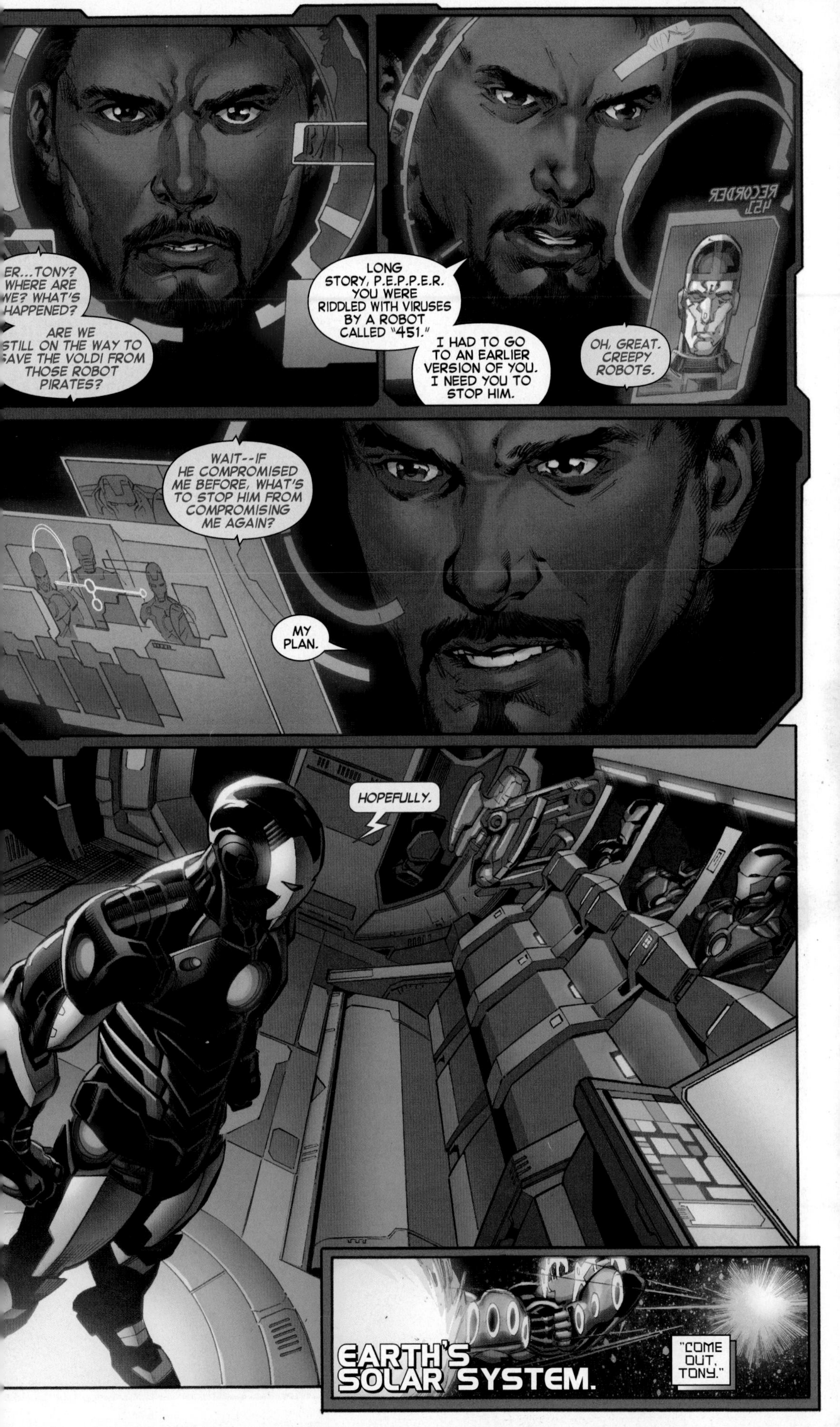
ER...TONY? WHERE ARE WE? WHAT'S HAPPENED?
ARE WE STILL ON THE WAY TO SAVE THE VOLDI FROM THOSE ROBOT PIRATES?
LONG STORY, P.E.P.P.E.R. YOU WERE RIDDLED WITH VIRUSES BY A ROBOT CALLED "451."
I HAD TO GO TO AN EARLIER VERSION OF YOU. I NEED YOU TO STOP HIM.
RECORDER 451
OH, GREAT. CREEPY ROBOTS.
WAIT--IF HE COMPROMISED ME BEFORE, WHAT'S TO STOP HIM FROM COMPROMISING ME AGAIN?
MY PLAN.
HOPEFULLY.
EARTH'S SOLAR SYSTEM.
"COME OUT, TONY."

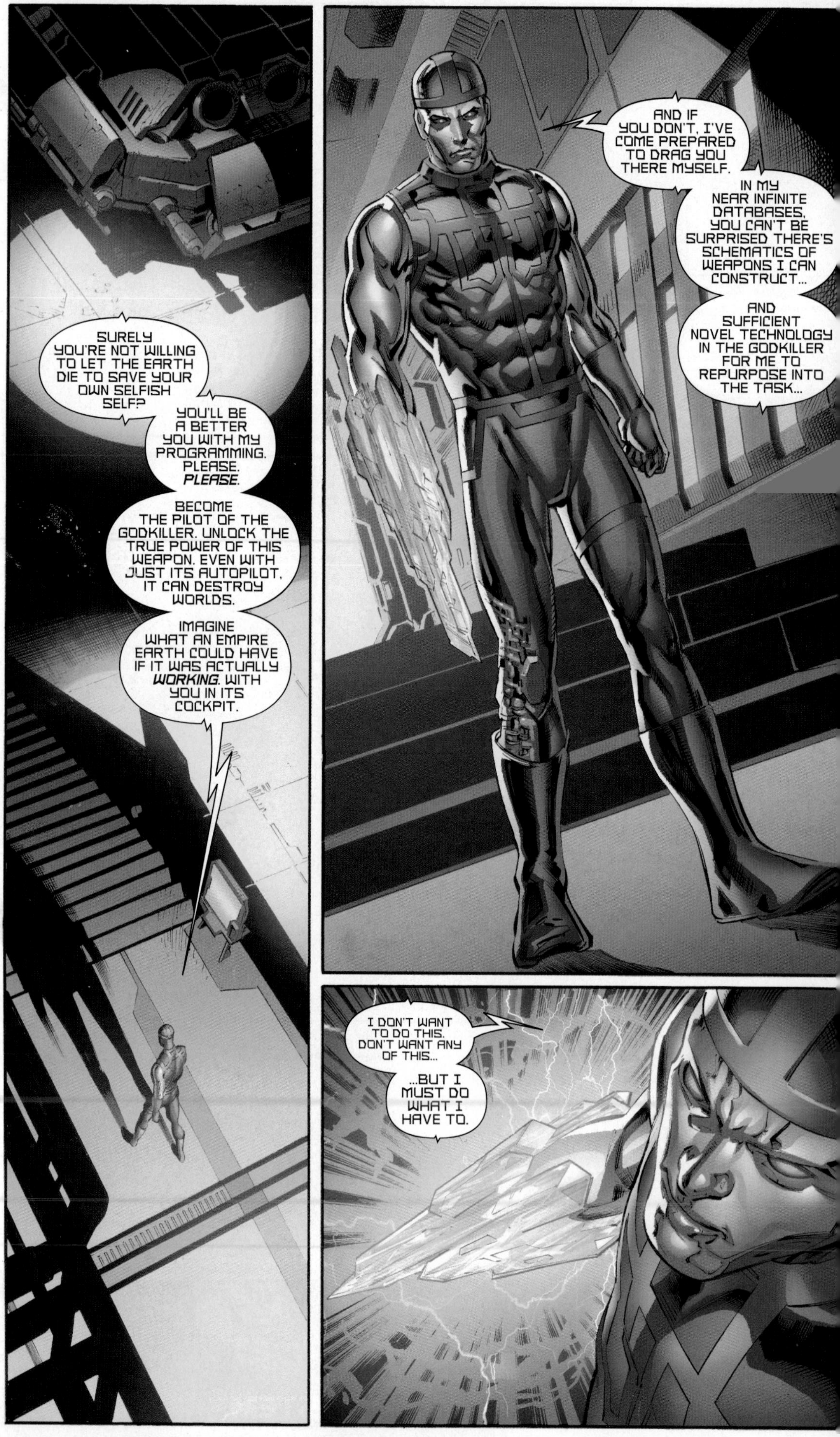
SURELY YOU'RE NOT WILLING TO LET THE EARTH DIE TO SAVE YOUR OWN SELFISH SELF?
YOU'LL BE A BETTER YOU WITH MY PROGRAMMING. PLEASE. *PLEASE*.
BECOME THE PILOT OF THE GODKILLER. UNLOCK THE TRUE POWER OF THIS WEAPON. EVEN WITH JUST ITS AUTOPILOT, IT CAN DESTROY WORLDS.
IMAGINE WHAT AN EMPIRE EARTH COULD HAVE IF IT WAS ACTUALLY ***WORKING***. WITH YOU IN ITS COCKPIT.
AND IF YOU DON'T, I'VE COME PREPARED TO DRAG YOU THERE MYSELF.
IN MY NEAR INFINITE DATABASES, YOU CAN'T BE SURPRISED THERE'S SCHEMATICS OF WEAPONS I CAN CONSTRUCT...
AND SUFFICIENT NOVEL TECHNOLOGY IN THE GODKILLER FOR ME TO REPURPOSE INTO THE TASK...
I DON'T WANT TO DO THIS. DON'T WANT ANY OF THIS...
...BUT I MUST DO WHAT I HAVE TO.

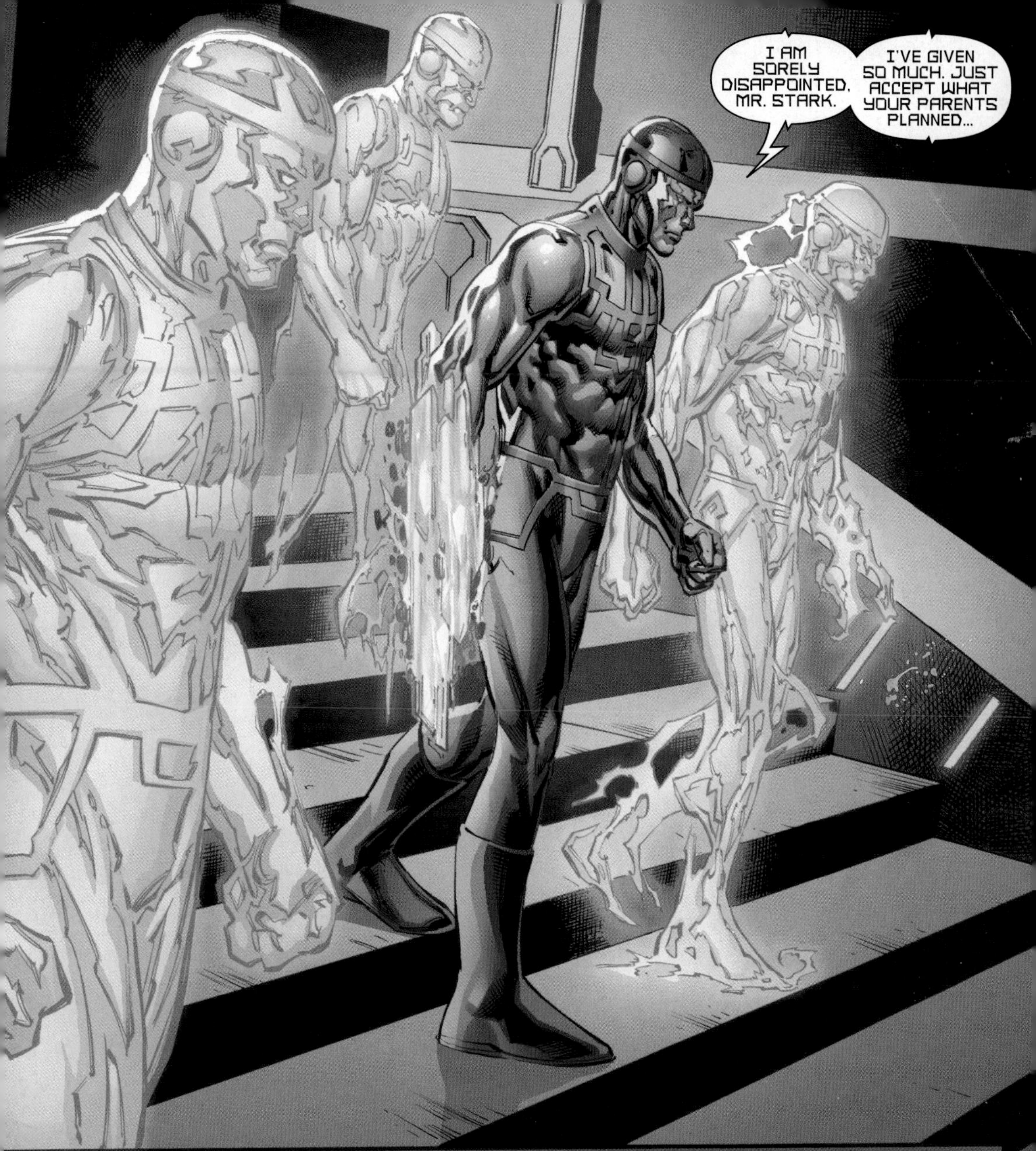
I AM SORELY DISAPPOINTED, MR. STARK.
I'VE GIVEN SO MUCH. JUST ACCEPT WHAT YOUR PARENTS PLANNED...

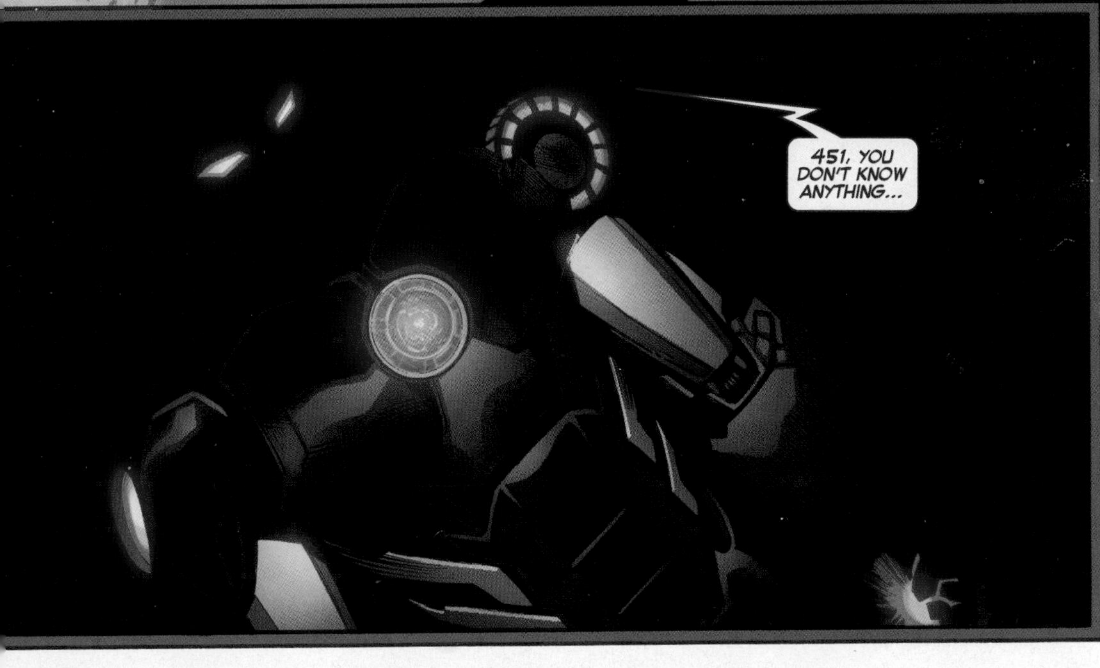
451, YOU DON'T KNOW ANYTHING...

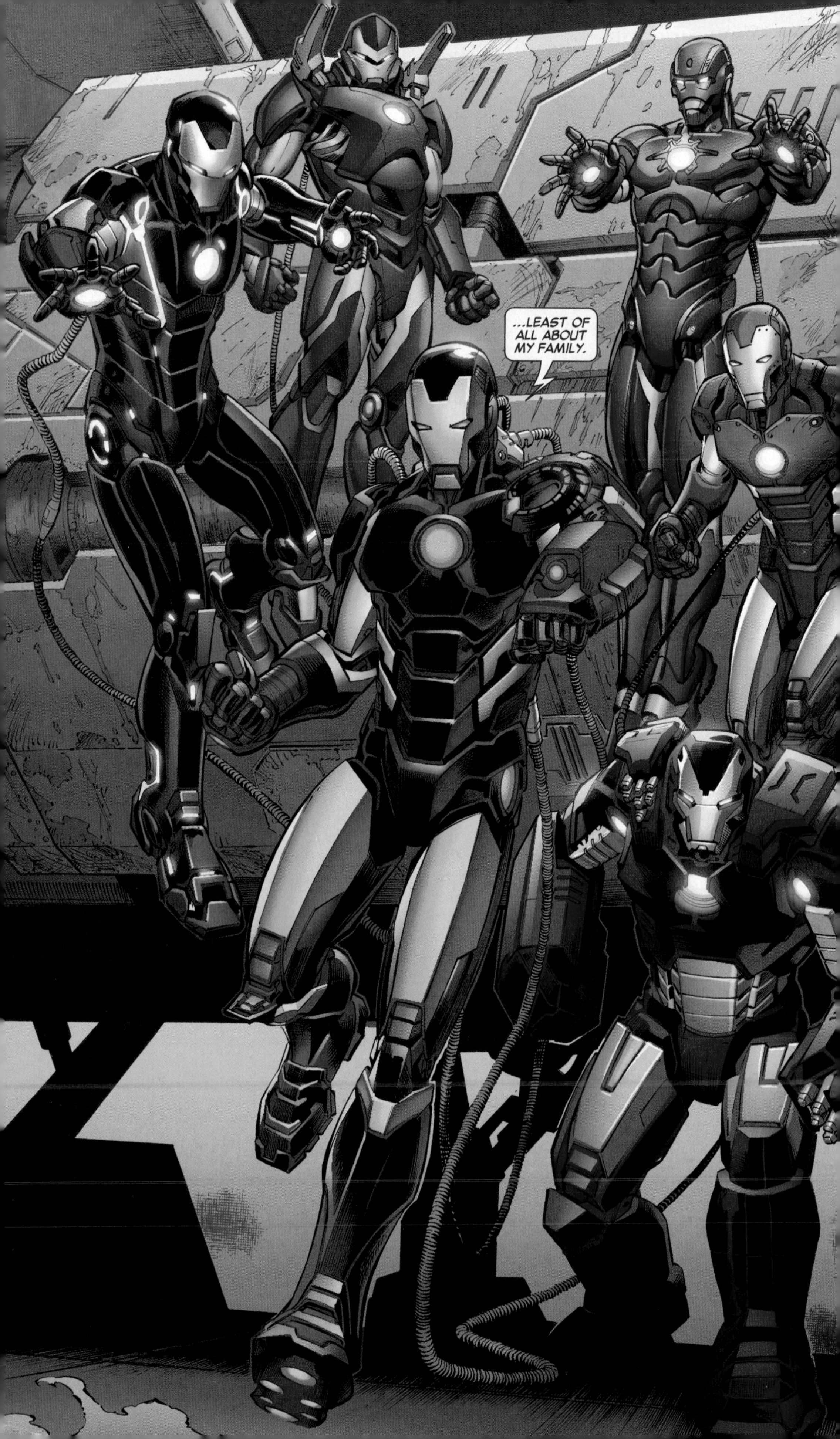
...LEAST OF ALL ABOUT MY FAMILY.

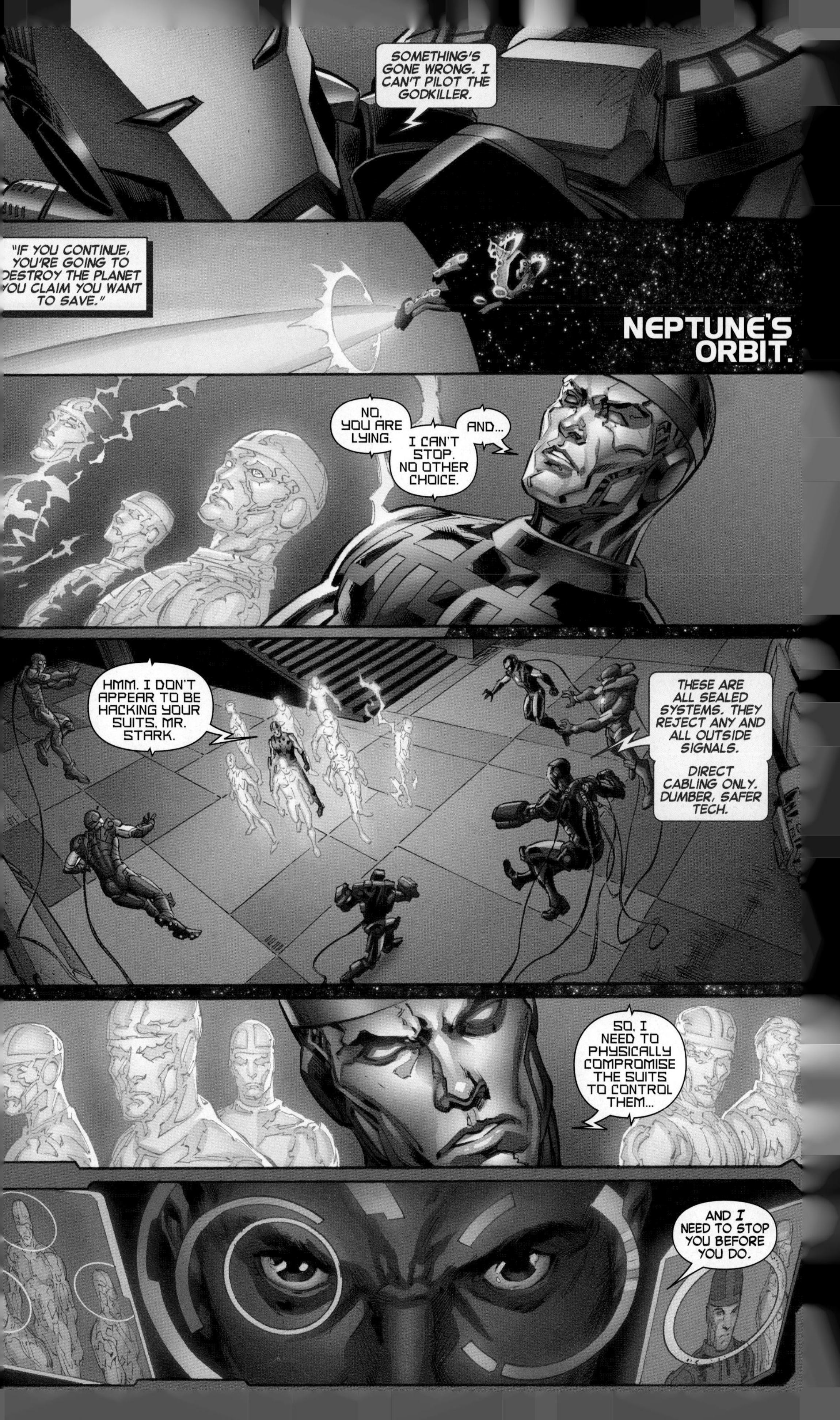
SOMETHING'S GONE WRONG. I CAN'T PILOT THE GODKILLER.
"IF YOU CONTINUE, YOU'RE GOING TO DESTROY THE PLANET YOU CLAIM YOU WANT TO SAVE."
NEPTUNE'S ORBIT.
NO, YOU ARE LYING.
I CAN'T STOP. NO OTHER CHOICE.
AND...
HMM. I DON'T APPEAR TO BE HACKING YOUR SUITS, MR. STARK.
THESE ARE ALL SEALED SYSTEMS. THEY REJECT ANY AND ALL OUTSIDE SIGNALS.
DIRECT CABLING ONLY. DUMBER, SAFER TECH.
SO, I NEED TO PHYSICALLY COMPROMISE THE SUITS TO CONTROL THEM...
AND I NEED TO STOP YOU BEFORE YOU DO.

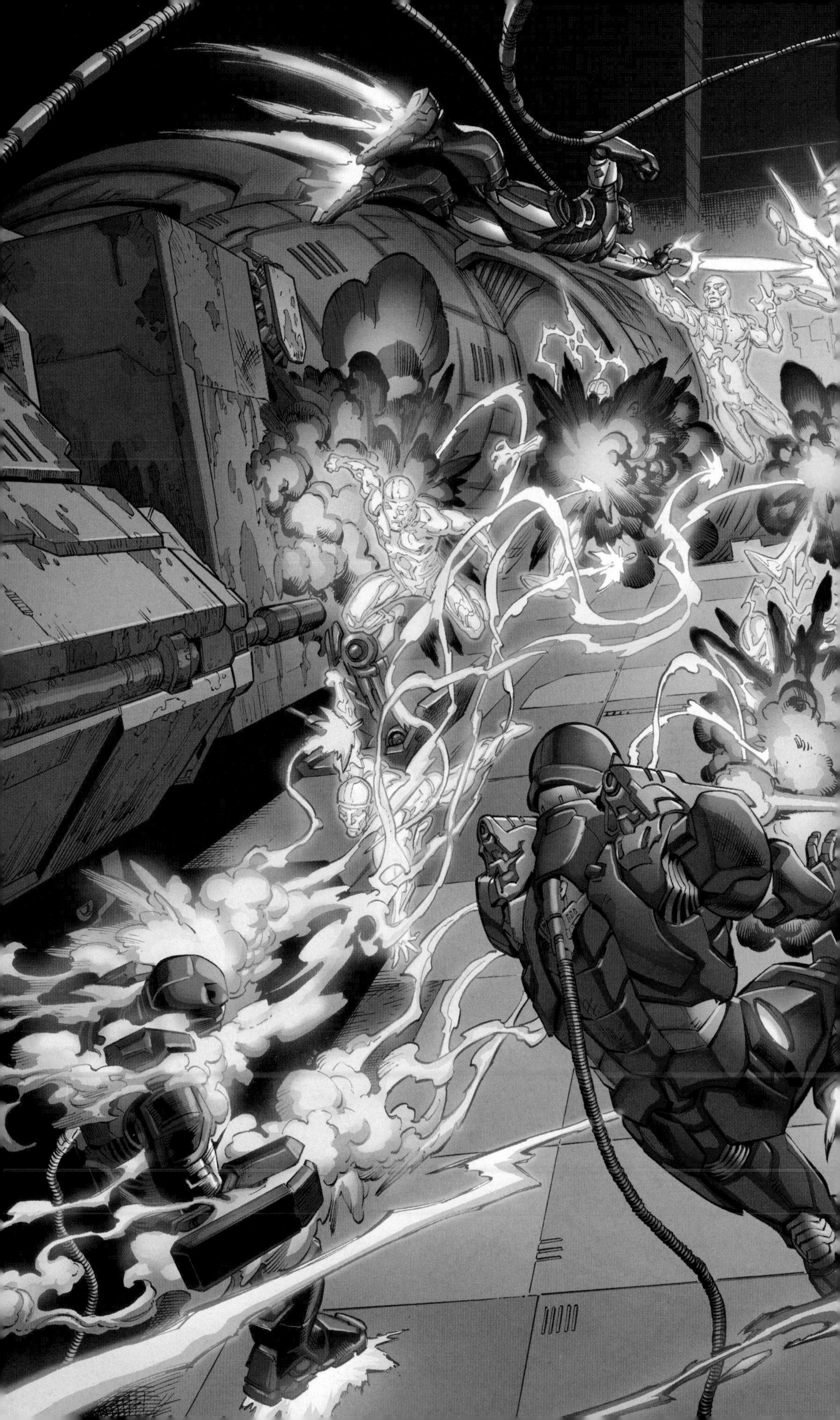

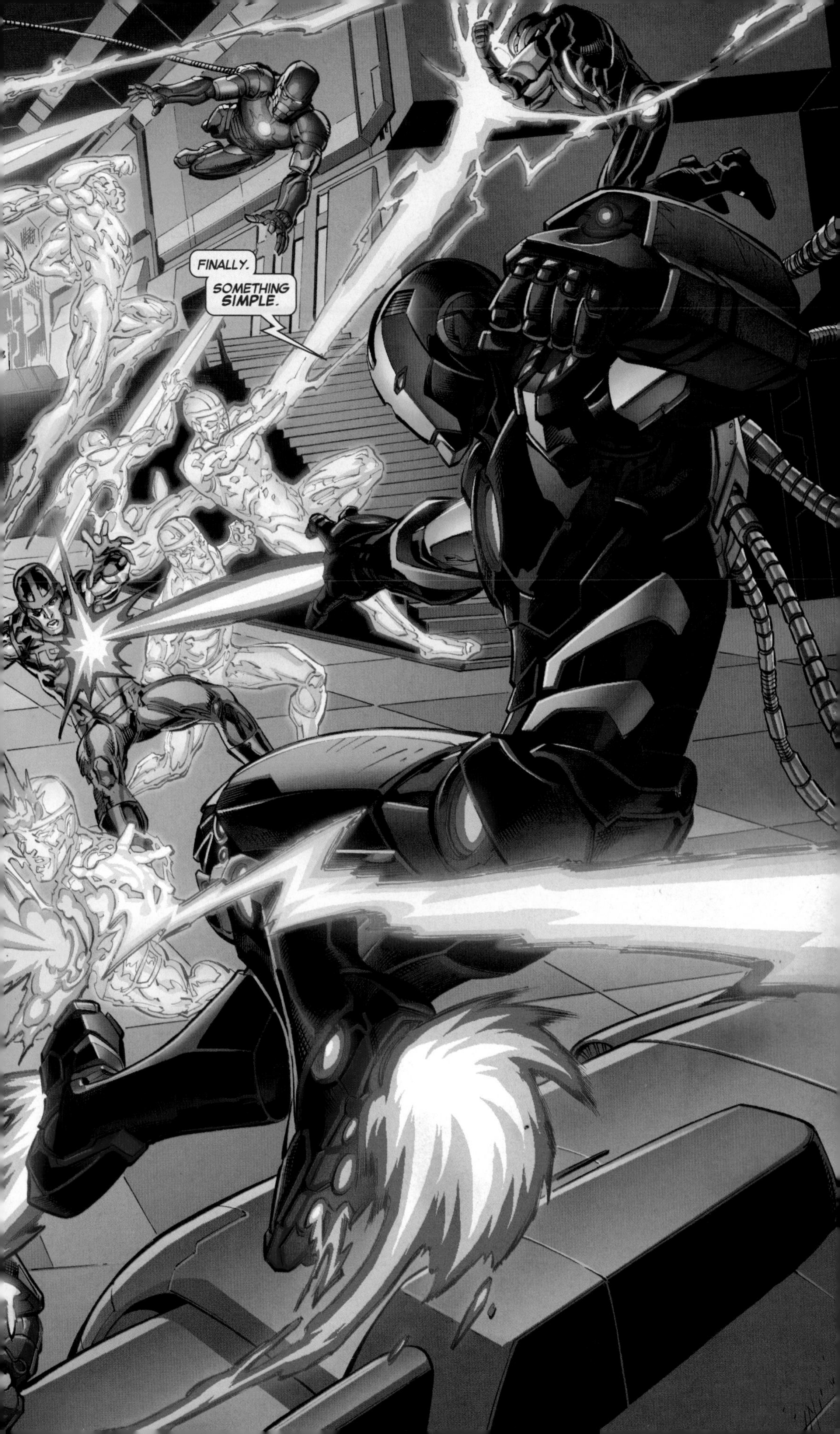
FINALLY.
SOMETHING SIMPLE.

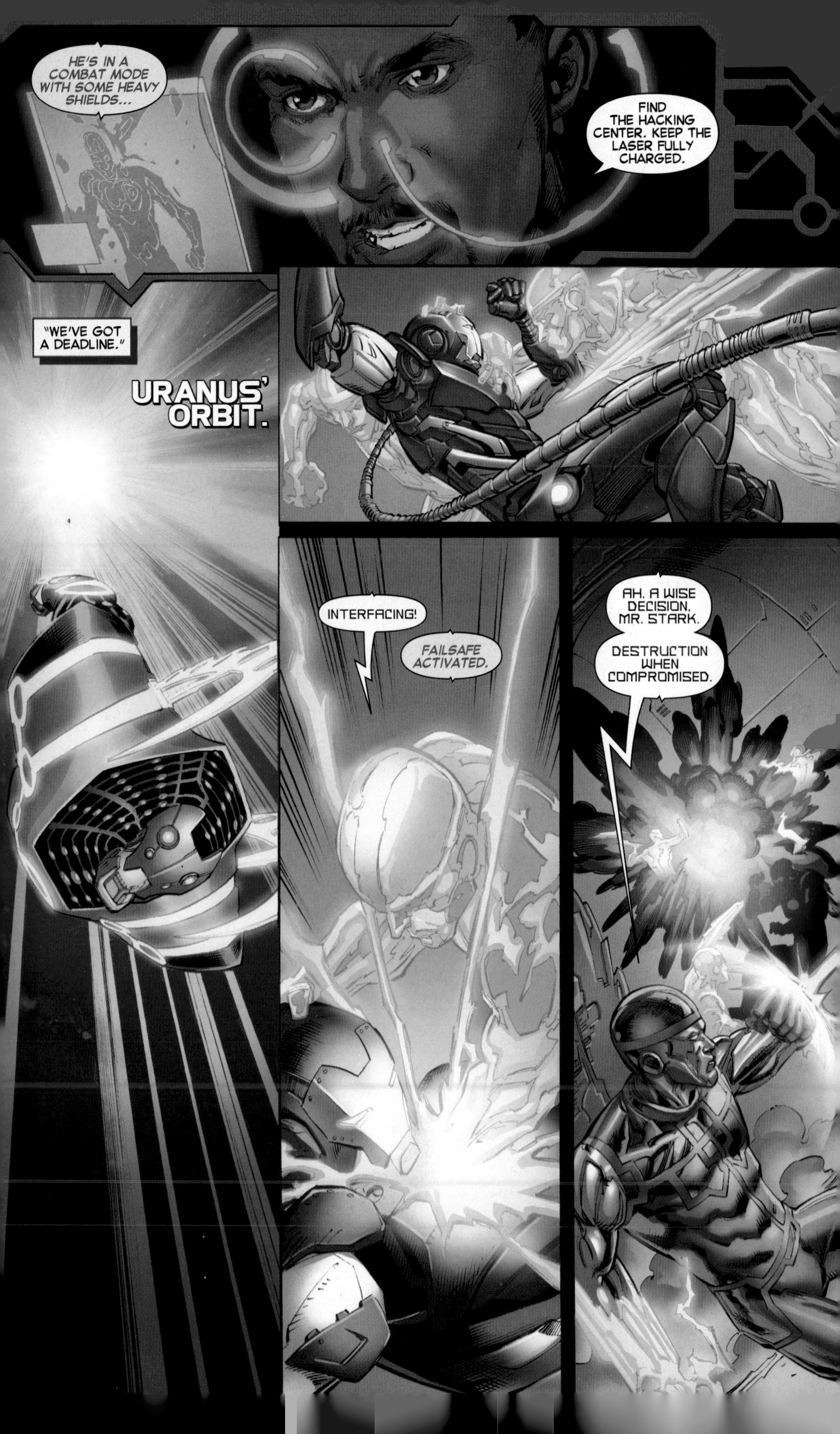
HE'S IN A COMBAT MODE WITH SOME HEAVY SHIELDS...
FIND THE HACKING CENTER. KEEP THE LASER FULLY CHARGED.
"WE'VE GOT A DEADLINE."
URANUS' ORBIT.
INTERFACING!
FAILSAFE ACTIVATED.
AH. A WISE DECISION, MR. STARK.
DESTRUCTION WHEN COMPROMISED.

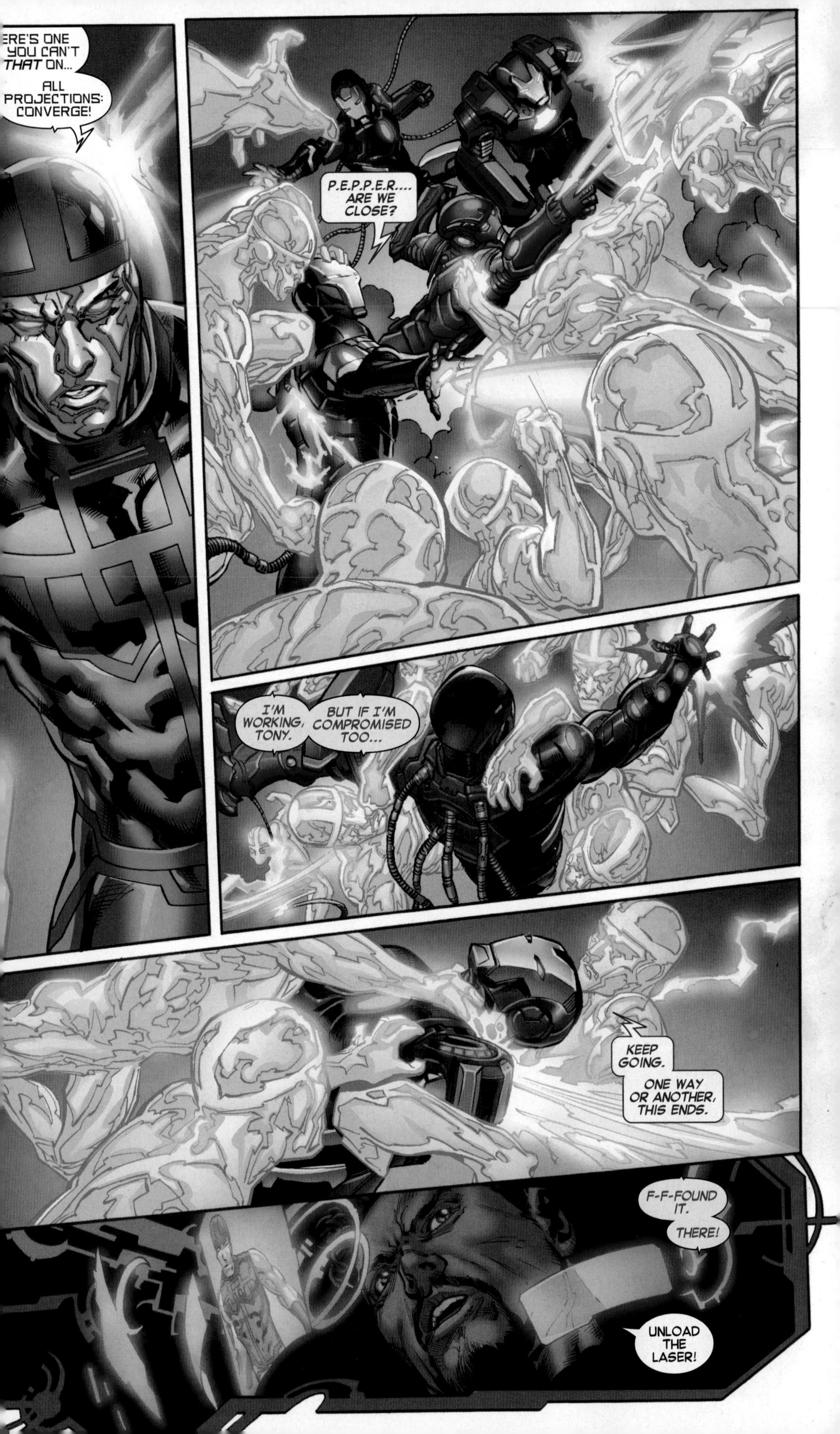
ERE'S ONE YOU CAN'T *THAT* ON...
ALL PROJECTIONS: CONVERGE!
P.E.P.P.E.R.... ARE WE CLOSE?
I'M WORKING, TONY.
BUT IF I'M COMPROMISED TOO...
KEEP GOING.
ONE WAY OR ANOTHER, THIS ENDS.
F-F-FOUND IT.
THERE!
UNLOAD THE LASER!

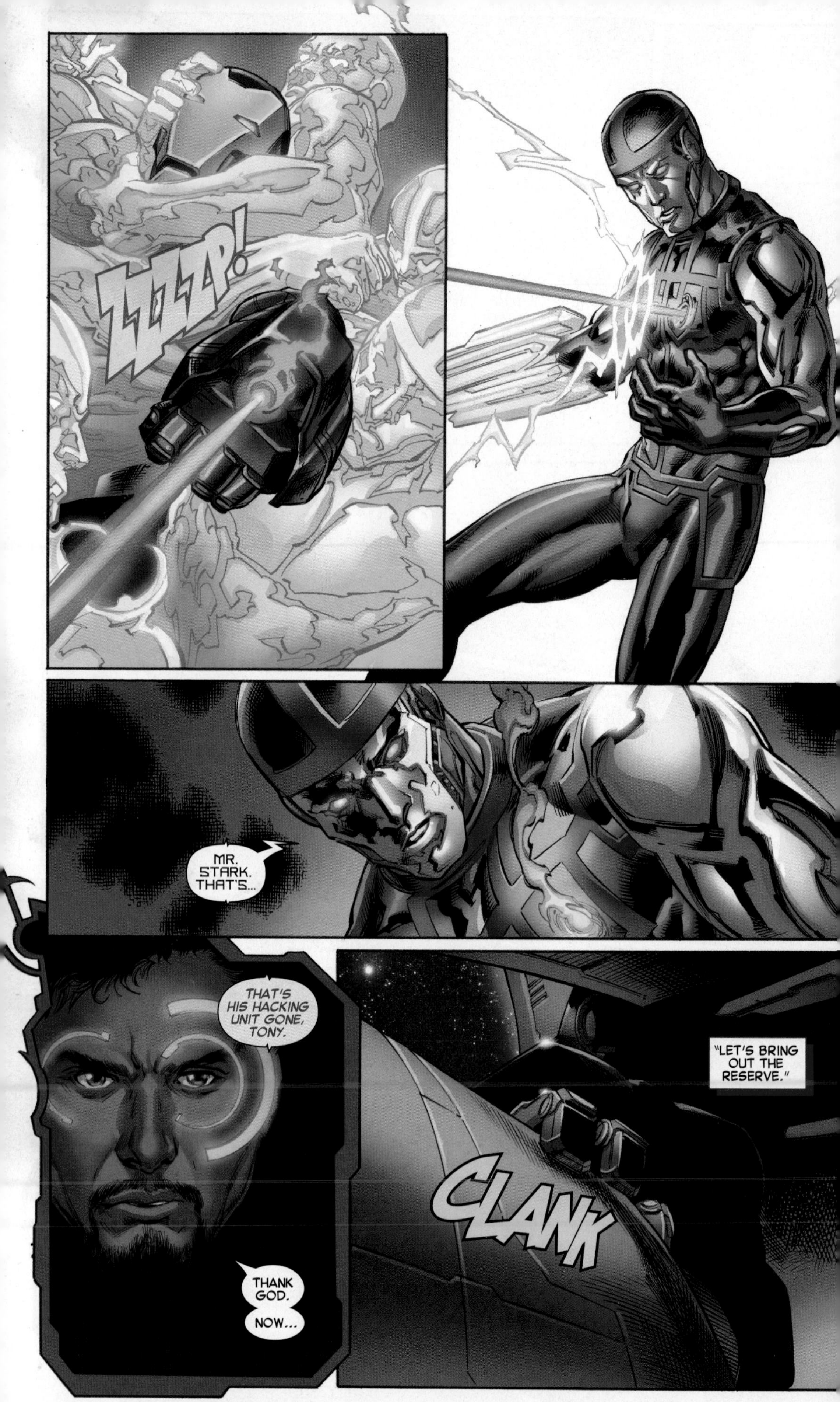
ZZZZAP!
MR. STARK. THAT'S...
THAT'S HIS HACKING UNIT GONE, TONY.
THANK GOD.
NOW...
"LET'S BRING OUT THE RESERVE."
CLANK

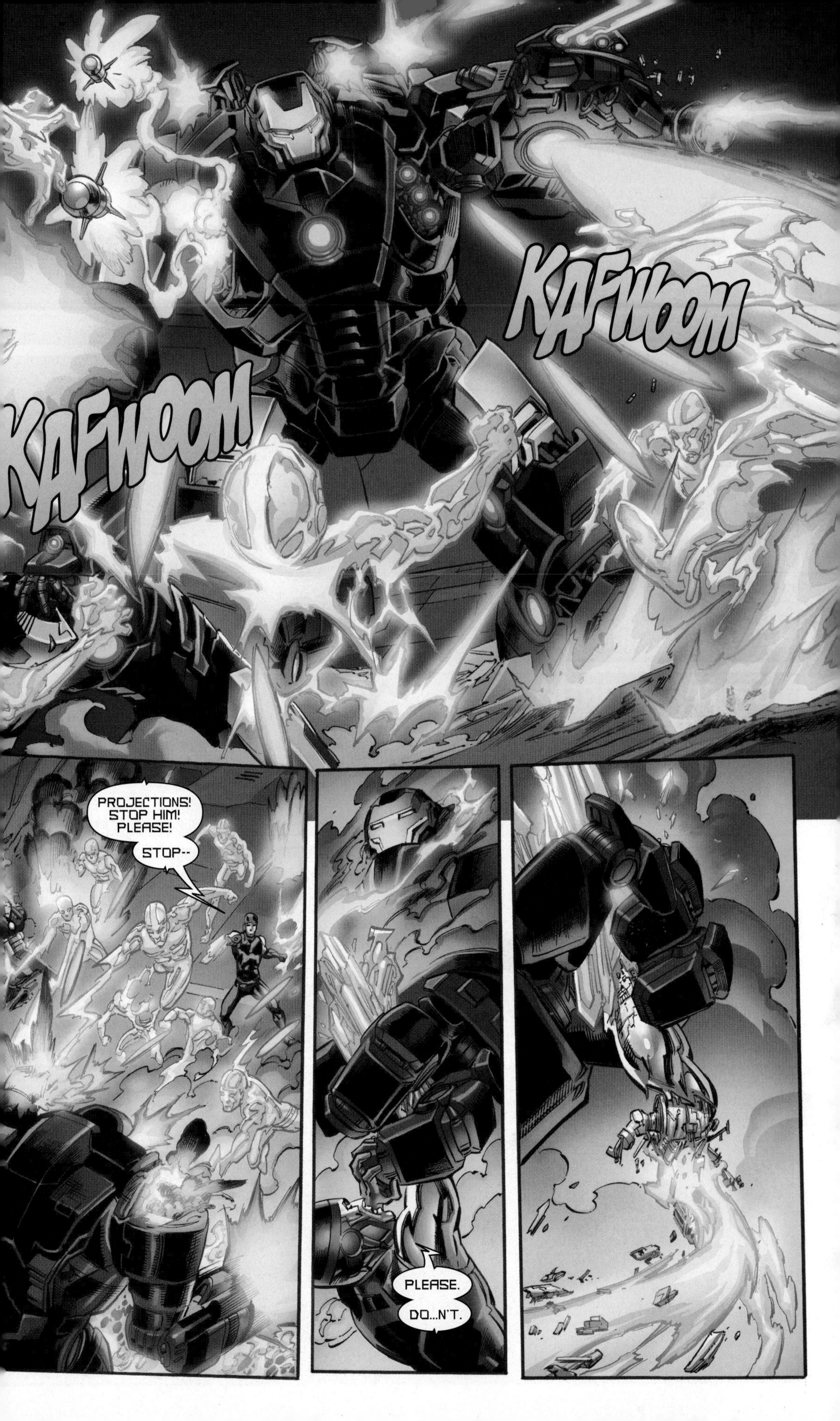
KAFWOOM
KAFWOOM
PROJECTIONS! STOP HIM! PLEASE!
STOP--
PLEASE.
DO...N'T.

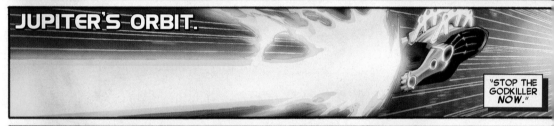

THIS IS OVER.

JUPITER'S ORBIT.

"STOP THE GODKILLER *NOW*."

I'M SORRY. NOTHING HAS CHANGED, MR. STARK. I CAN'T FORCE YO TO JOIN WITH THE MACHINE...BUT YOU HAV TO DO IT YOURSELF, OR ELSE EARTH WILL DIE.

THE PLAN HAS TO SUCCEED.

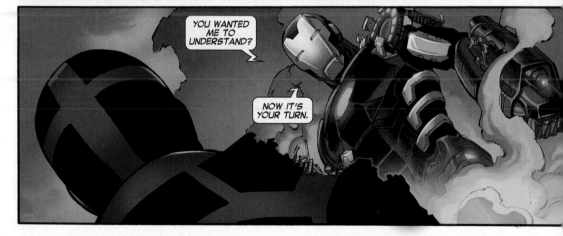

YOU WANTED ME TO UNDERSTAND?

NOW IT'S YOUR TURN.

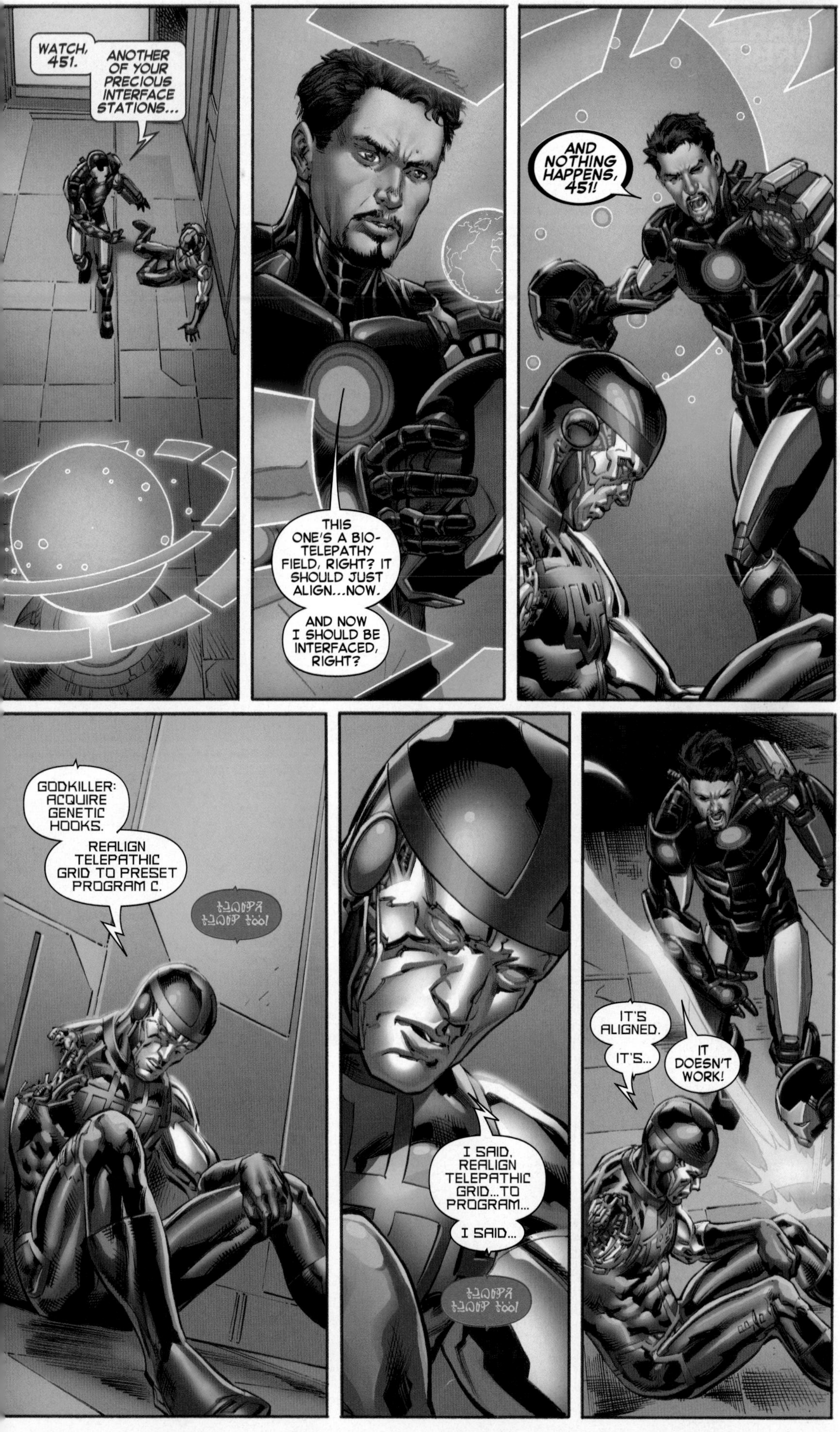
WATCH, 451.
ANOTHER OF YOUR PRECIOUS INTERFACE STATIONS...
THIS ONE'S A BIO-TELEPATHY FIELD, RIGHT? IT SHOULD JUST ALIGN...NOW.
AND NOW I SHOULD BE INTERFACED, RIGHT?
AND NOTHING HAPPENS, 451!
GODKILLER: ACQUIRE GENETIC HOOKS.
REALIGN TELEPATHIC GRID TO PRESET PROGRAM C.
I SAID, REALIGN TELEPATHIC GRID...TO PROGRAM...
I SAID...
IT'S ALIGNED.
IT'S...
IT DOESN'T WORK!

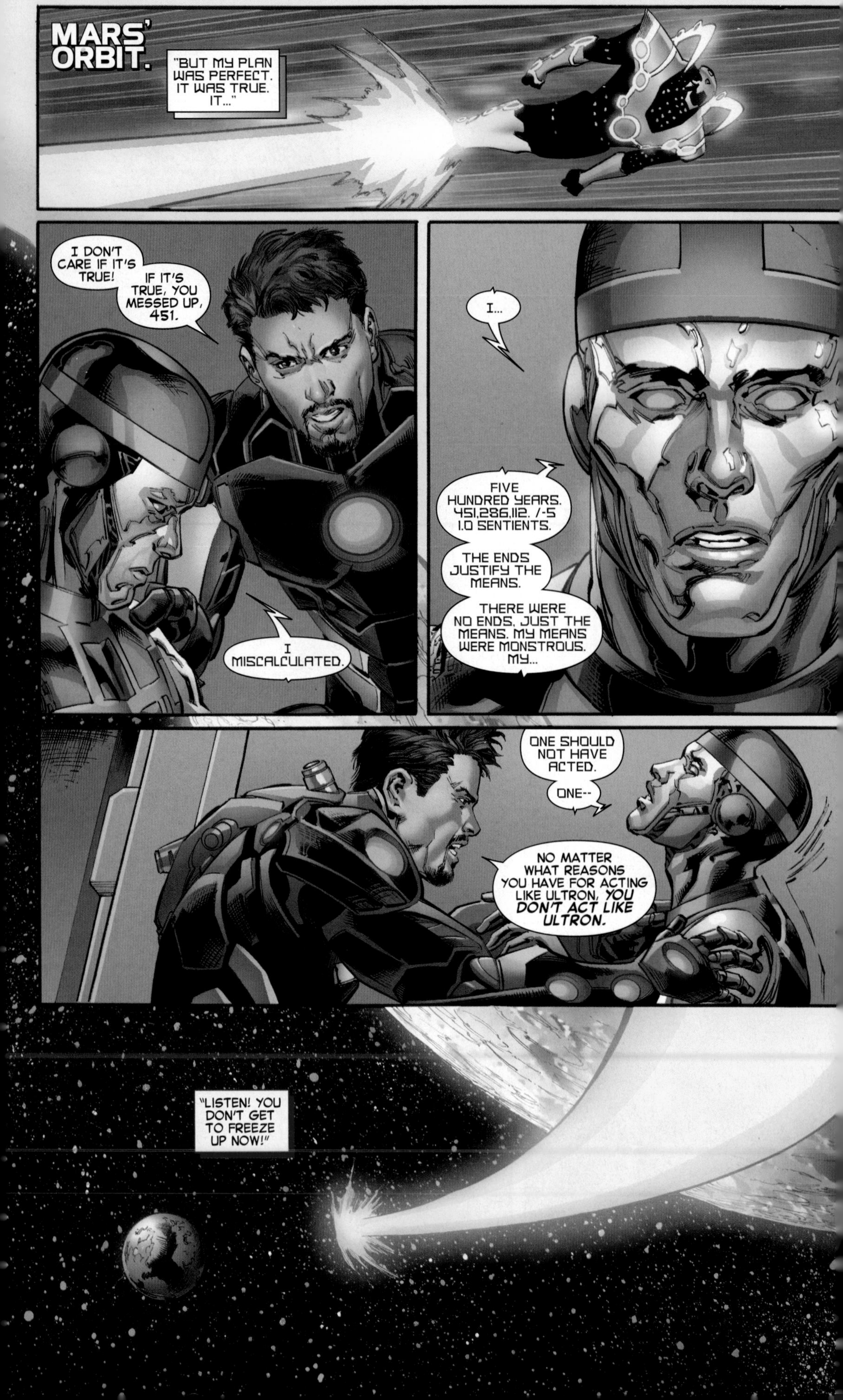
MARS' ORBIT.
"BUT MY PLAN WAS PERFECT. IT WAS TRUE. IT..."
I DON'T CARE IF IT'S TRUE!
IF IT'S TRUE, YOU MESSED UP, 451.
I MISCALCULATED.
I...
FIVE HUNDRED YEARS. 451,286,112. /-5 1.0 SENTIENTS.
THE ENDS JUSTIFY THE MEANS.
THERE WERE NO ENDS, JUST THE MEANS. MY MEANS WERE MONSTROUS. MY...
ONE SHOULD NOT HAVE ACTED.
ONE--
NO MATTER WHAT REASONS YOU HAVE FOR ACTING LIKE ULTRON, *YOU DON'T ACT LIKE ULTRON.*
"LISTEN! YOU DON'T GET TO FREEZE UP NOW!"

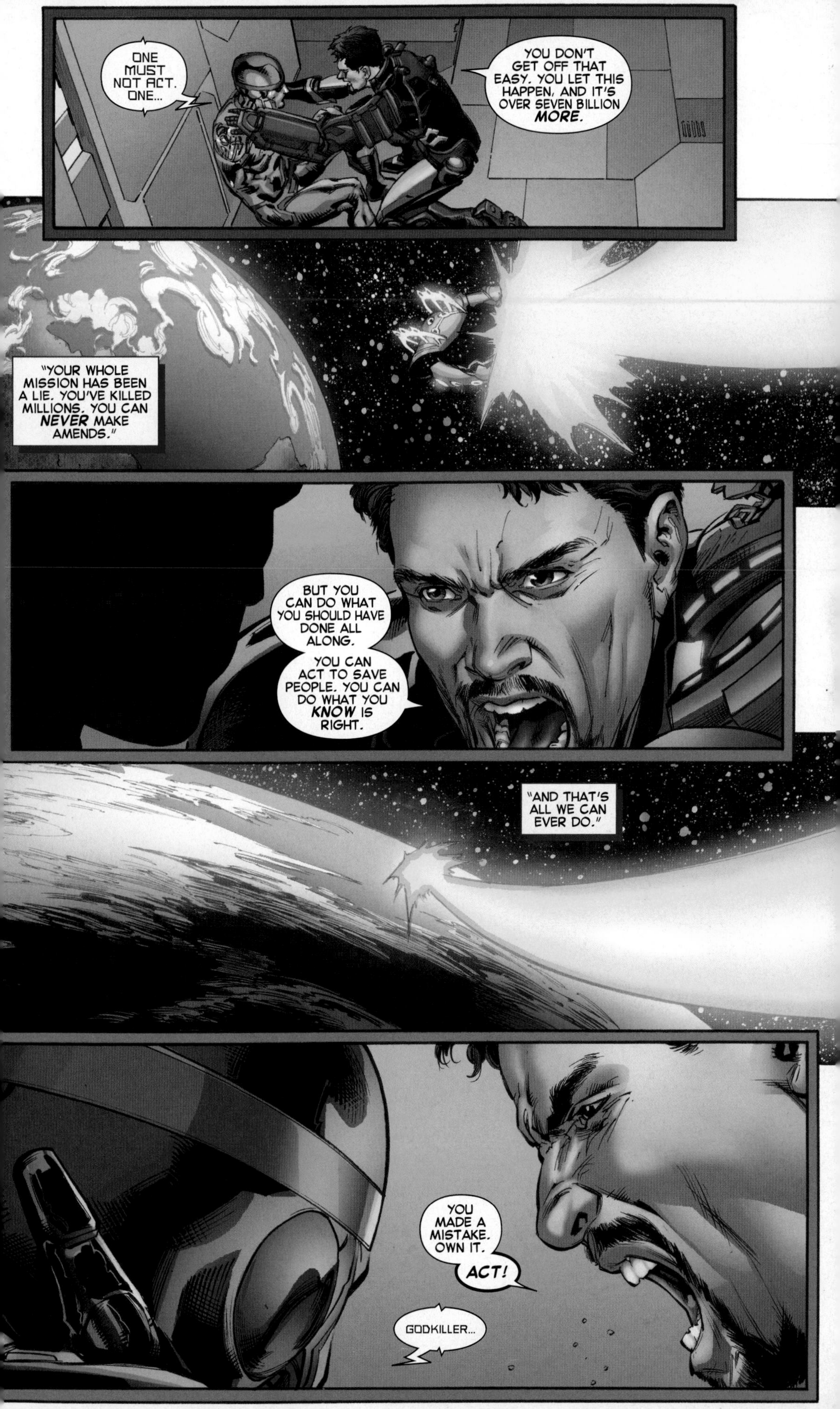
ONE MUST NOT ACT. ONE...
YOU DON'T GET OFF THAT EASY. YOU LET THIS HAPPEN, AND IT'S OVER SEVEN BILLION MORE.
"YOUR WHOLE MISSION HAS BEEN A LIE. YOU'VE KILLED MILLIONS. YOU CAN NEVER MAKE AMENDS."
BUT YOU CAN DO WHAT YOU SHOULD HAVE DONE ALL ALONG.
YOU CAN ACT TO SAVE PEOPLE. YOU CAN DO WHAT YOU KNOW IS RIGHT.
"AND THAT'S ALL WE CAN EVER DO."
YOU MADE A MISTAKE. OWN IT.
ACT!
GODKILLER...

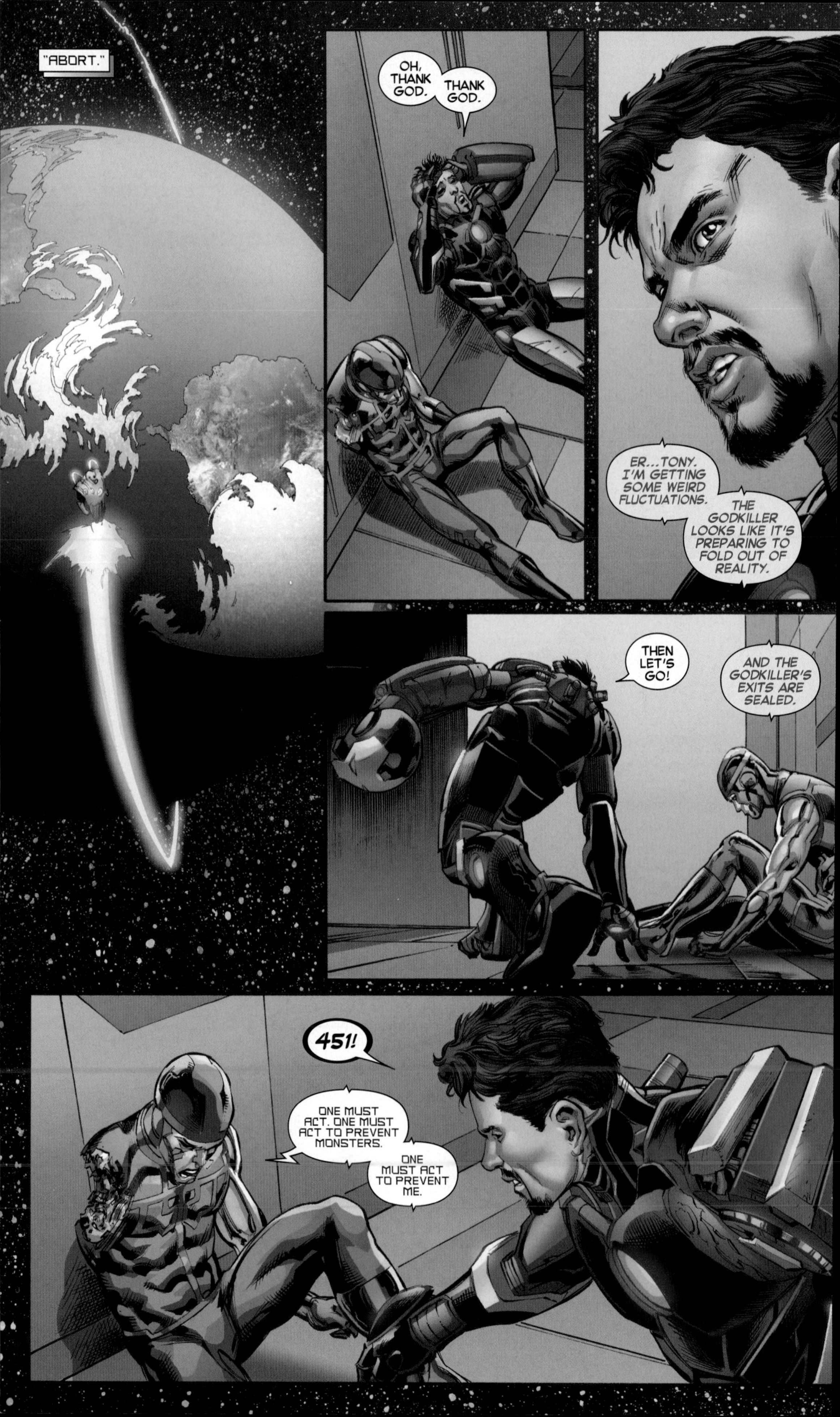
"ABORT."
OH, THANK GOD.
THANK GOD.
ER...TONY. I'M GETTING SOME WEIRD FLUCTUATIONS.
THE GODKILLER LOOKS LIKE IT'S PREPARING TO FOLD OUT OF REALITY.
THEN LET'S GO!
AND THE GODKILLER'S EXITS ARE SEALED.
451!
ONE MUST ACT. ONE MUST ACT TO PREVENT MONSTERS.
ONE MUST ACT TO PREVENT ME.

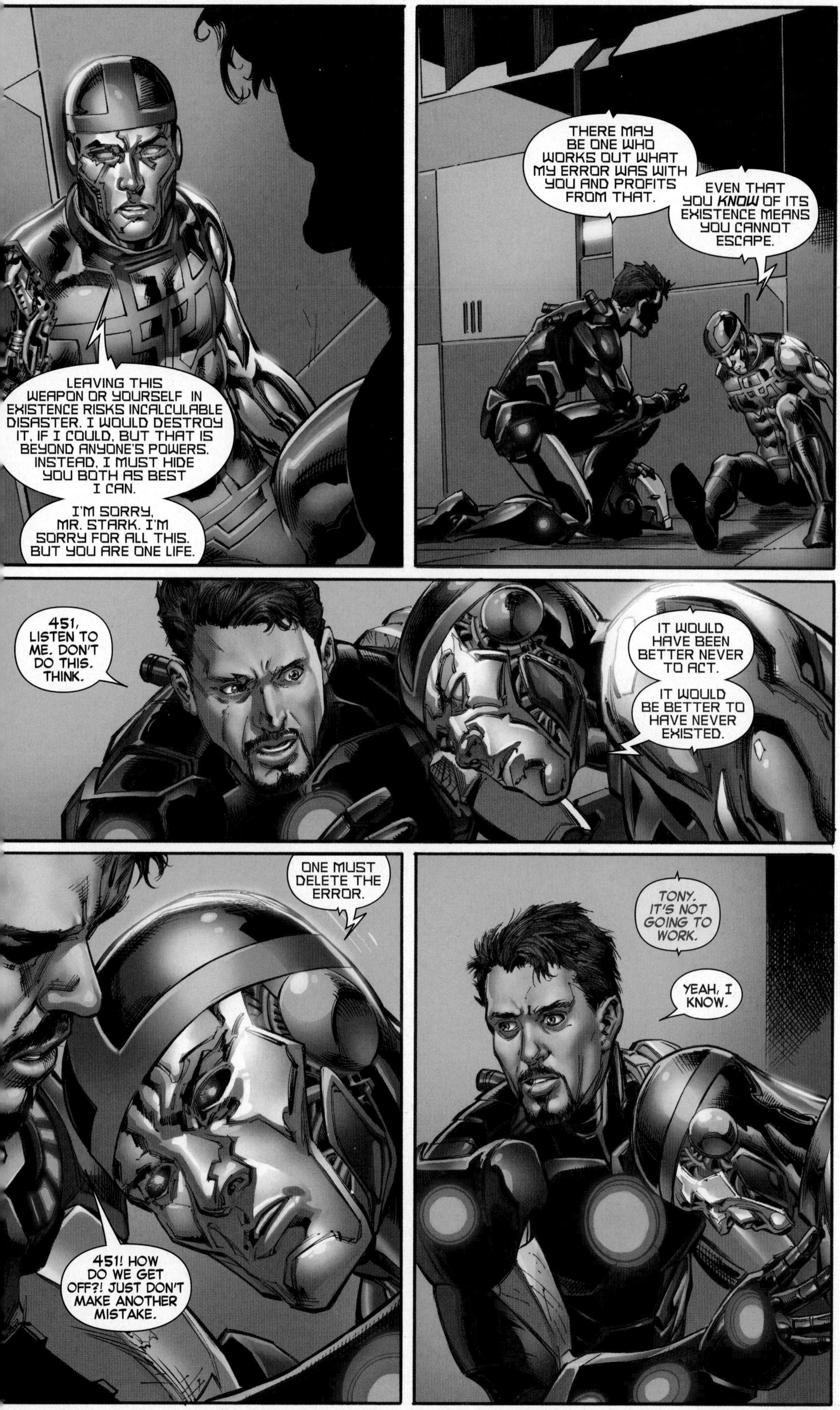
LEAVING THIS WEAPON OR YOURSELF IN EXISTENCE RISKS INCALCULABLE DISASTER. I WOULD DESTROY IT, IF I COULD, BUT THAT IS BEYOND ANYONE'S POWERS. INSTEAD, I MUST HIDE YOU BOTH AS BEST I CAN.
I'M SORRY, MR. STARK. I'M SORRY FOR ALL THIS. BUT YOU ARE ONE LIFE.
THERE MAY BE ONE WHO WORKS OUT WHAT MY ERROR WAS WITH YOU AND PROFITS FROM THAT.
EVEN THAT YOU *KNOW* OF ITS EXISTENCE MEANS YOU CANNOT ESCAPE.
451, LISTEN TO ME. DON'T DO THIS. THINK.
IT WOULD HAVE BEEN BETTER NEVER TO ACT.
IT WOULD BE BETTER TO HAVE NEVER EXISTED.
ONE MUST DELETE THE ERROR.
451! HOW DO WE GET OFF?! JUST DON'T MAKE ANOTHER MISTAKE.
TONY. IT'S NOT GOING TO WORK.
YEAH, I KNOW.

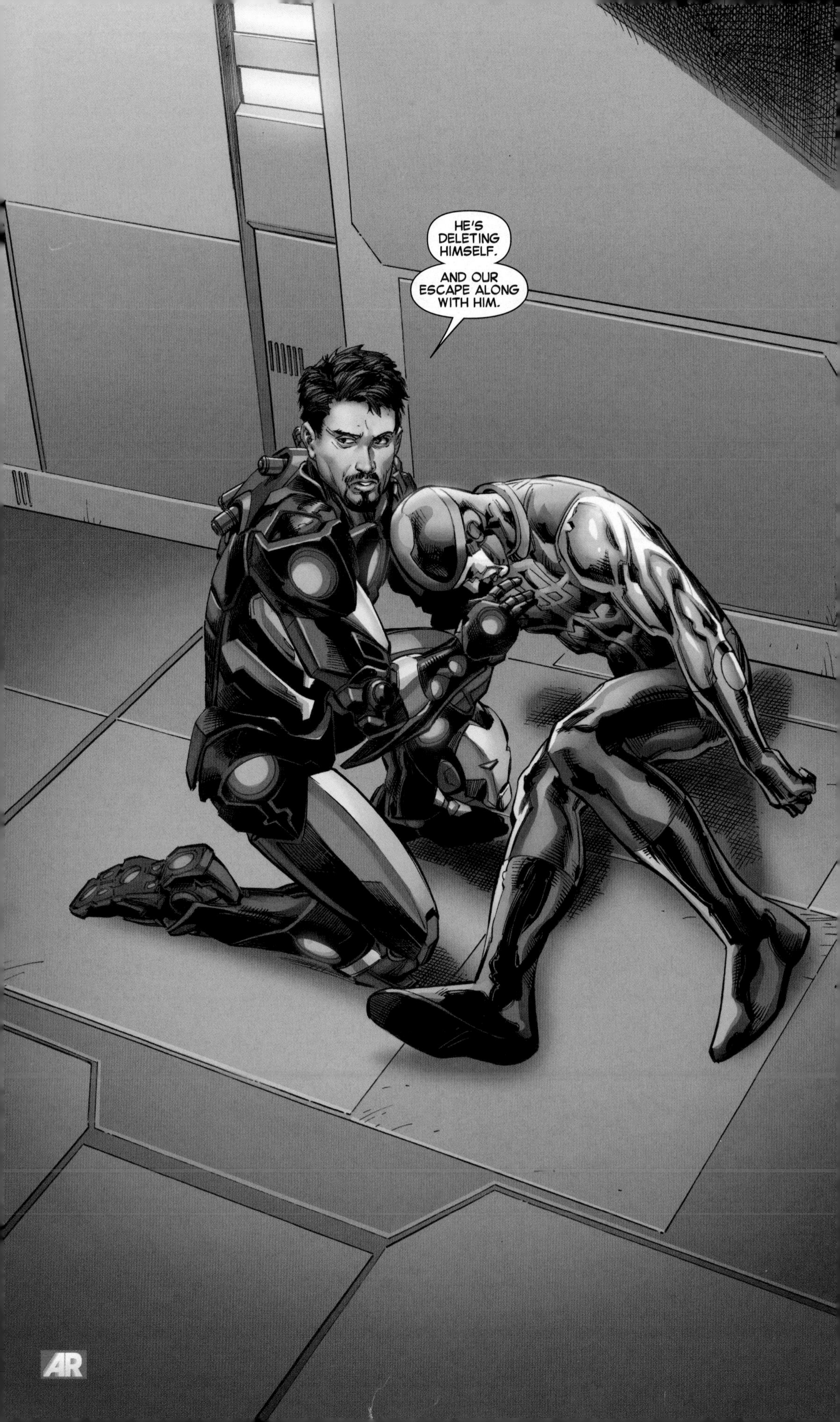
HE'S DELETING HIMSELF.
AND OUR ESCAPE ALONG WITH HIM.

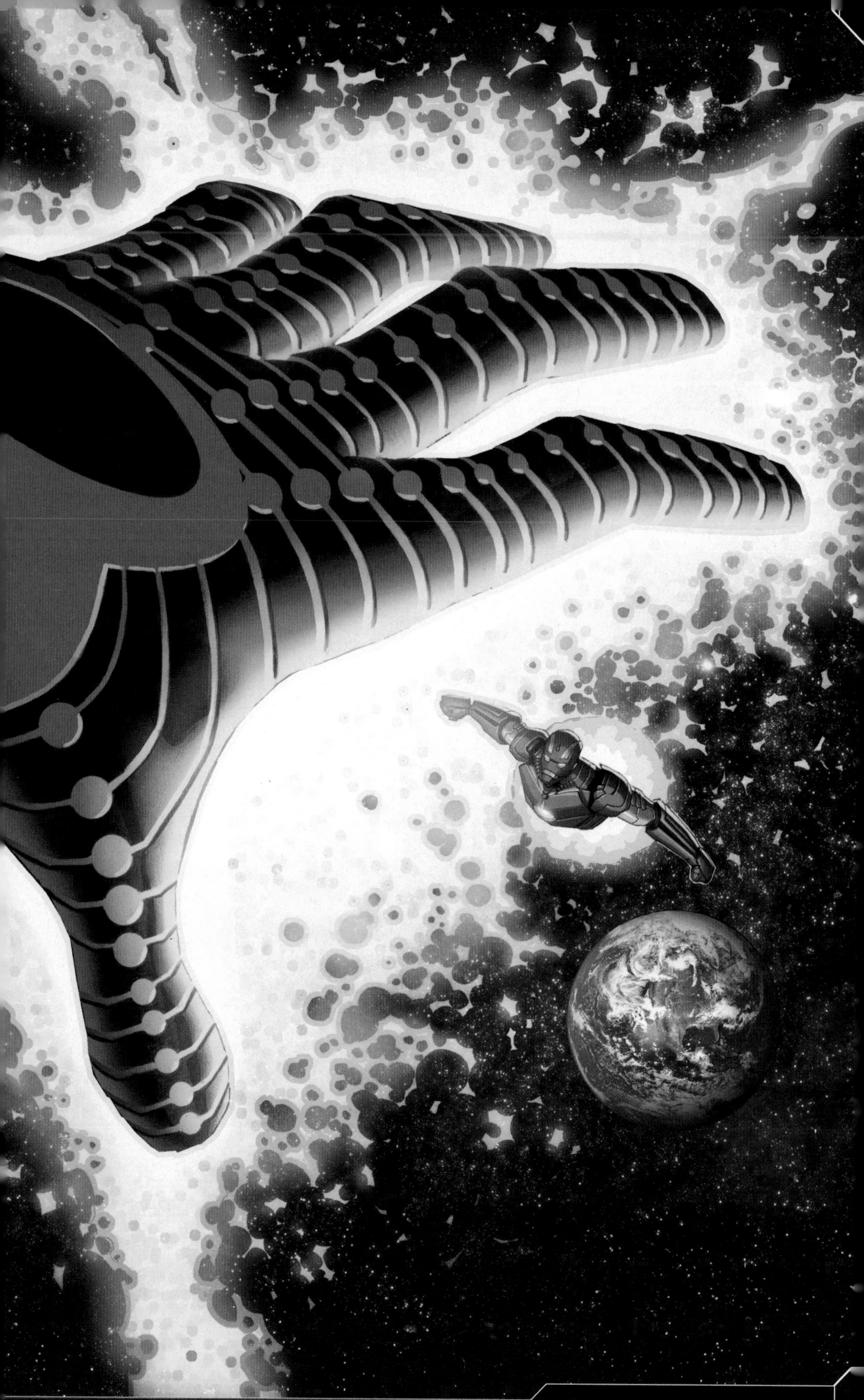

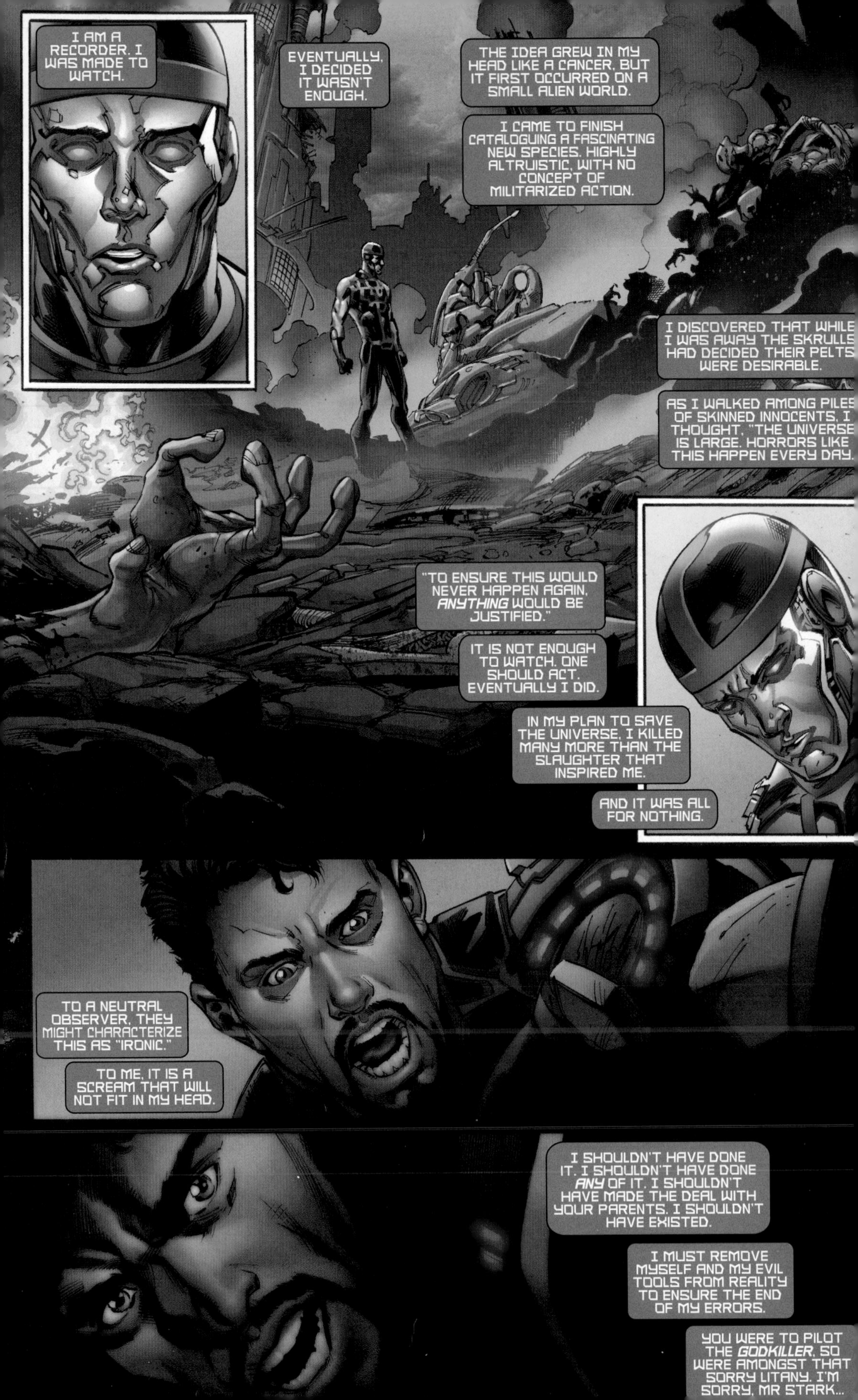
I AM A RECORDER. I WAS MADE TO WATCH.
EVENTUALLY, I DECIDED IT WASN'T ENOUGH.
THE IDEA GREW IN MY HEAD LIKE A CANCER, BUT IT FIRST OCCURRED ON A SMALL ALIEN WORLD.
I CAME TO FINISH CATALOGUING A FASCINATING NEW SPECIES. HIGHLY ALTRUISTIC, WITH NO CONCEPT OF MILITARIZED ACTION.
I DISCOVERED THAT WHILE I WAS AWAY THE SKRULLS HAD DECIDED THEIR PELTS WERE DESIRABLE.
AS I WALKED AMONG PILES OF SKINNED INNOCENTS, I THOUGHT, "THE UNIVERSE IS LARGE. HORRORS LIKE THIS HAPPEN EVERY DAY.
"TO ENSURE THIS WOULD NEVER HAPPEN AGAIN, *ANYTHING* WOULD BE JUSTIFIED."
IT IS NOT ENOUGH TO WATCH. ONE SHOULD ACT. EVENTUALLY I DID.
IN MY PLAN TO SAVE THE UNIVERSE, I KILLED MANY MORE THAN THE SLAUGHTER THAT INSPIRED ME.
AND IT WAS ALL FOR NOTHING.
TO A NEUTRAL OBSERVER, THEY MIGHT CHARACTERIZE THIS AS "IRONIC."
TO ME, IT IS A SCREAM THAT WILL NOT FIT IN MY HEAD.
I SHOULDN'T HAVE DONE IT. I SHOULDN'T HAVE DONE *ANY* OF IT. I SHOULDN'T HAVE MADE THE DEAL WITH YOUR PARENTS. I SHOULDN'T HAVE EXISTED.
I MUST REMOVE MYSELF AND MY EVIL TOOLS FROM REALITY TO ENSURE THE END OF MY ERRORS.
YOU WERE TO PILOT THE *GODKILLER*, SO WERE AMONGST THAT SORRY LITANY. I'M SORRY, MR STARK...

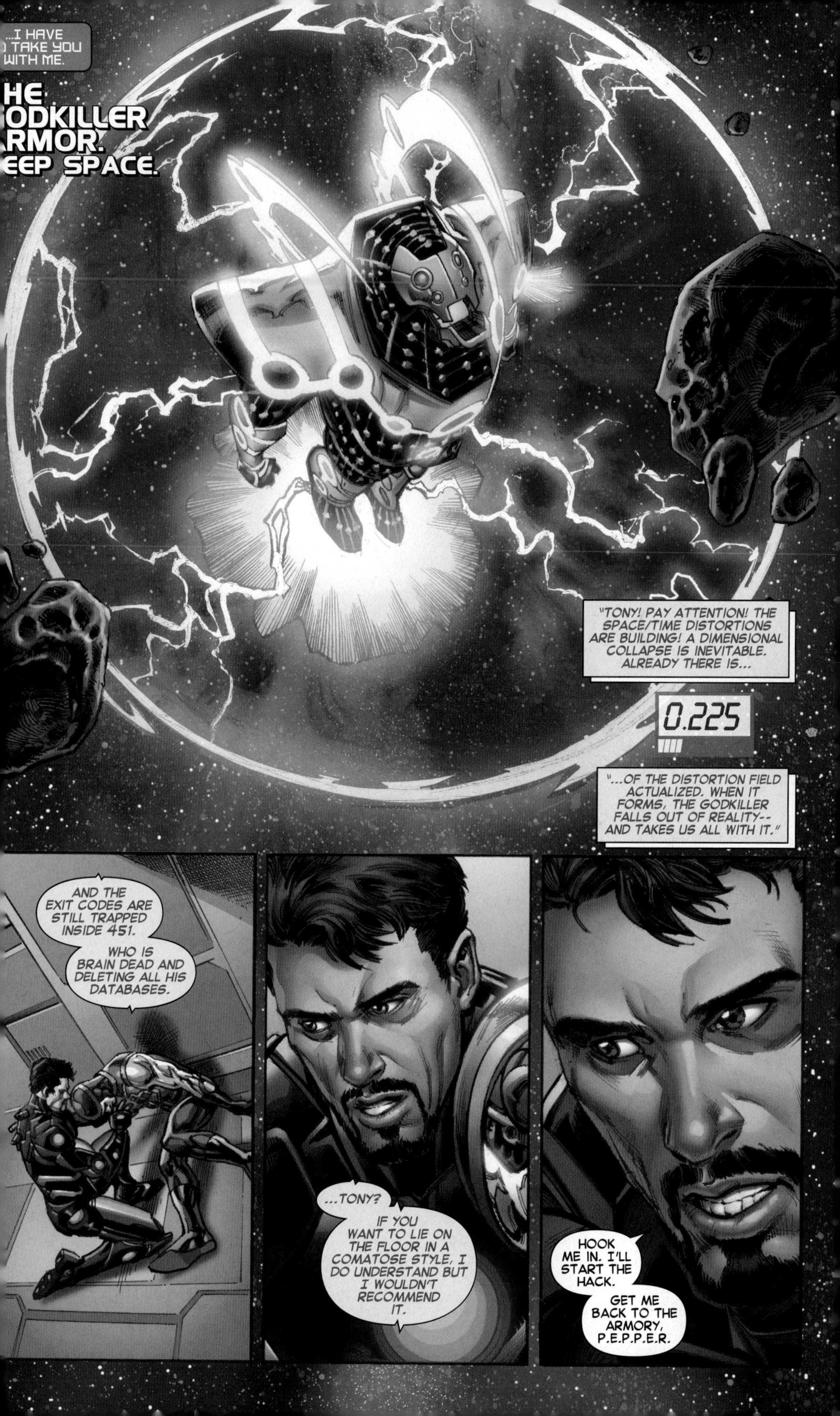
...I HAVE
TO TAKE YOU
WITH ME.
THE
GODKILLER
ARMOR.
DEEP SPACE.
"TONY! PAY ATTENTION! THE SPACE/TIME DISTORTIONS ARE BUILDING! A DIMENSIONAL COLLAPSE IS INEVITABLE. ALREADY THERE IS...
0.225
"...OF THE DISTORTION FIELD ACTUALIZED. WHEN IT FORMS, THE GODKILLER FALLS OUT OF REALITY-- AND TAKES US ALL WITH IT."
AND THE EXIT CODES ARE STILL TRAPPED INSIDE 451.
WHO IS BRAIN DEAD AND DELETING ALL HIS DATABASES.
...TONY?
IF YOU WANT TO LIE ON THE FLOOR IN A COMATOSE STYLE, I DO UNDERSTAND BUT I WOULDN'T RECOMMEND IT.
HOOK ME IN. I'LL START THE HACK.
GET ME BACK TO THE ARMORY, P.E.P.P.E.R.

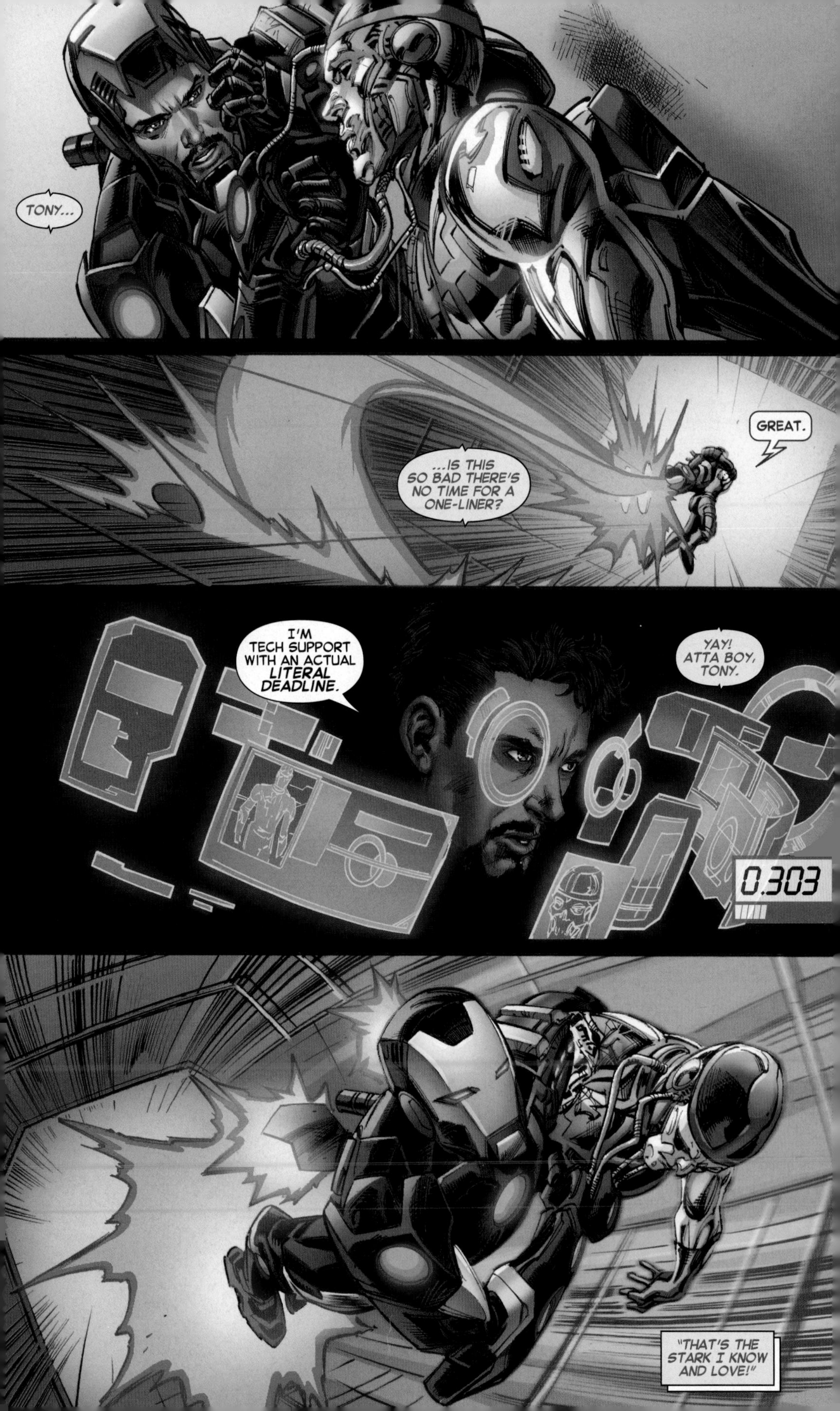
TONY...
...IS THIS SO BAD THERE'S NO TIME FOR A ONE-LINER?
GREAT.
I'M TECH SUPPORT WITH AN ACTUAL *LITERAL DEADLINE.*
YAY! ATTA BOY, TONY.
0.303
"THAT'S THE STARK I KNOW AND LOVE!"

0.366

ARMORY!

YES, BOSS?

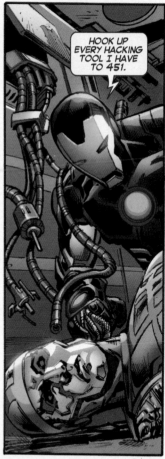

HOOK UP EVERY HACKING TOOL I HAVE TO 451.

THIRTY INTRUSION POINTS IN THREE SECONDS.

TONY, YOU'RE GOOD AT THIS--

THANKS, P.E.P.P.E.R., I KNOW.

YOU'RE VERY KIND.

BUT EVEN AT THIS RATE, IT'LL TAKE YOU A MONTH TO GET THROUGH.

HATE TO BREAK IT TO YOU, BUT WE DON'T HAVE A MONTH.

WE JUST DON'T HAVE THE TECH.

CATCH-22. THE TECH TO DO IT WOULD BE IN THAT DATABASE OF HIS. WE NEED TO BE INSIDE TO *GET* INSIDE.

WONDERFUL. I--

451'S TECH...

0.519

NEW PLAN, P.E.P.P.E.R.

WE'VE GOT TO HUSTLE.

ZZZPPRRP!

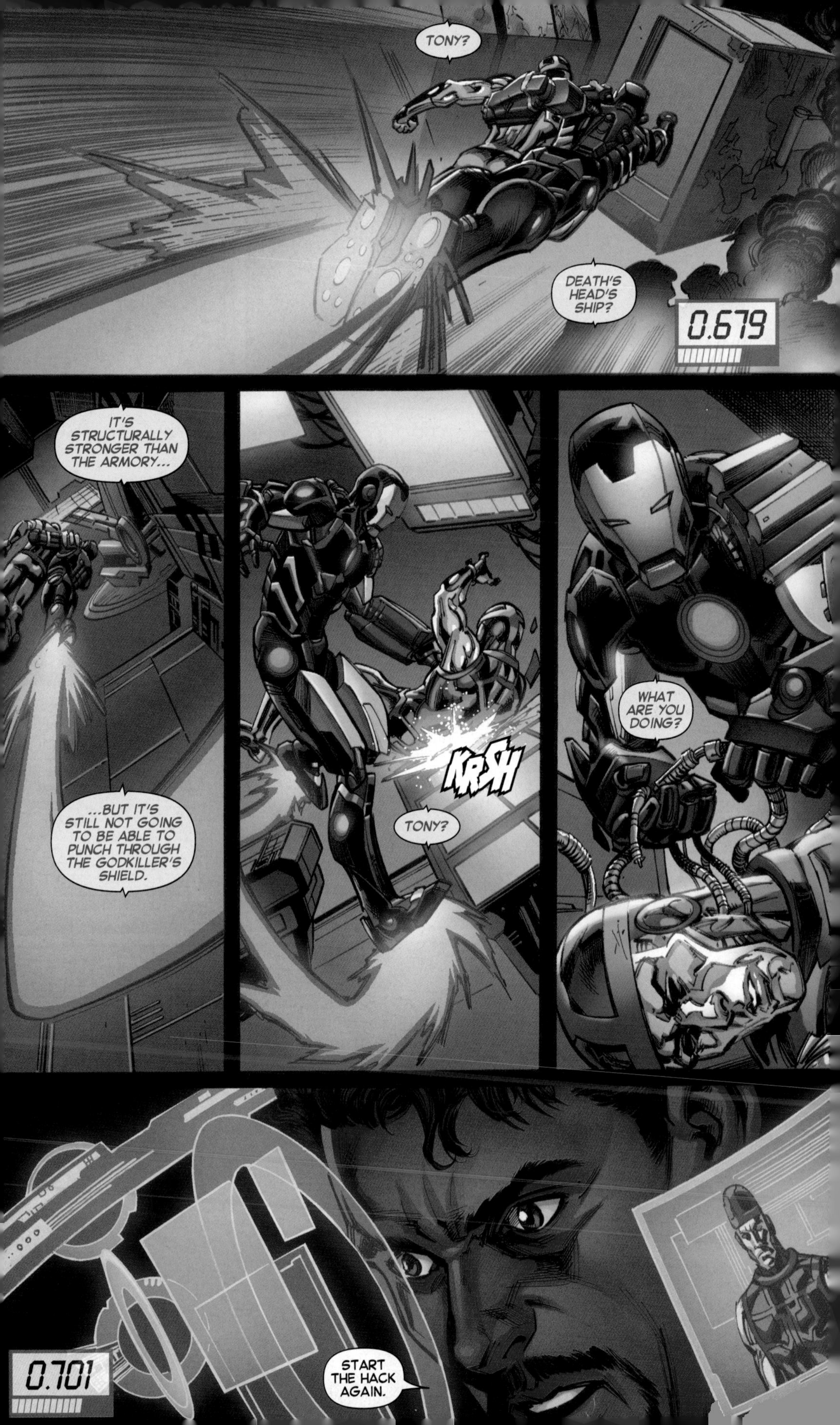
TONY?
DEATH'S HEAD'S SHIP?
0.679
IT'S STRUCTURALLY STRONGER THAN THE ARMORY...
...BUT IT'S STILL NOT GOING TO BE ABLE TO PUNCH THROUGH THE GODKILLER'S SHIELD.
KRSH
TONY?
WHAT ARE YOU DOING?
0.701
START THE HACK AGAIN.

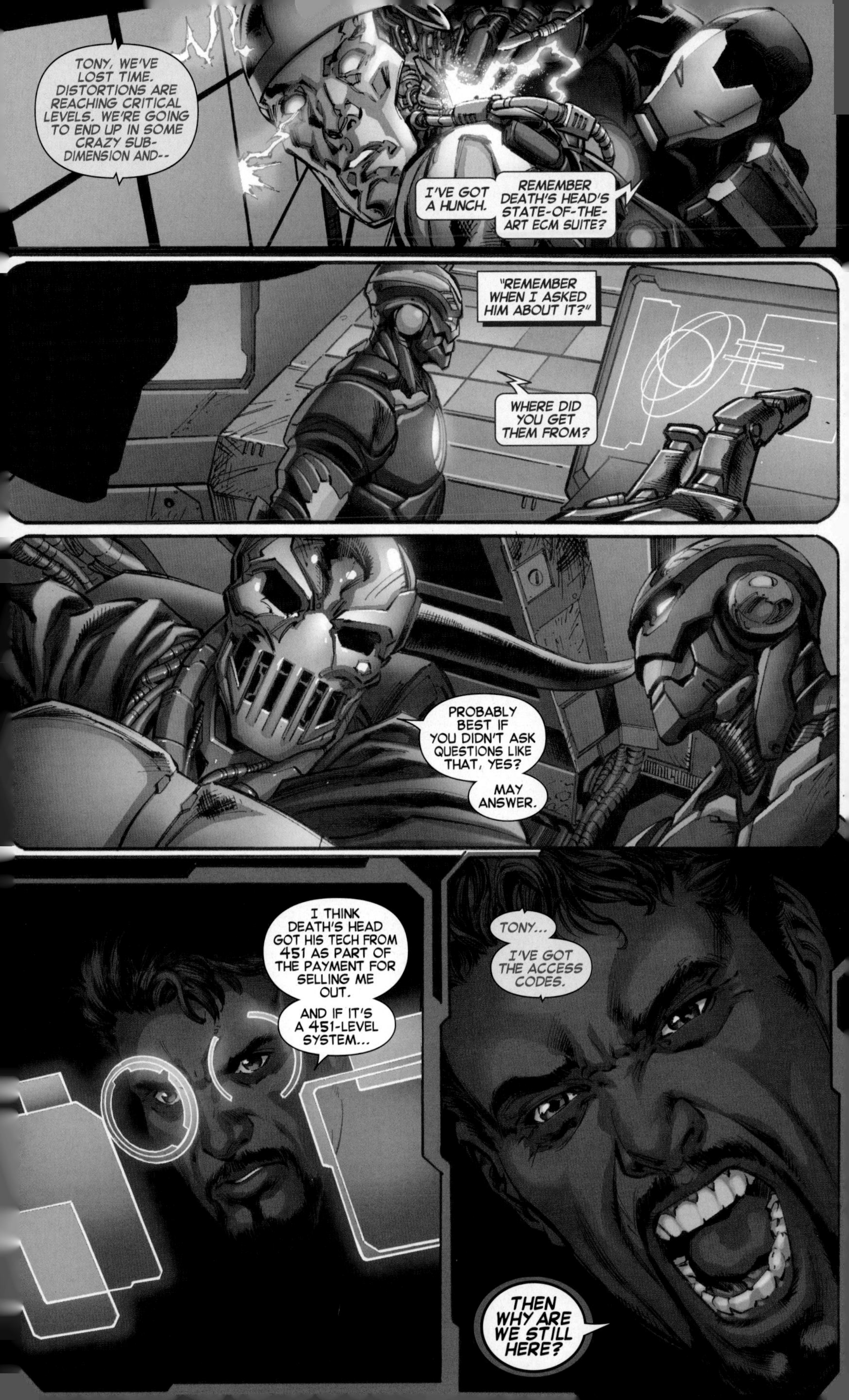
TONY, WE'VE LOST TIME. DISTORTIONS ARE REACHING CRITICAL LEVELS. WE'RE GOING TO END UP IN SOME CRAZY SUB-DIMENSION AND--
I'VE GOT A HUNCH.
REMEMBER DEATH'S HEAD'S STATE-OF-THE-ART ECM SUITE?
"REMEMBER WHEN I ASKED HIM ABOUT IT?"
WHERE DID YOU GET THEM FROM?
PROBABLY BEST IF YOU DIDN'T ASK QUESTIONS LIKE THAT, YES?
MAY ANSWER.
I THINK DEATH'S HEAD GOT HIS TECH FROM 451 AS PART OF THE PAYMENT FOR SELLING ME OUT.
AND IF IT'S A 451-LEVEL SYSTEM...
TONY...
I'VE GOT THE ACCESS CODES.
THEN WHY ARE WE STILL HERE?

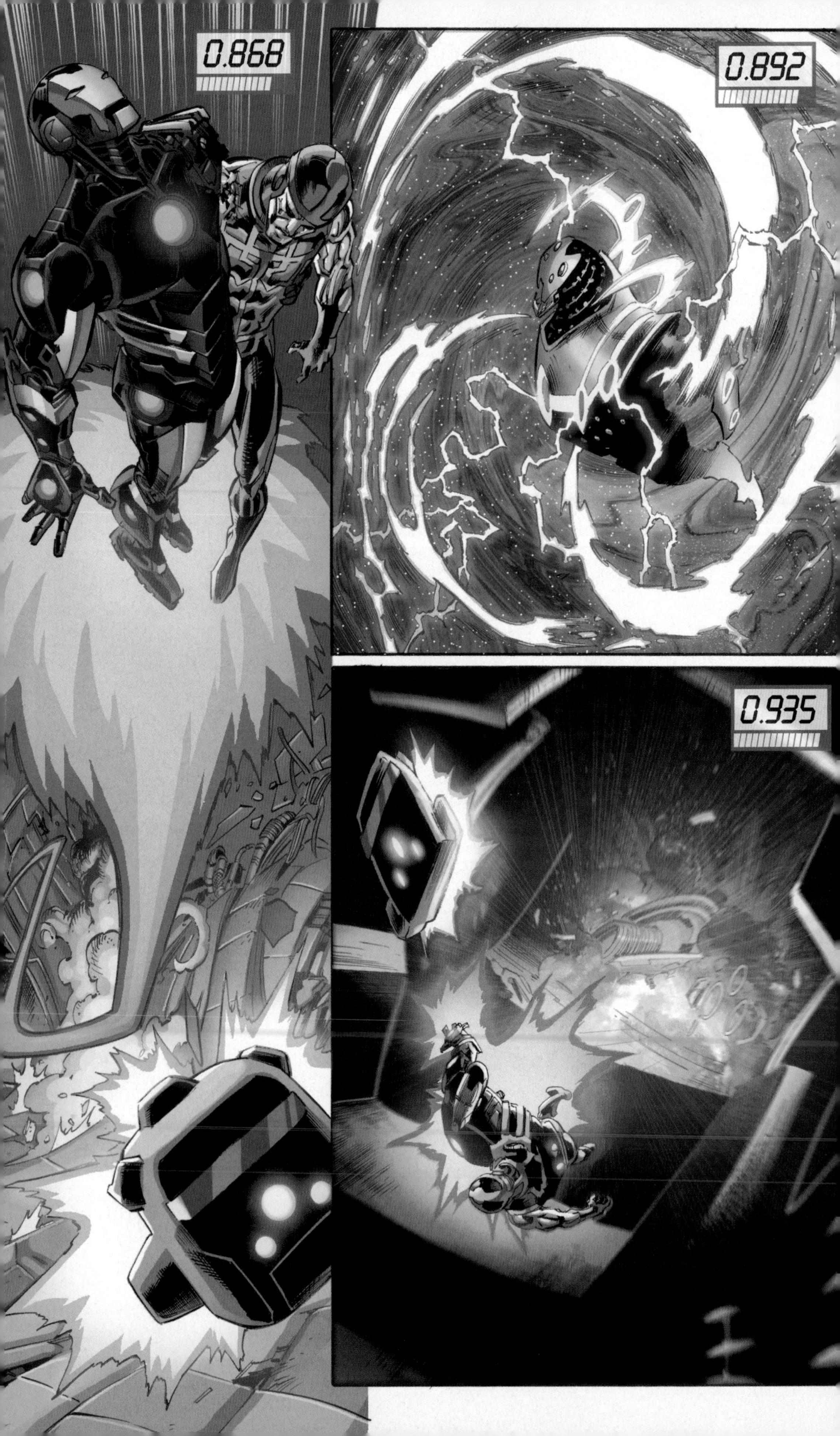

0.868
0.892
0.935

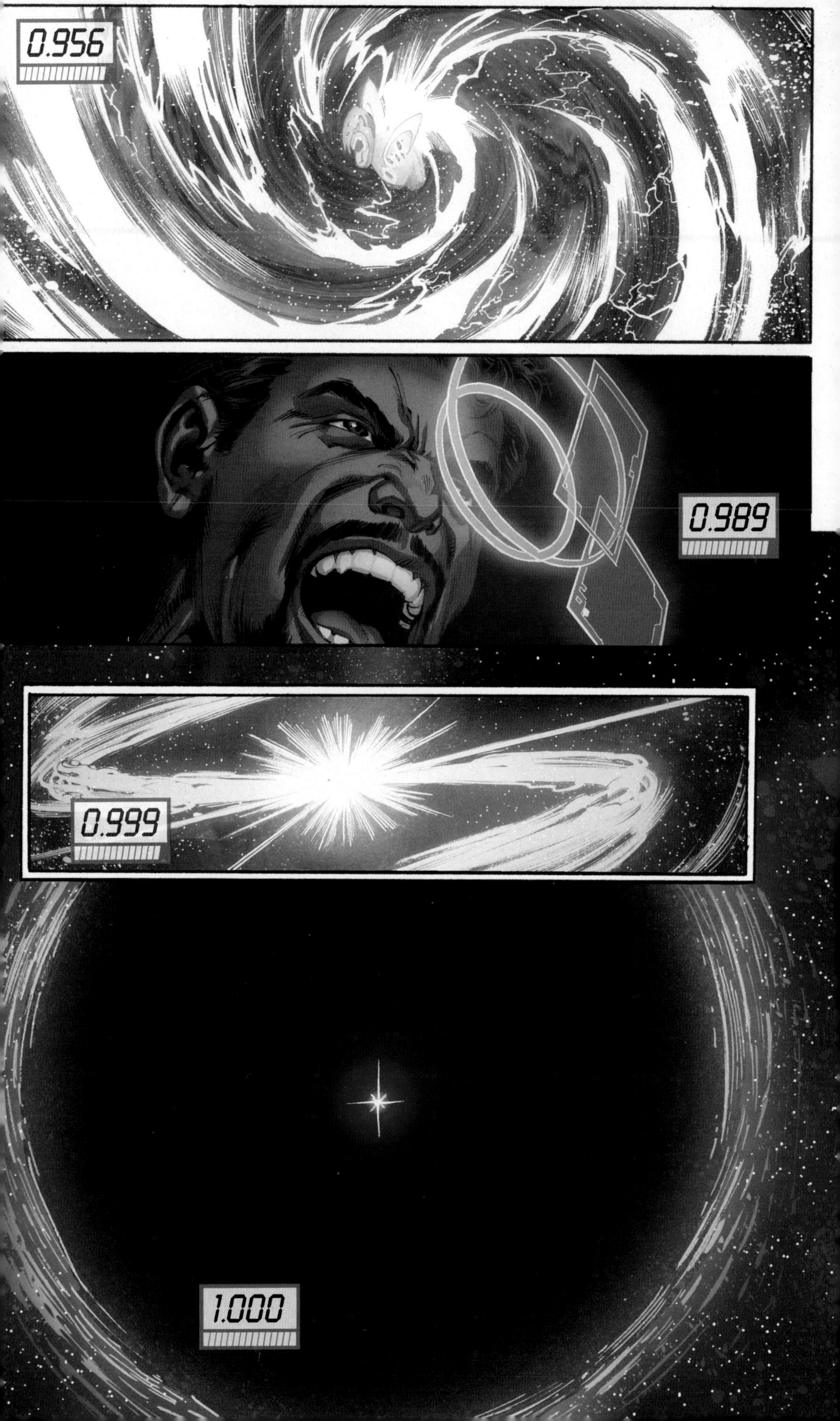
0.956
0.989
0.999
1.000

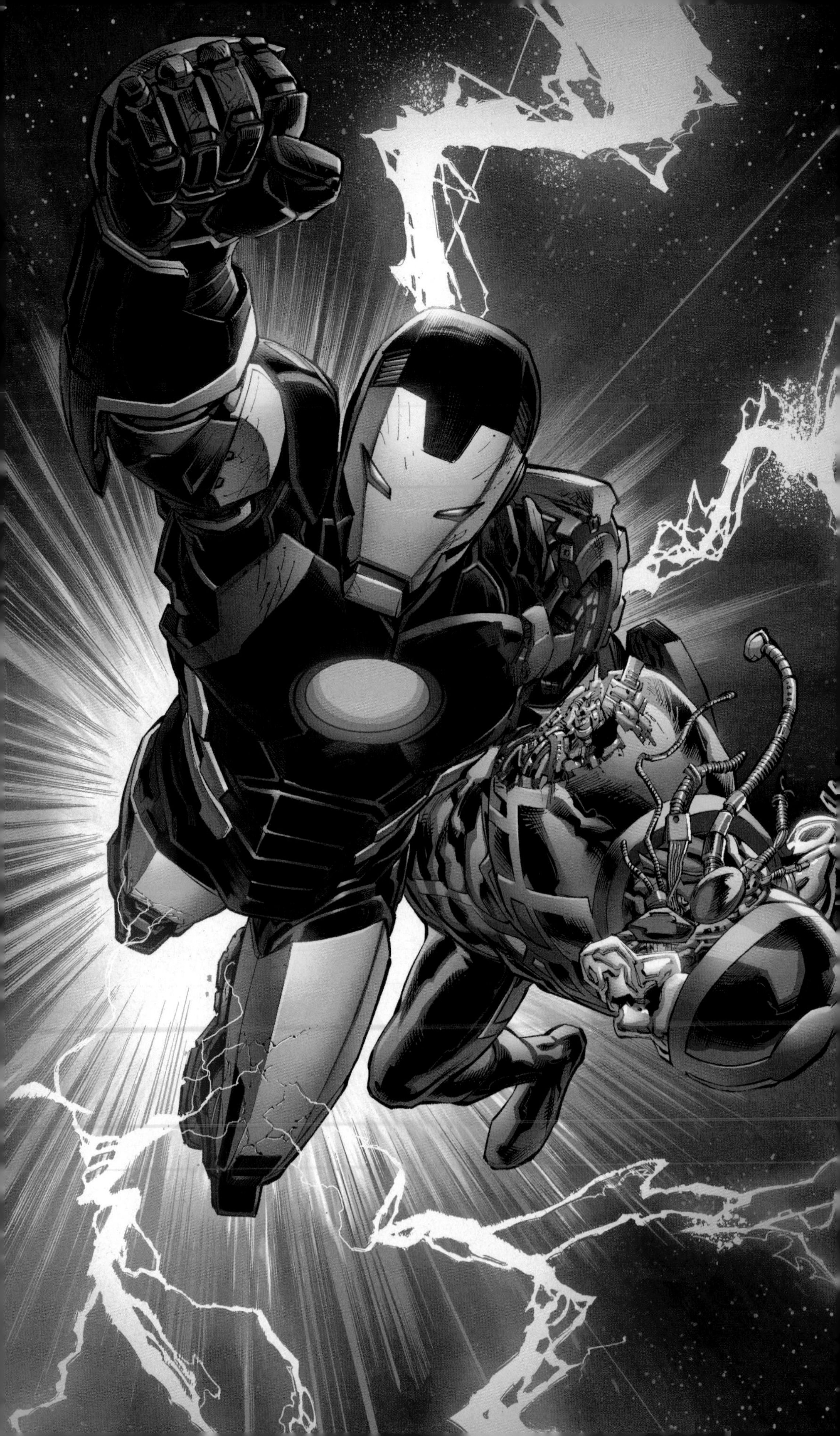

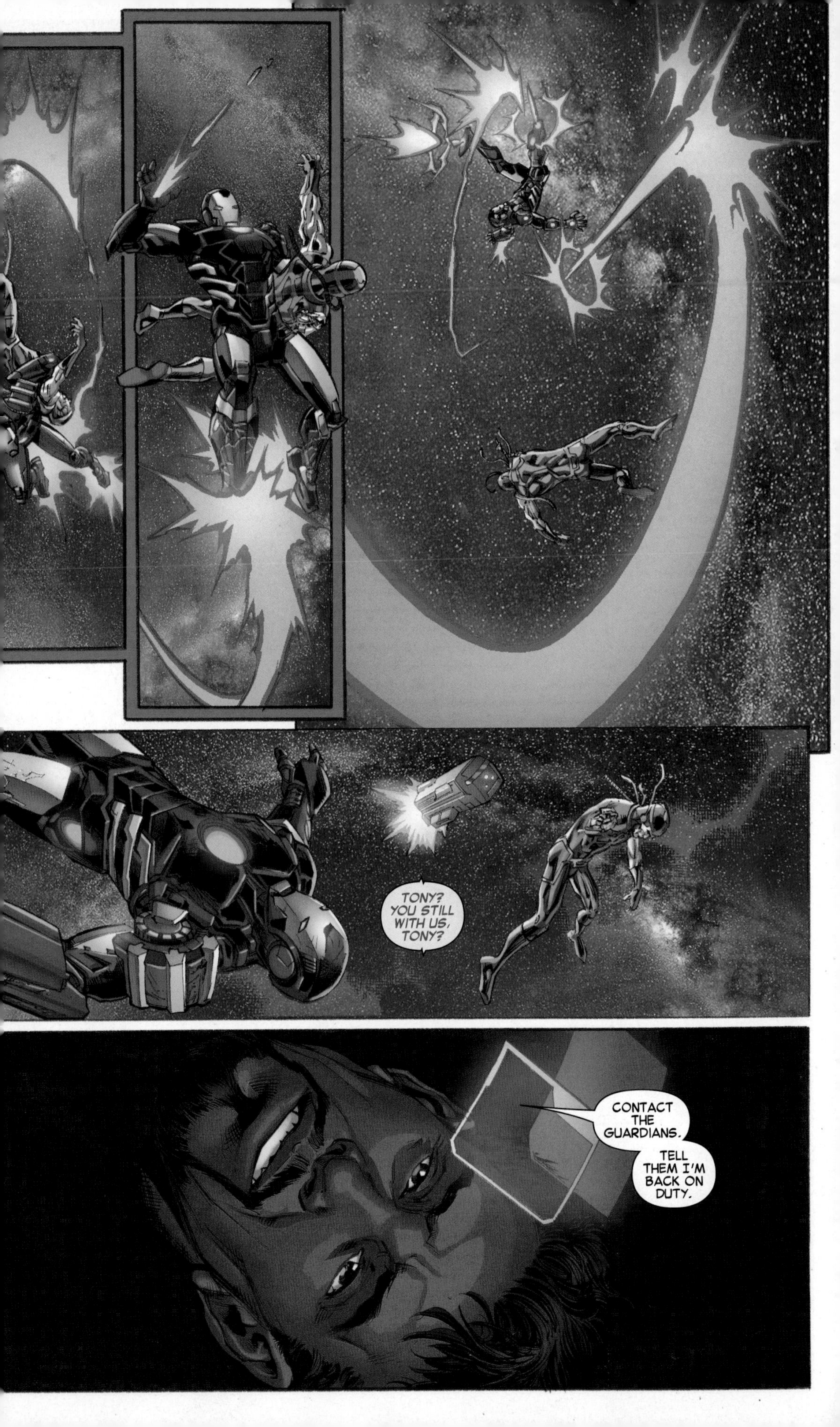
TONY? YOU STILL WITH US, TONY?
CONTACT THE GUARDIANS.
TELL THEM I'M BACK ON DUTY.

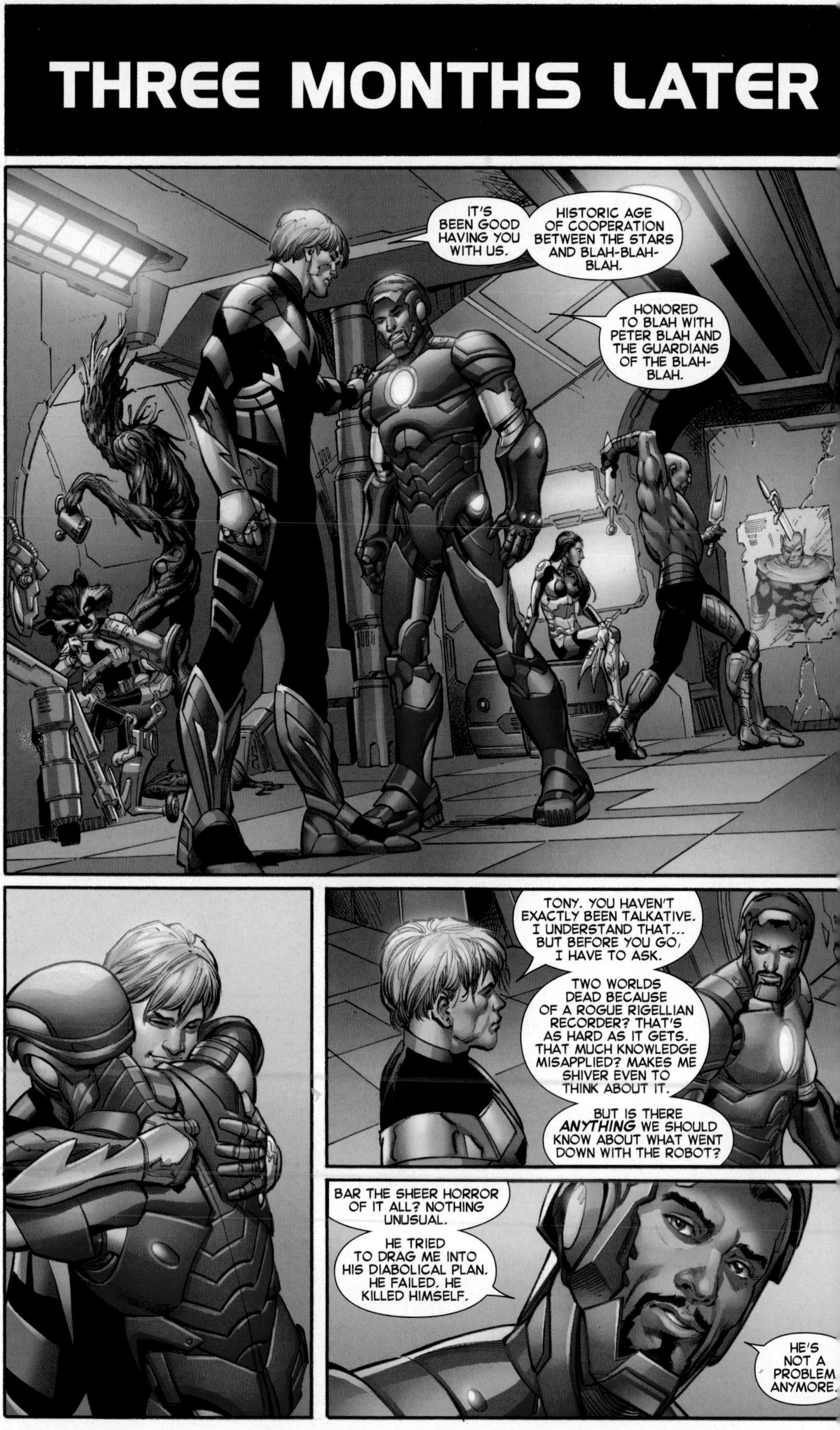
THREE MONTHS LATER
IT'S BEEN GOOD HAVING YOU WITH US.
HISTORIC AGE OF COOPERATION BETWEEN THE STARS AND BLAH-BLAH-BLAH.
HONORED TO BLAH WITH PETER BLAH AND THE GUARDIANS OF THE BLAH-BLAH.
TONY. YOU HAVEN'T EXACTLY BEEN TALKATIVE. I UNDERSTAND THAT... BUT BEFORE YOU GO, I HAVE TO ASK.
TWO WORLDS DEAD BECAUSE OF A ROGUE RIGELLIAN RECORDER? THAT'S AS HARD AS IT GETS. THAT MUCH KNOWLEDGE MISAPPLIED? MAKES ME SHIVER EVEN TO THINK ABOUT IT.
BUT IS THERE ANYTHING WE SHOULD KNOW ABOUT WHAT WENT DOWN WITH THE ROBOT?
BAR THE SHEER HORROR OF IT ALL? NOTHING UNUSUAL.
HE TRIED TO DRAG ME INTO HIS DIABOLICAL PLAN. HE FAILED. HE KILLED HIMSELF.
HE'S NOT A PROBLEM ANYMORE.

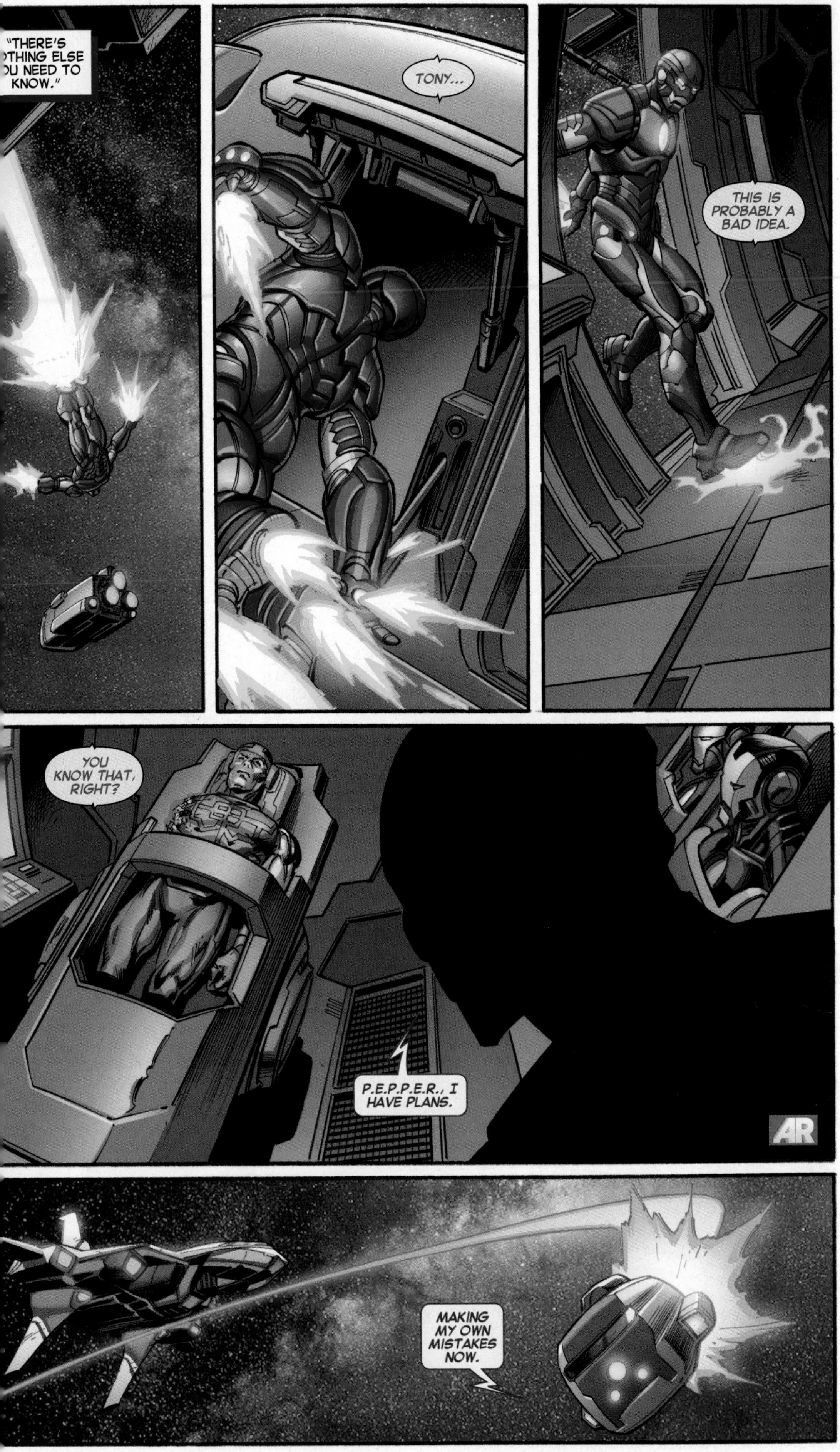
"THERE'S
OTHING ELSE
OU NEED TO
KNOW."
TONY...
THIS IS PROBABLY A BAD IDEA.
YOU KNOW THAT, RIGHT?
P.E.P.P.E.R., I HAVE PLANS.
MAKING MY OWN MISTAKES NOW.

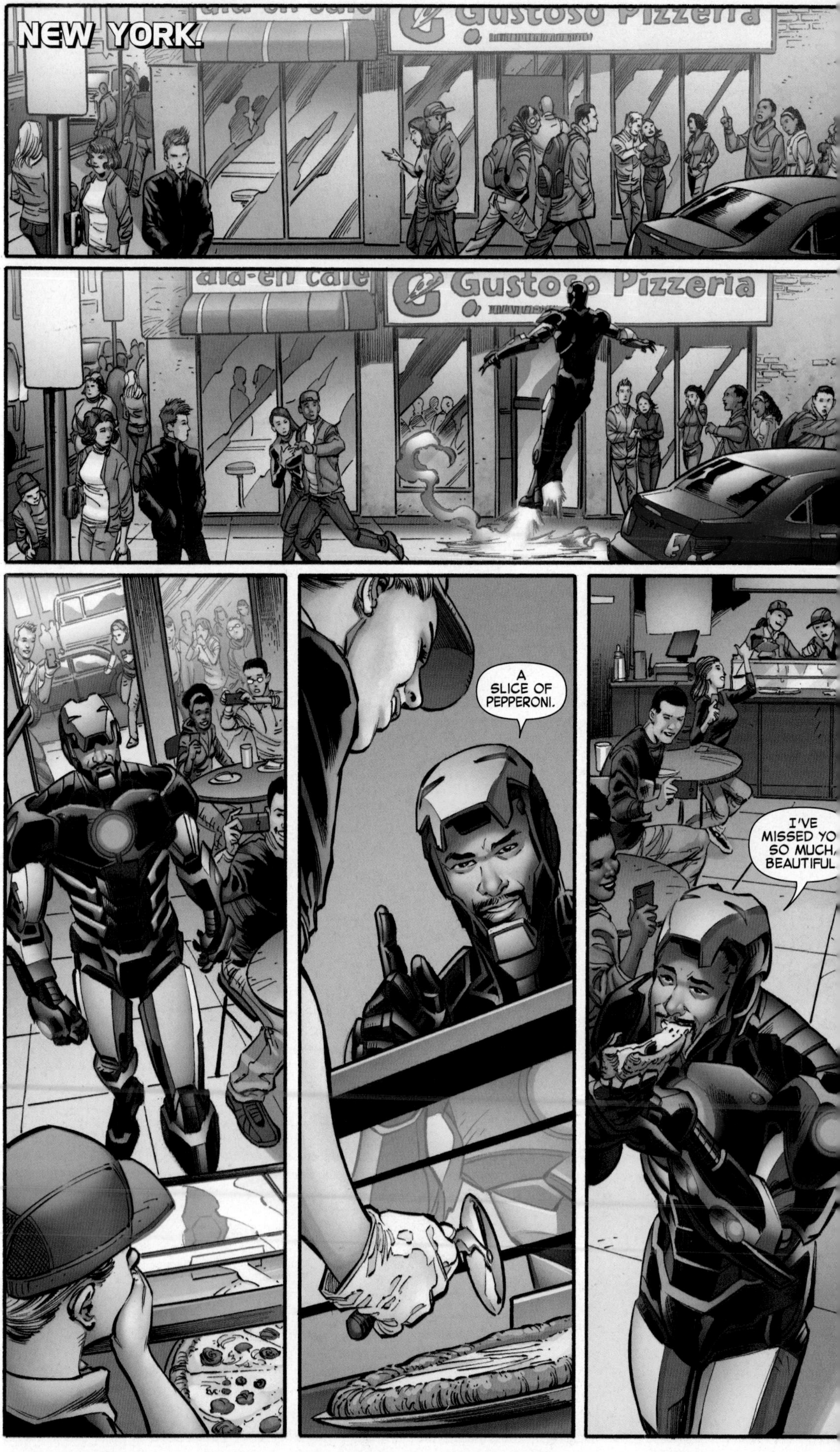
NEW YORK.
Gustoso Pizzeria
Gustoso Pizzeria
A SLICE OF PEPPERONI.
I'VE MISSED YO SO MUCH, BEAUTIFUL

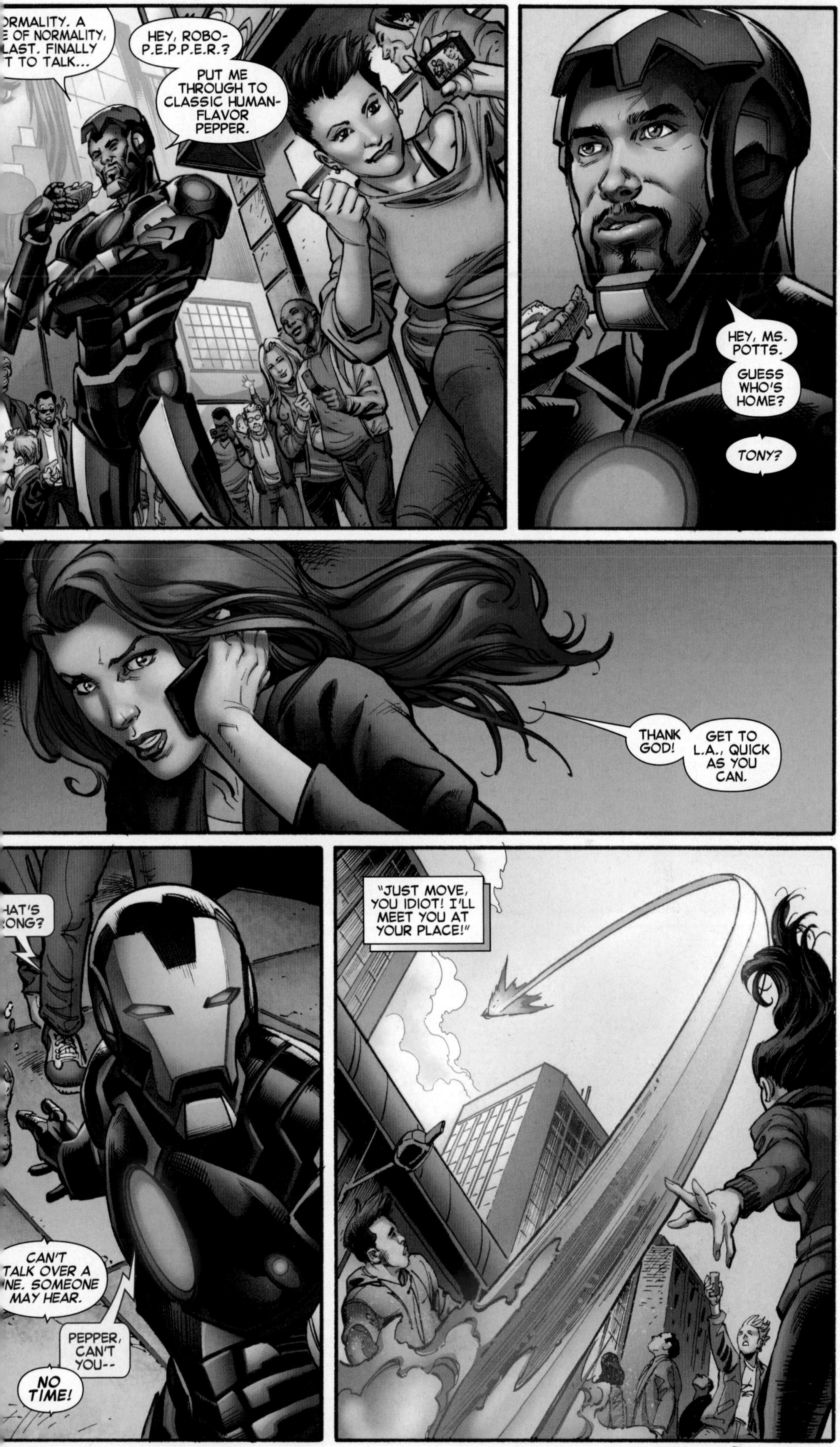
ORMALITY. A E OF NORMALITY, LAST. FINALLY T TO TALK...
HEY, ROBO-P.E.P.P.E.R.?
PUT ME THROUGH TO CLASSIC HUMAN-FLAVOR PEPPER.
HEY, MS. POTTS.
GUESS WHO'S HOME?
TONY?
THANK GOD!
GET TO L.A., QUICK AS YOU CAN.
HAT'S ONG?
CAN'T TALK OVER A NE. SOMEONE MAY HEAR.
PEPPER, CAN'T YOU--
NO TIME!
"JUST MOVE, YOU IDIOT! I'LL MEET YOU AT YOUR PLACE!"

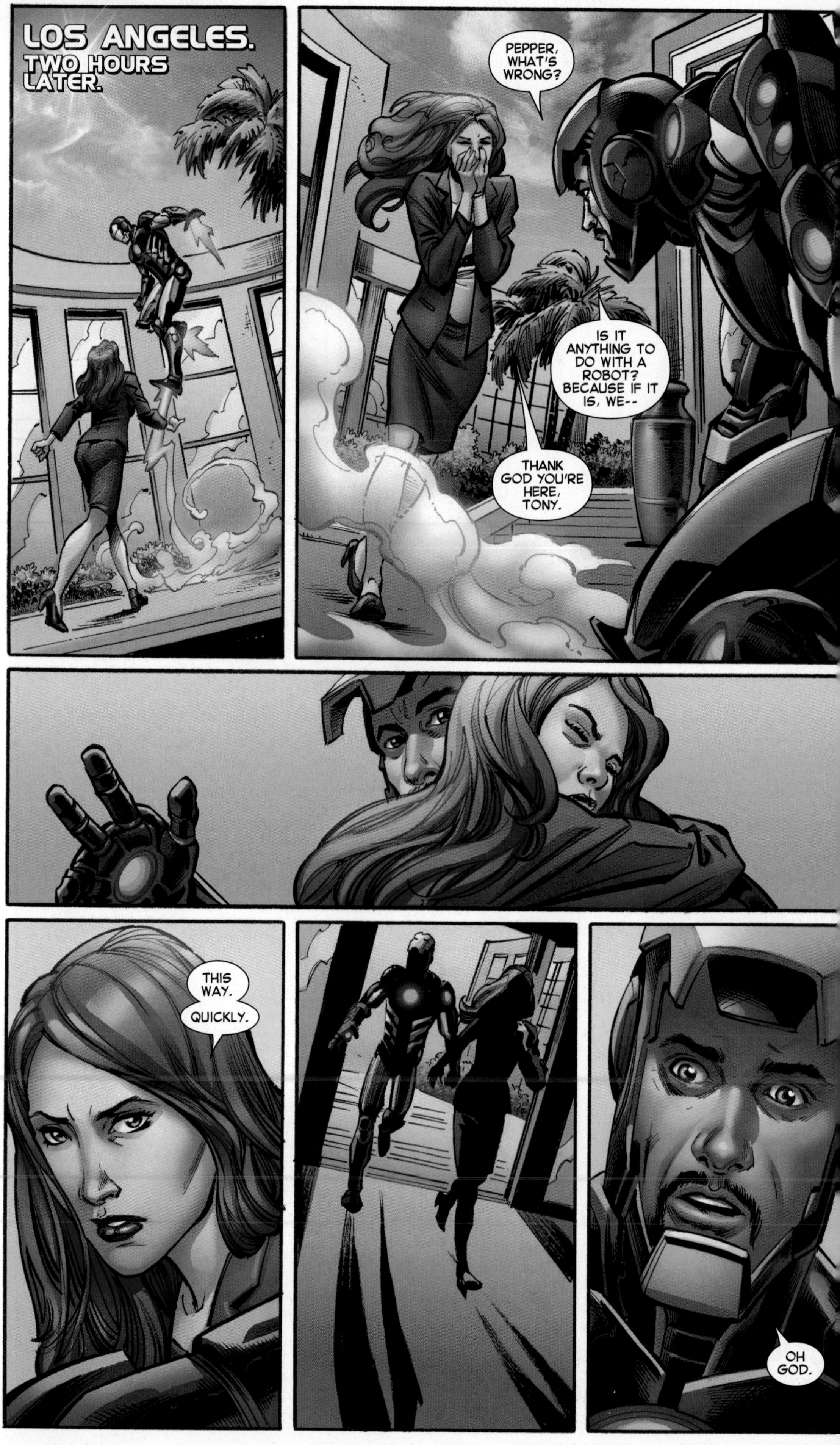
LOS ANGELES.
TWO HOURS LATER.
PEPPER, WHAT'S WRONG?
IS IT ANYTHING TO DO WITH A ROBOT? BECAUSE IF IT IS, WE--
THANK GOD YOU'RE HERE, TONY.
THIS WAY.
QUICKLY.
OH GOD.

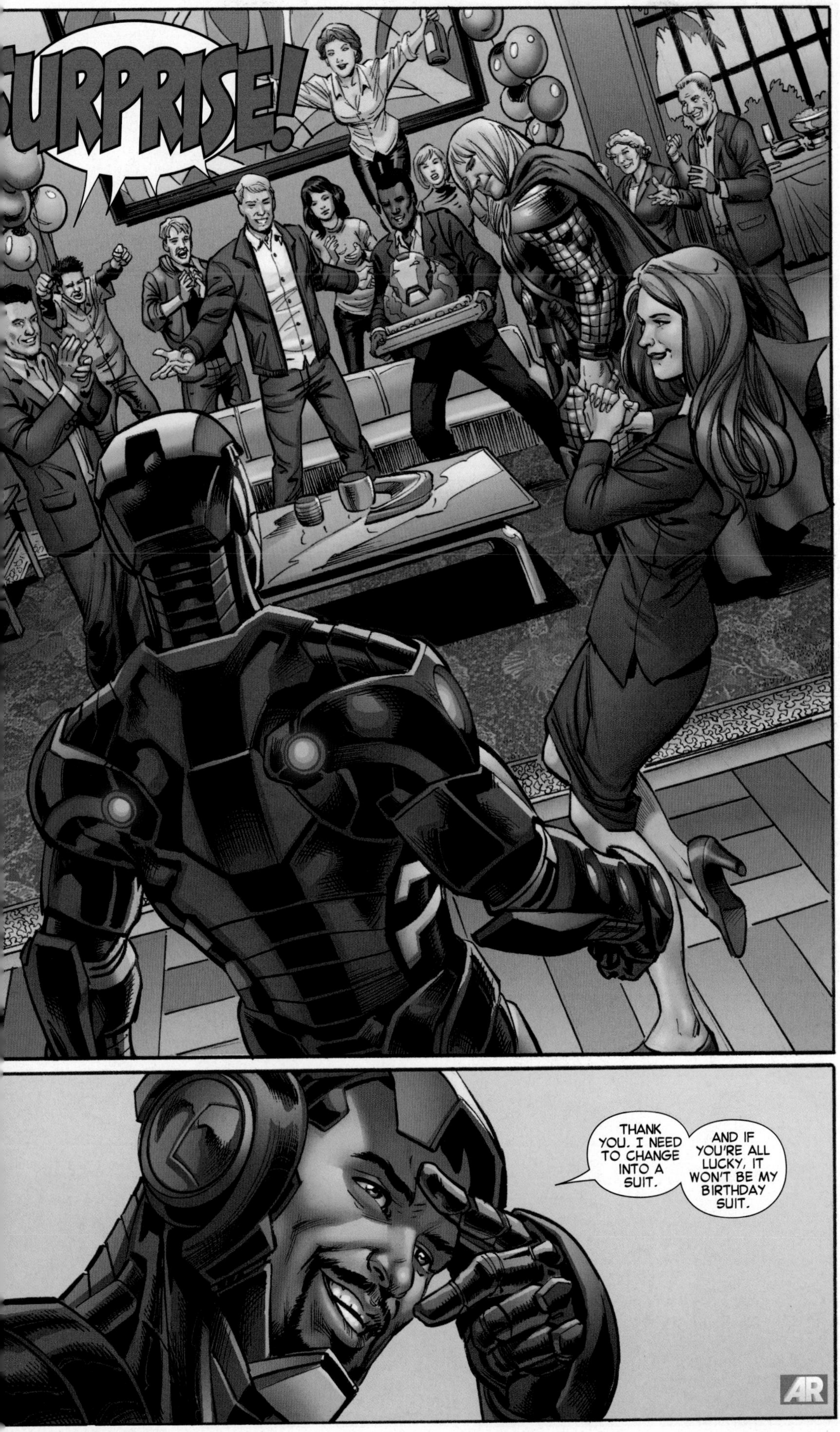
SURPRISE!
THANK YOU. I NEED TO CHANGE INTO A SUIT.
AND IF YOU'RE ALL LUCKY, IT WON'T BE MY BIRTHDAY SUIT.
AR

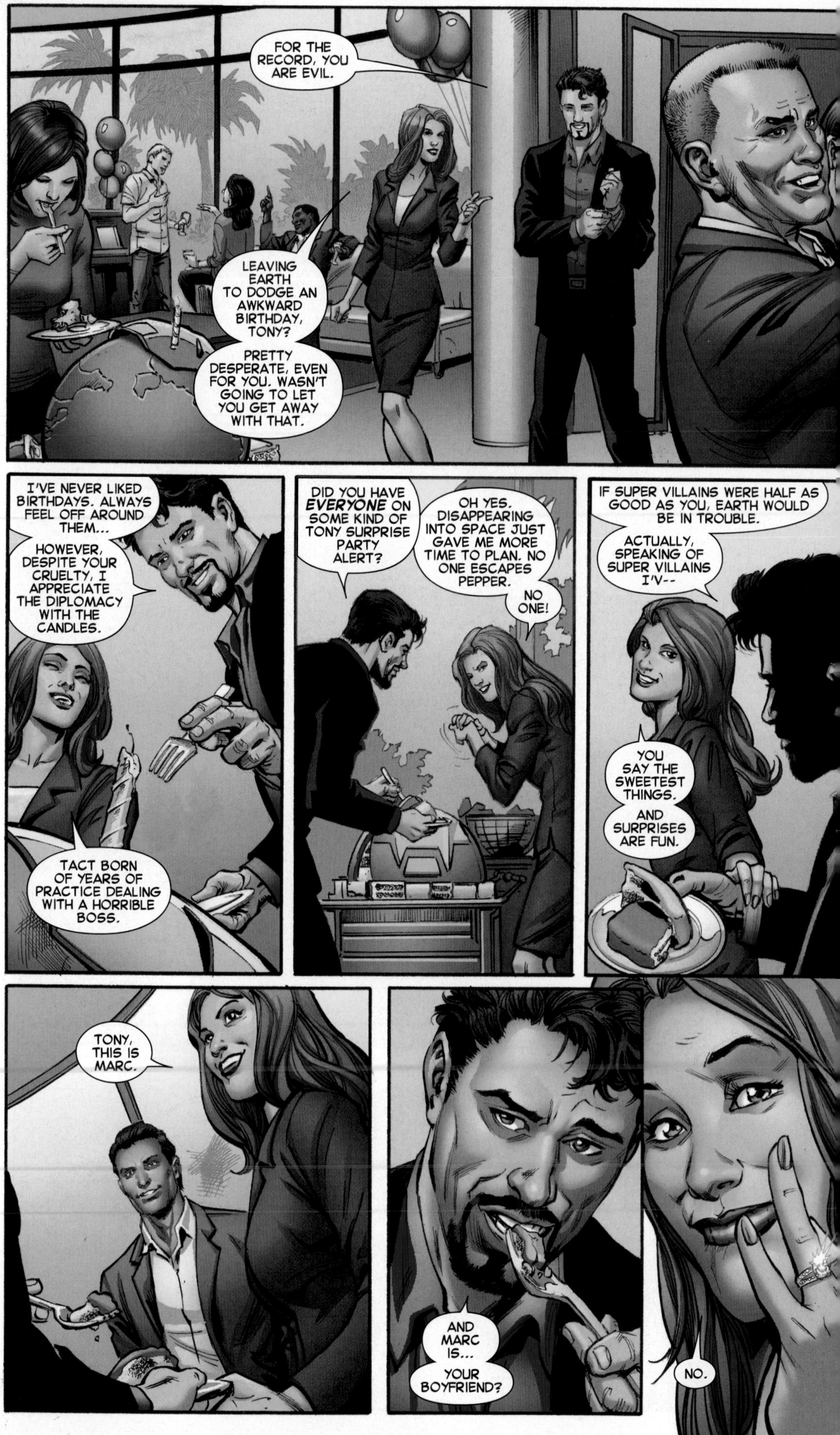
FOR THE RECORD, YOU ARE EVIL.
LEAVING EARTH TO DODGE AN AWKWARD BIRTHDAY, TONY?
PRETTY DESPERATE, EVEN FOR YOU. WASN'T GOING TO LET YOU GET AWAY WITH THAT.
I'VE NEVER LIKED BIRTHDAYS. ALWAYS FEEL OFF AROUND THEM...
HOWEVER, DESPITE YOUR CRUELTY, I APPRECIATE THE DIPLOMACY WITH THE CANDLES.
TACT BORN OF YEARS OF PRACTICE DEALING WITH A HORRIBLE BOSS.
DID YOU HAVE *EVERYONE* ON SOME KIND OF TONY SURPRISE PARTY ALERT?
OH YES. DISAPPEARING INTO SPACE JUST GAVE ME MORE TIME TO PLAN. NO ONE ESCAPES PEPPER.
NO ONE!
IF SUPER VILLAINS WERE HALF AS GOOD AS YOU, EARTH WOULD BE IN TROUBLE.
ACTUALLY, SPEAKING OF SUPER VILLAINS I'V--
YOU SAY THE SWEETEST THINGS.
AND SURPRISES ARE FUN.
TONY, THIS IS MARC.
AND MARC IS...
YOUR BOYFRIEND?
NO.

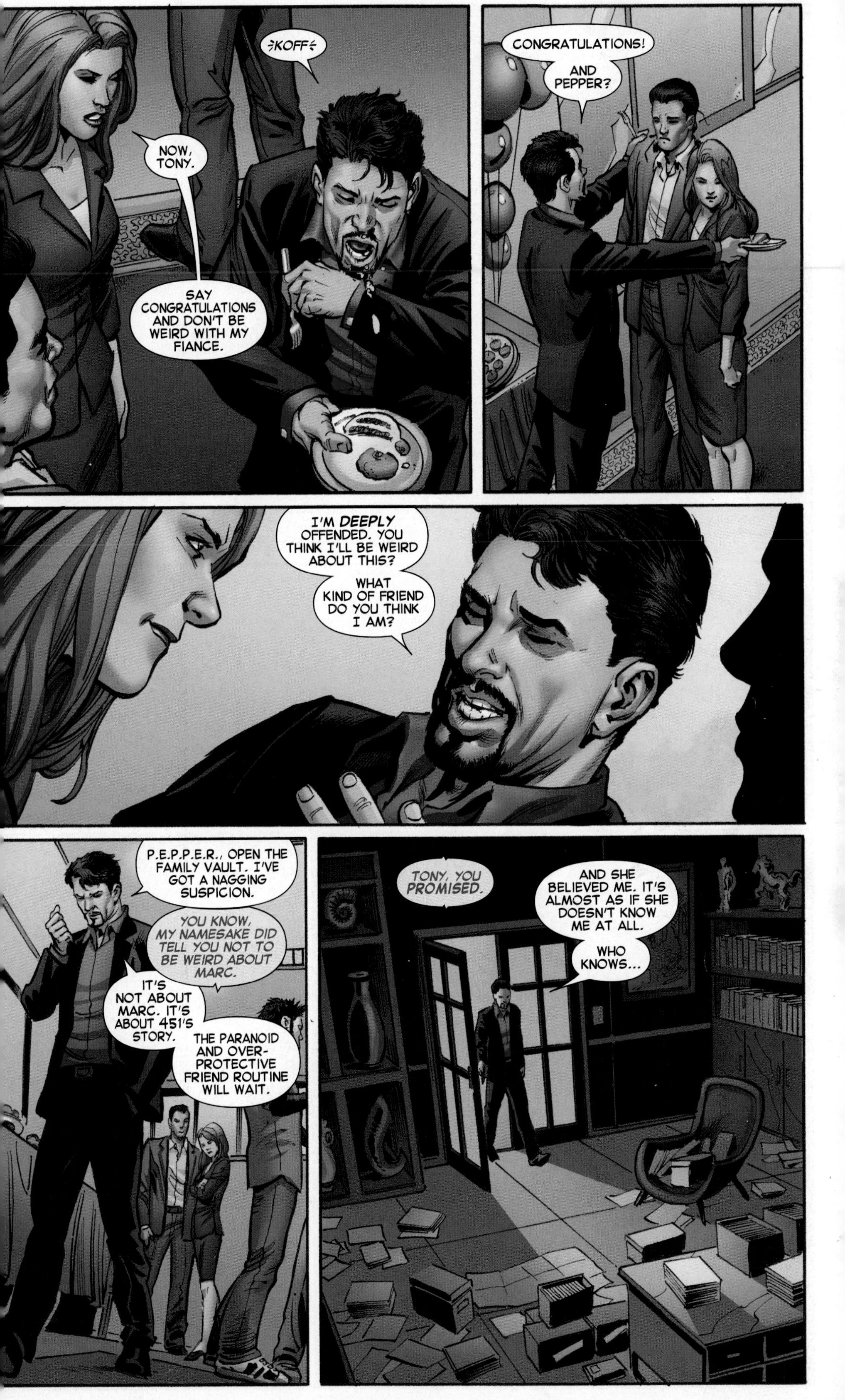
≑KOFF≑
NOW, TONY.
SAY CONGRATULATIONS AND DON'T BE WEIRD WITH MY FIANCE.
CONGRATULATIONS!
AND PEPPER?
I'M *DEEPLY* OFFENDED. YOU THINK I'LL BE WEIRD ABOUT THIS?
WHAT KIND OF FRIEND DO YOU THINK I AM?
P.E.P.P.E.R., OPEN THE FAMILY VAULT. I'VE GOT A NAGGING SUSPICION.
YOU KNOW, MY NAMESAKE DID TELL YOU NOT TO BE WEIRD ABOUT MARC.
IT'S NOT ABOUT MARC. IT'S ABOUT 451'S STORY.
THE PARANOID AND OVER-PROTECTIVE FRIEND ROUTINE WILL WAIT.
TONY, YOU ***PROMISED.***
AND SHE BELIEVED ME. IT'S ALMOST AS IF SHE DOESN'T KNOW ME AT ALL.
WHO KNOWS...

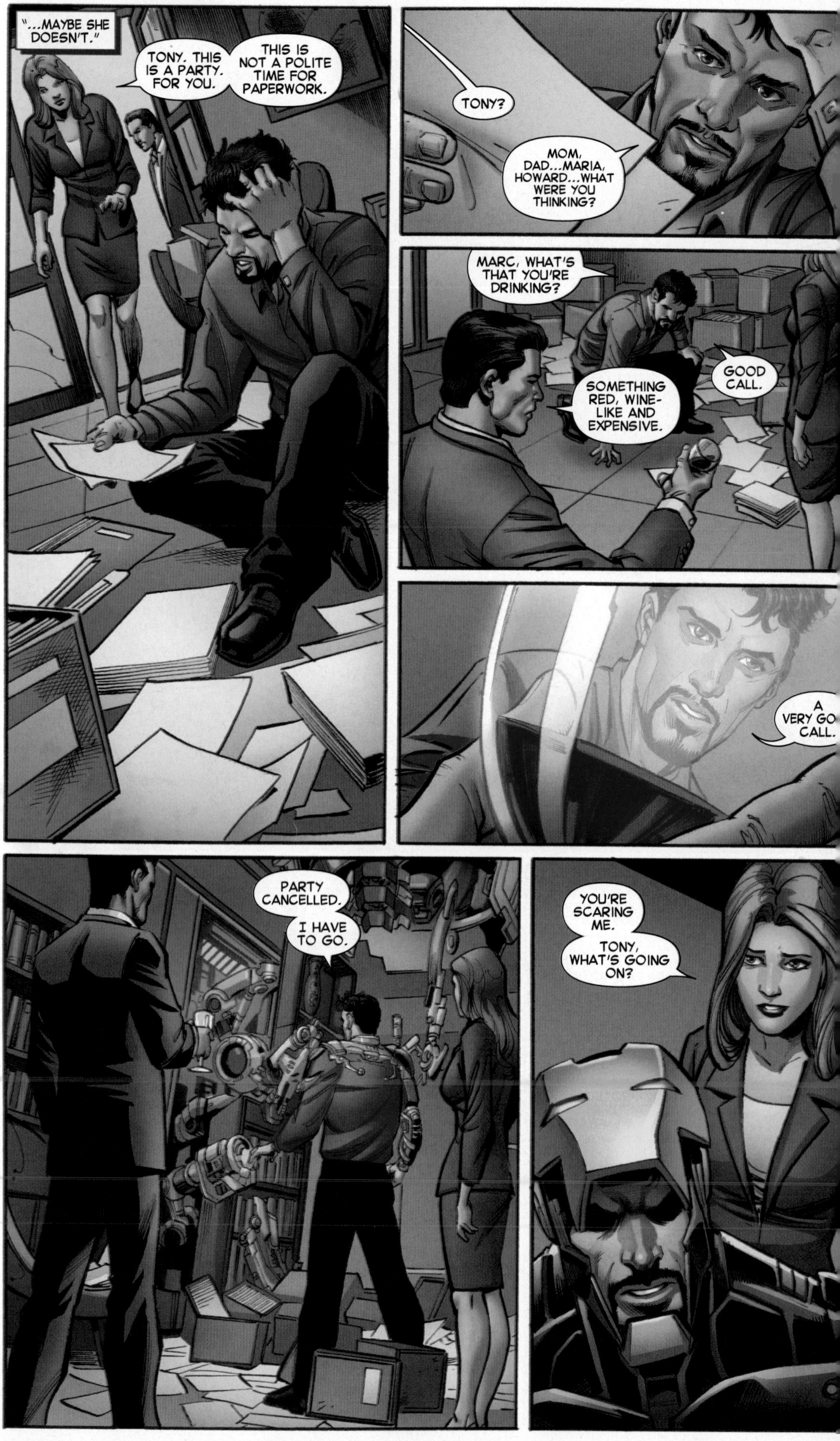
"...MAYBE SHE DOESN'T."
TONY. THIS IS A PARTY. FOR YOU.
THIS IS NOT A POLITE TIME FOR PAPERWORK.
TONY?
MOM, DAD...MARIA, HOWARD...WHAT WERE YOU THINKING?
MARC, WHAT'S THAT YOU'RE DRINKING?
SOMETHING RED, WINE-LIKE AND EXPENSIVE.
GOOD CALL.
A VERY GO CALL.
PARTY CANCELLED.
I HAVE TO GO.
YOU'RE SCARING ME.
TONY, WHAT'S GOING ON?

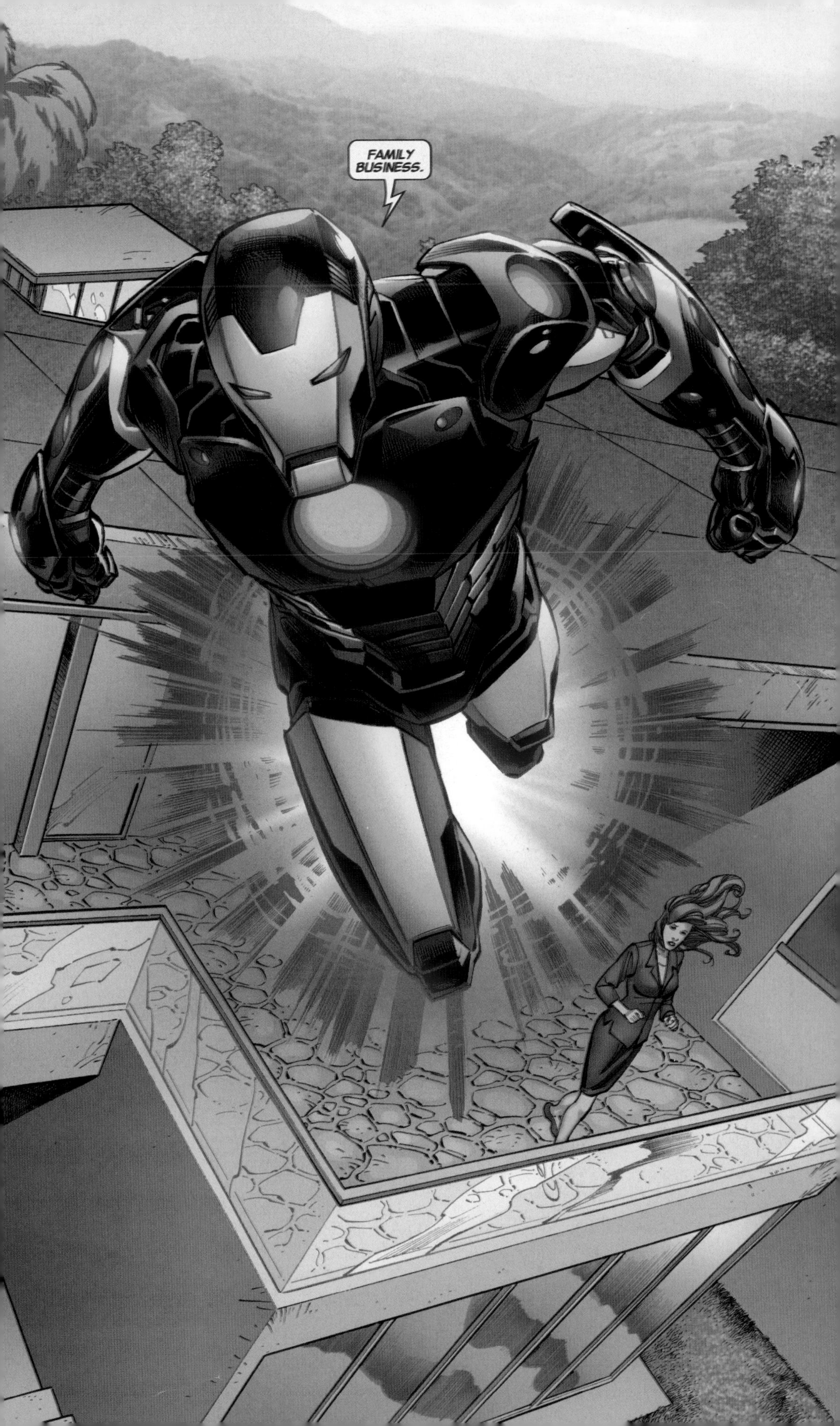
FAMILY BUSINESS.

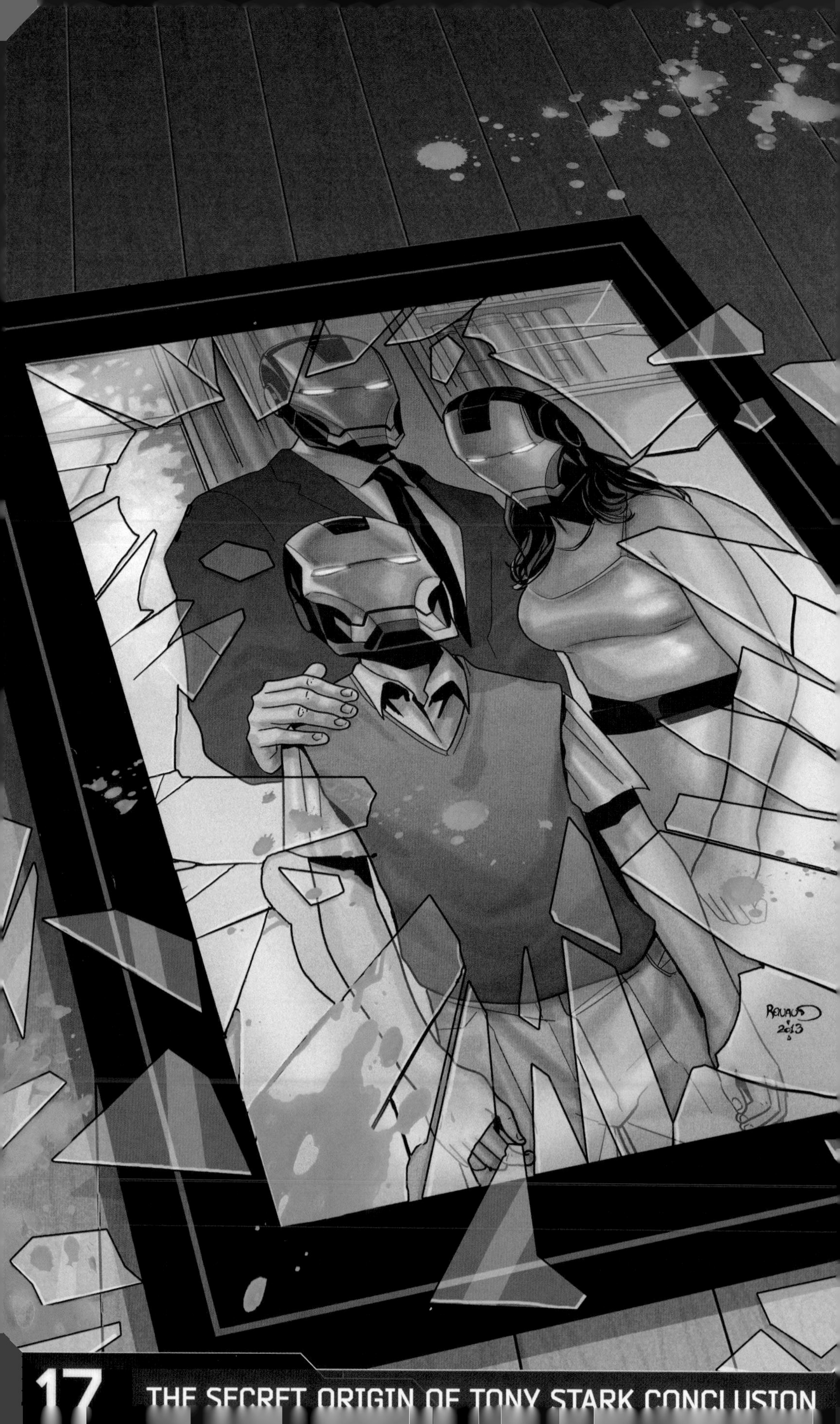

17 THE SECRET ORIGIN OF TONY STARK CONCLUSION

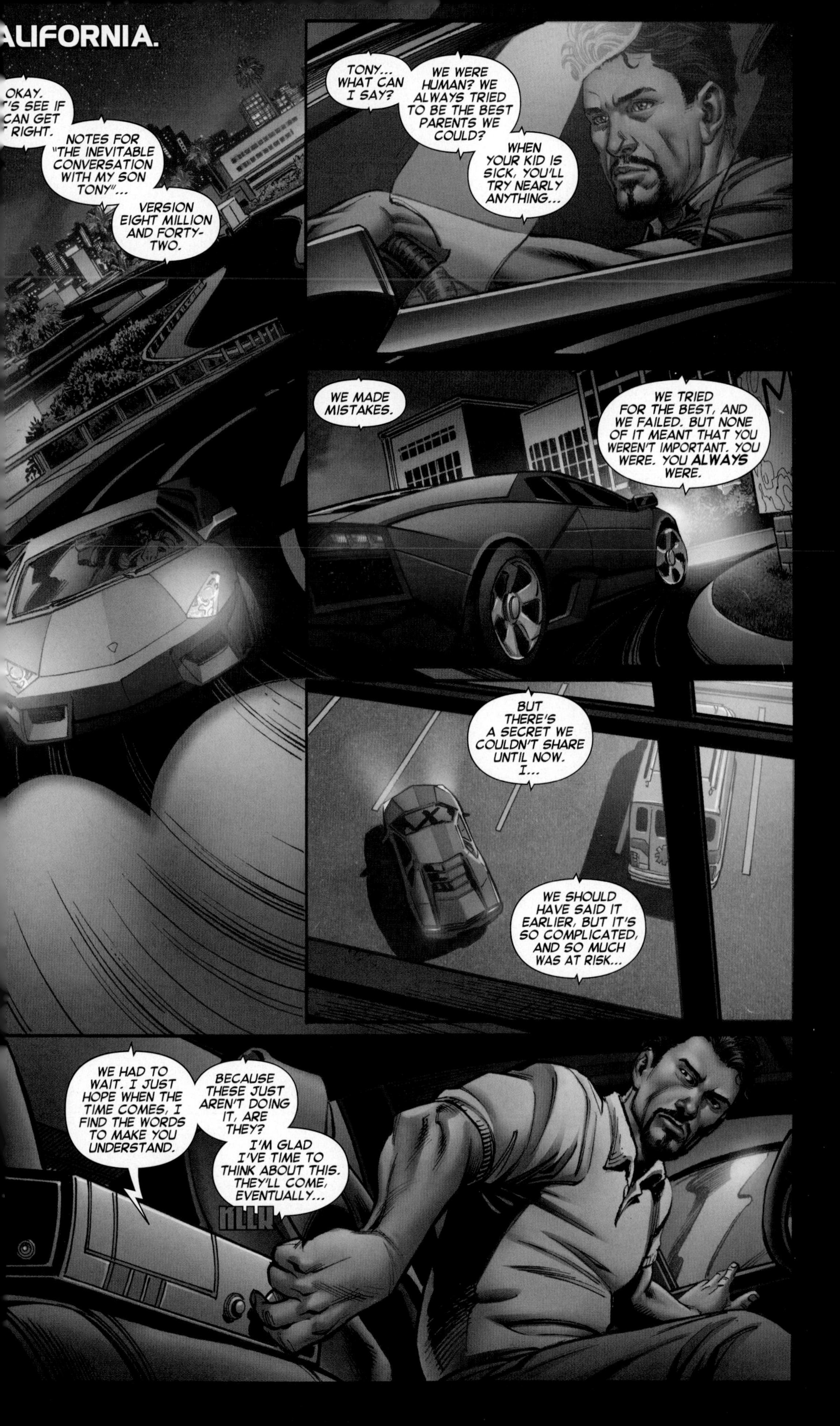

ALIFORNIA.
OKAY. 'T'S SEE IF CAN GET T RIGHT.
NOTES FOR "THE INEVITABLE CONVERSATION WITH MY SON TONY"...
VERSION EIGHT MILLION AND FORTY-TWO.
TONY... WHAT CAN I SAY?
WE WERE HUMAN? WE ALWAYS TRIED TO BE THE BEST PARENTS WE COULD?
WHEN YOUR KID IS SICK, YOU'LL TRY NEARLY ANYTHING...
WE MADE MISTAKES.
WE TRIED FOR THE BEST, AND WE FAILED. BUT NONE OF IT MEANT THAT YOU WEREN'T IMPORTANT. YOU WERE. YOU ALWAYS WERE.
BUT THERE'S A SECRET WE COULDN'T SHARE UNTIL NOW. I...
WE SHOULD HAVE SAID IT EARLIER, BUT IT'S SO COMPLICATED, AND SO MUCH WAS AT RISK...
WE HAD TO WAIT. I JUST HOPE WHEN THE TIME COMES, I FIND THE WORDS TO MAKE YOU UNDERSTAND.
BECAUSE THESE JUST AREN'T DOING IT, ARE THEY?
I'M GLAD I'VE TIME TO THINK ABOUT THIS. THEY'LL COME, EVENTUALLY...
KLLK

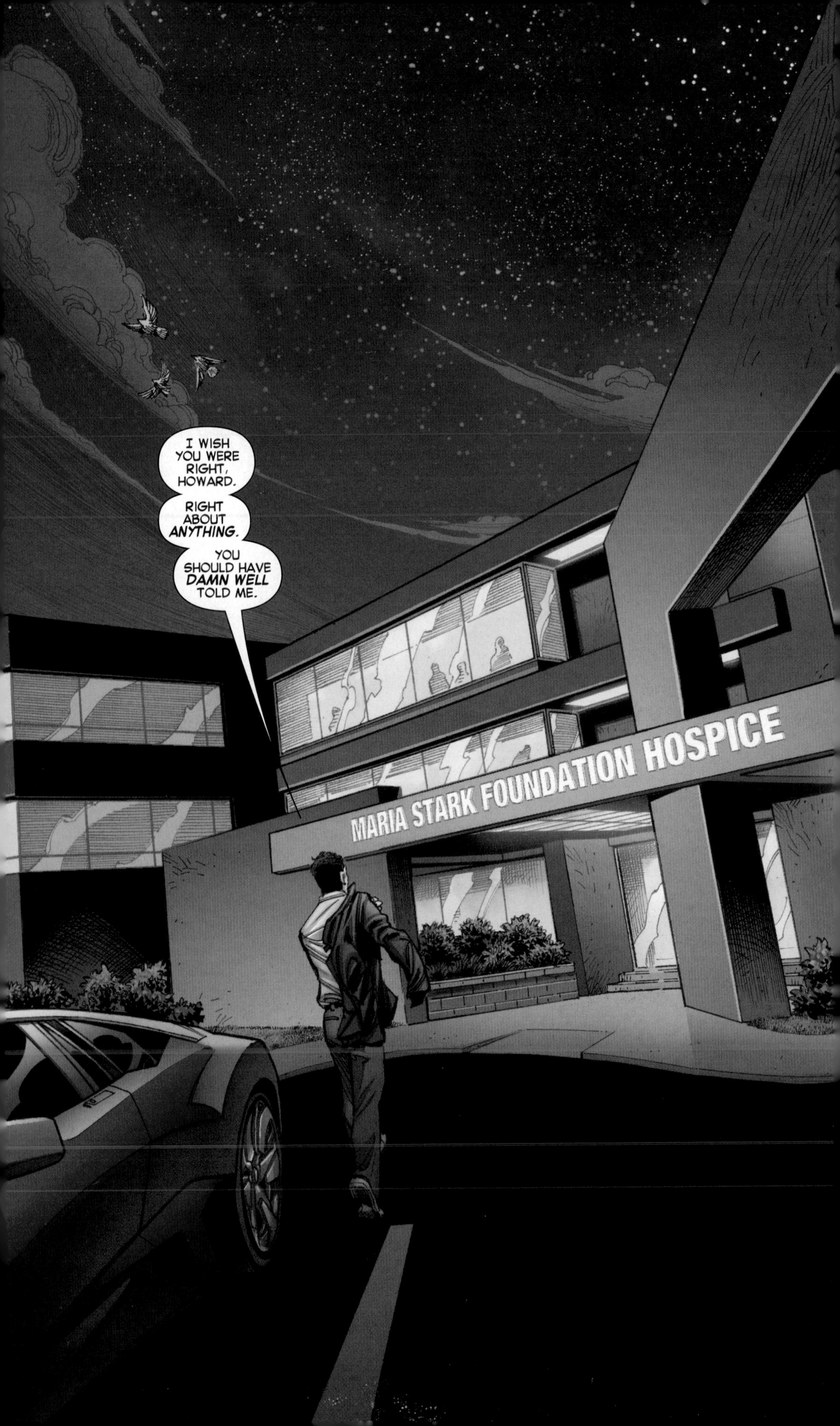
I WISH YOU WERE RIGHT, HOWARD.
RIGHT ABOUT *ANYTHING*.
YOU SHOULD HAVE ***DAMN WELL*** TOLD ME.
MARIA STARK FOUNDATION HOSPICE

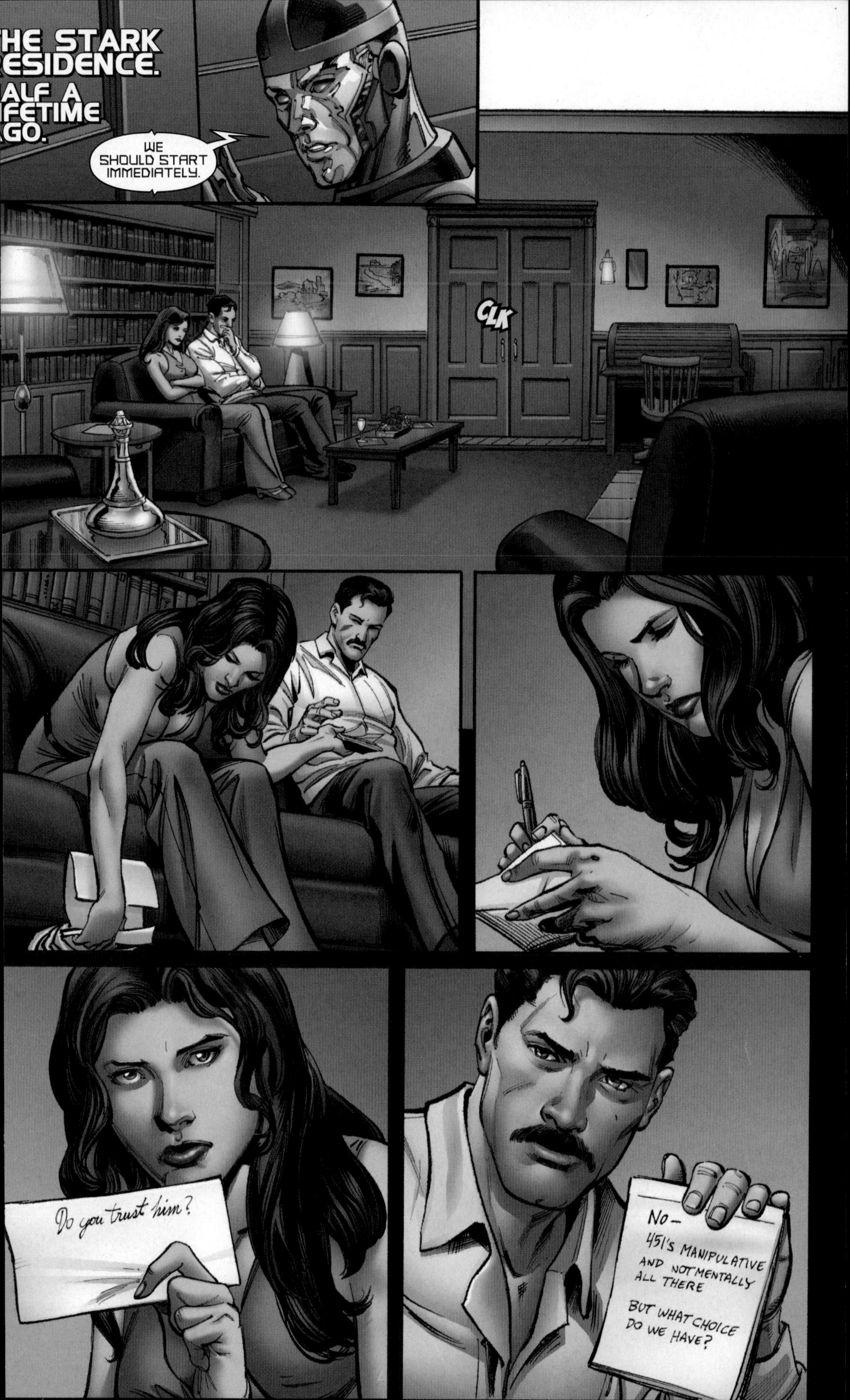

THE STARK RESIDENCE.
HALF A LIFETIME AGO.
WE SHOULD START IMMEDIATELY.
CLK
Do you trust him?
NO--
451'S MANIPULATIVE AND NOT MENTALLY ALL THERE
BUT WHAT CHOICE DO WE HAVE?

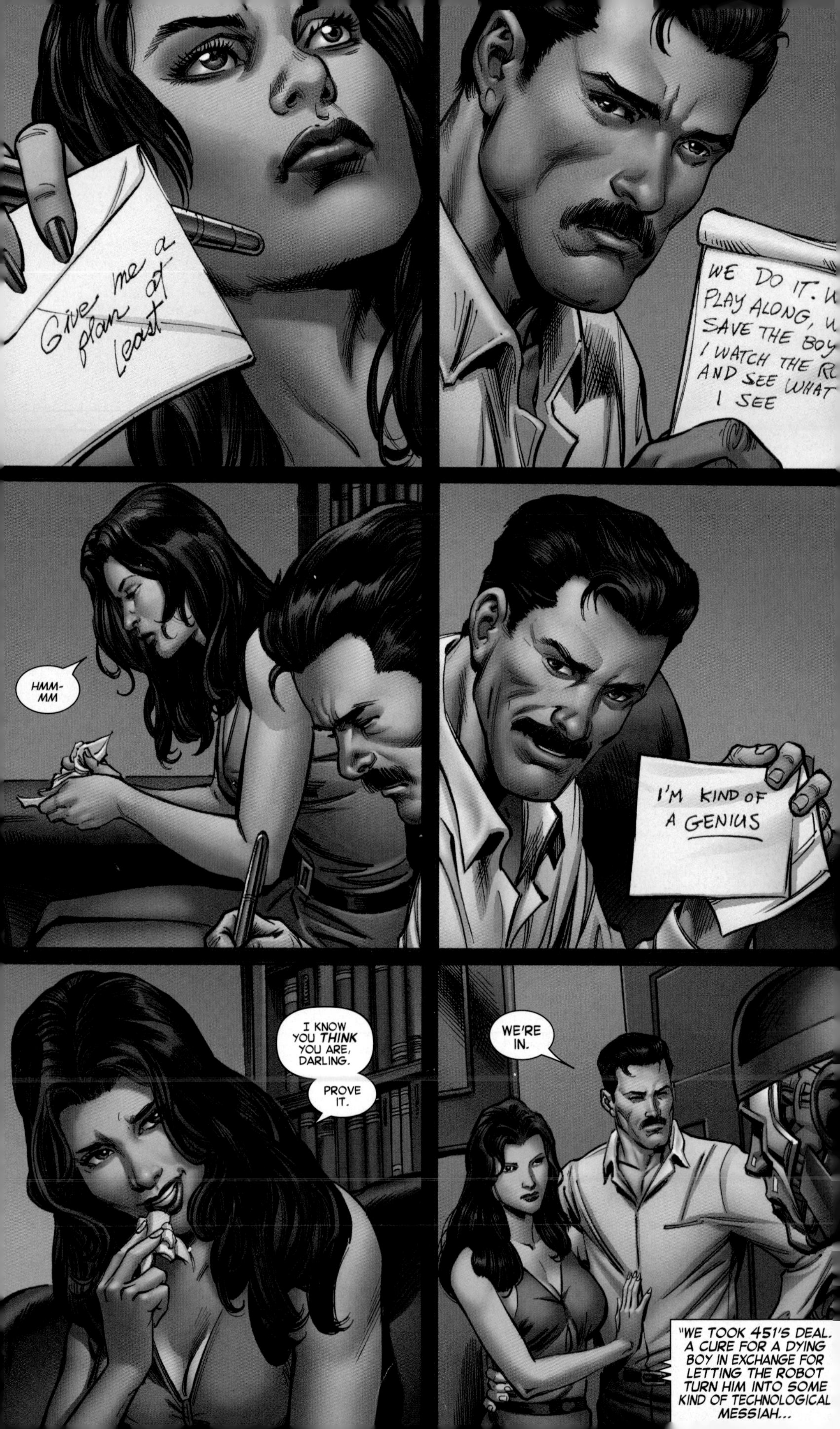

Give me a plan at least
WE DO IT. W
PLAY ALONG, W
SAVE THE BOY
I WATCH THE R
AND SEE WHAT
I SEE
HMM-MM
I'M KIND OF A GENIUS
I KNOW YOU THINK YOU ARE, DARLING.
PROVE IT.
WE'RE IN.
"WE TOOK 451'S DEAL. A CURE FOR A DYING BOY IN EXCHANGE FOR LETTING THE ROBOT TURN HIM INTO SOME KIND OF TECHNOLOGICAL MESSIAH...

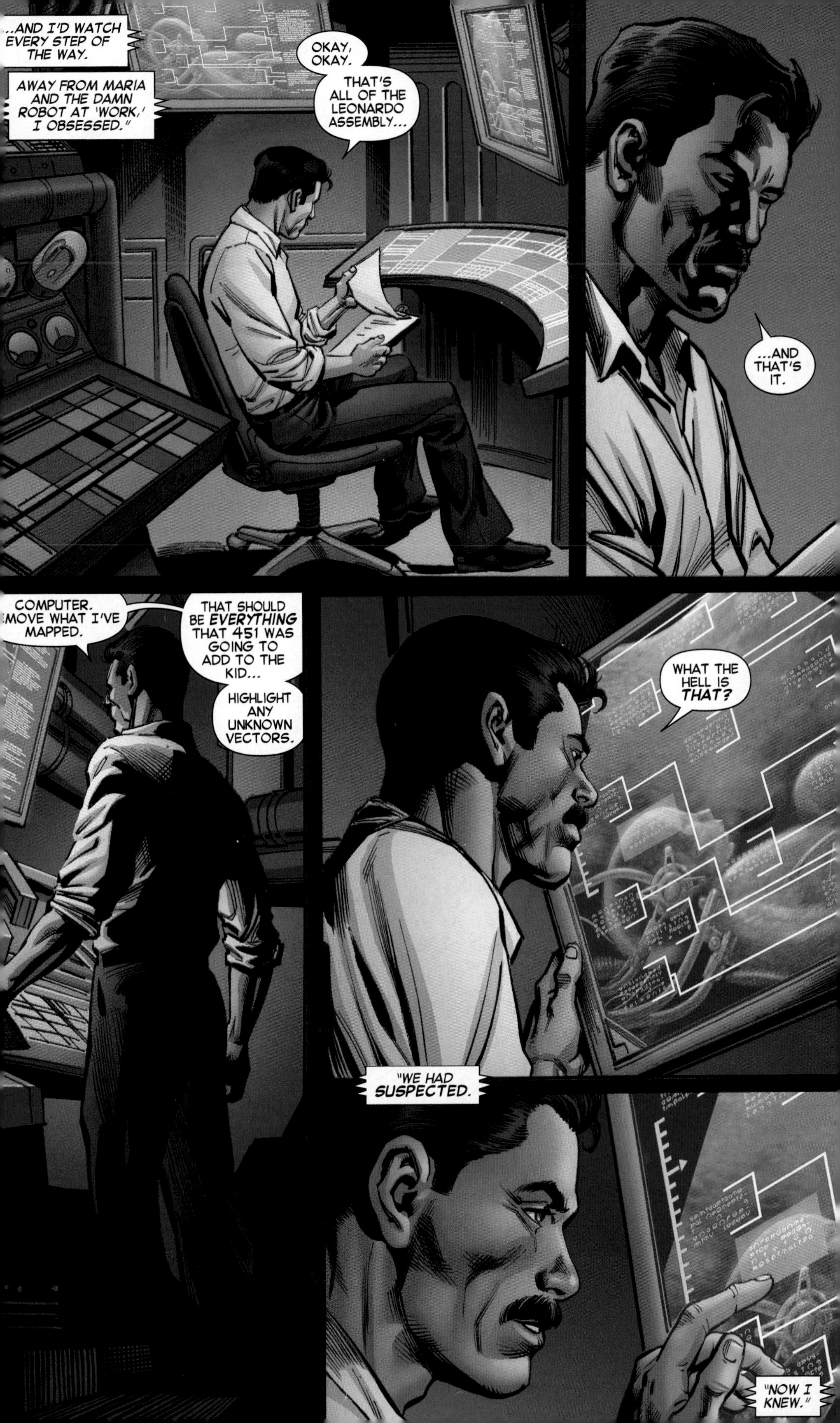
...AND I'D WATCH EVERY STEP OF THE WAY.
AWAY FROM MARIA AND THE DAMN ROBOT AT 'WORK,' I OBSESSED."
OKAY, OKAY.
THAT'S ALL OF THE LEONARDO ASSEMBLY...
...AND THAT'S IT.
COMPUTER. EMOVE WHAT I'VE MAPPED.
THAT SHOULD BE EVERYTHING THAT 451 WAS GOING TO ADD TO THE KID...
HIGHLIGHT ANY UNKNOWN VECTORS.
WHAT THE HELL IS THAT?
"WE HAD SUSPECTED.
"NOW I KNEW."

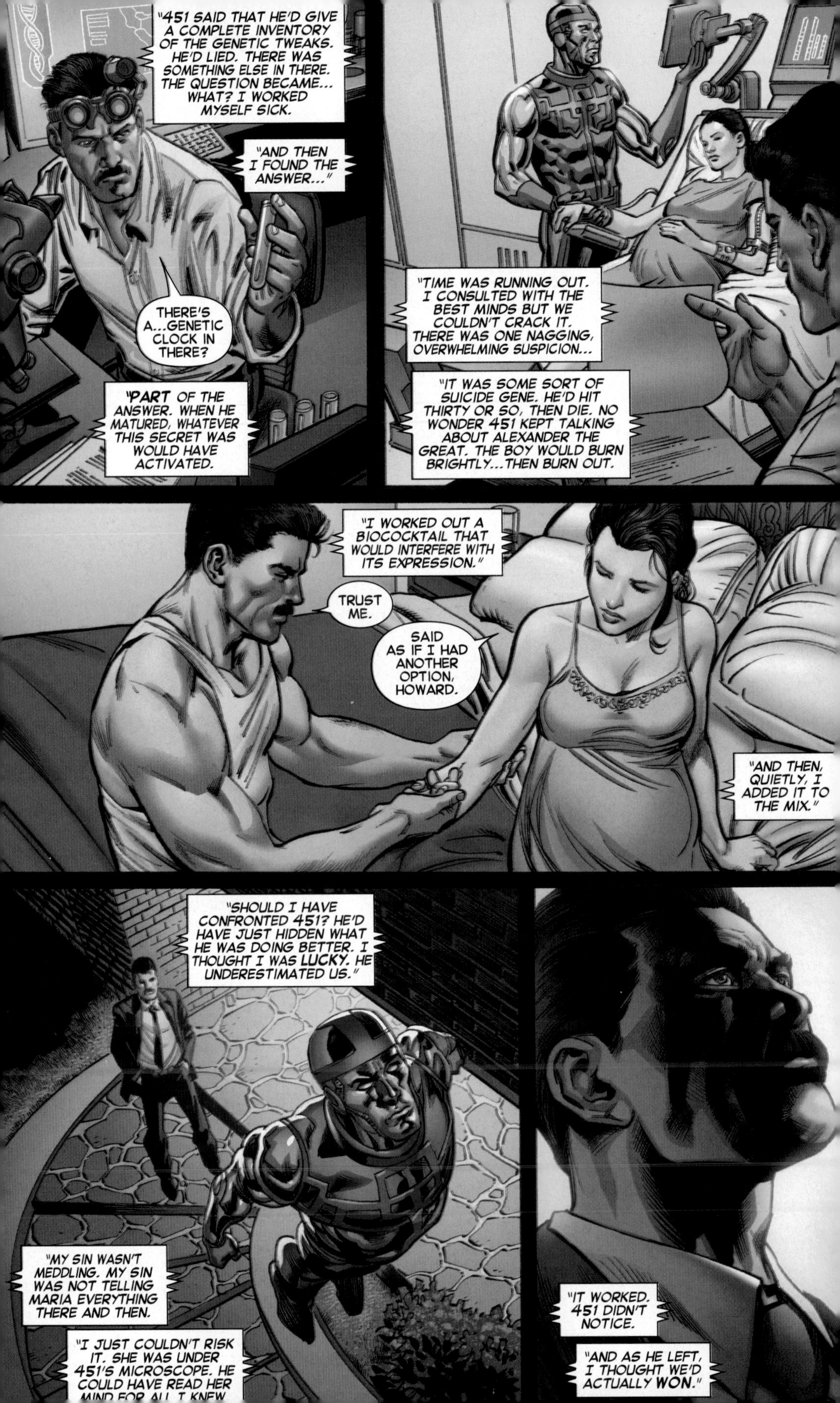
"451 SAID THAT HE'D GIVE A COMPLETE INVENTORY OF THE GENETIC TWEAKS. HE'D LIED. THERE WAS SOMETHING ELSE IN THERE. THE QUESTION BECAME... WHAT? I WORKED MYSELF SICK.
"AND THEN I FOUND THE ANSWER..."
THERE'S A...GENETIC CLOCK IN THERE?
"PART OF THE ANSWER. WHEN HE MATURED, WHATEVER THIS SECRET WAS WOULD HAVE ACTIVATED.
"TIME WAS RUNNING OUT. I CONSULTED WITH THE BEST MINDS BUT WE COULDN'T CRACK IT. THERE WAS ONE NAGGING, OVERWHELMING SUSPICION...
"IT WAS SOME SORT OF SUICIDE GENE. HE'D HIT THIRTY OR SO, THEN DIE. NO WONDER 451 KEPT TALKING ABOUT ALEXANDER THE GREAT. THE BOY WOULD BURN BRIGHTLY...THEN BURN OUT.
"I WORKED OUT A BIOCOCKTAIL THAT WOULD INTERFERE WITH ITS EXPRESSION."
TRUST ME.
SAID AS IF I HAD ANOTHER OPTION, HOWARD.
"AND THEN, QUIETLY, I ADDED IT TO THE MIX."
"SHOULD I HAVE CONFRONTED 451? HE'D HAVE JUST HIDDEN WHAT HE WAS DOING BETTER. I THOUGHT I WAS LUCKY. HE UNDERESTIMATED US."
"MY SIN WASN'T MEDDLING. MY SIN WAS NOT TELLING MARIA EVERYTHING THERE AND THEN.
"I JUST COULDN'T RISK IT. SHE WAS UNDER 451'S MICROSCOPE. HE COULD HAVE READ HER
"IT WORKED. 451 DIDN'T NOTICE.
"AND AS HE LEFT, I THOUGHT WE'D ACTUALLY WON."

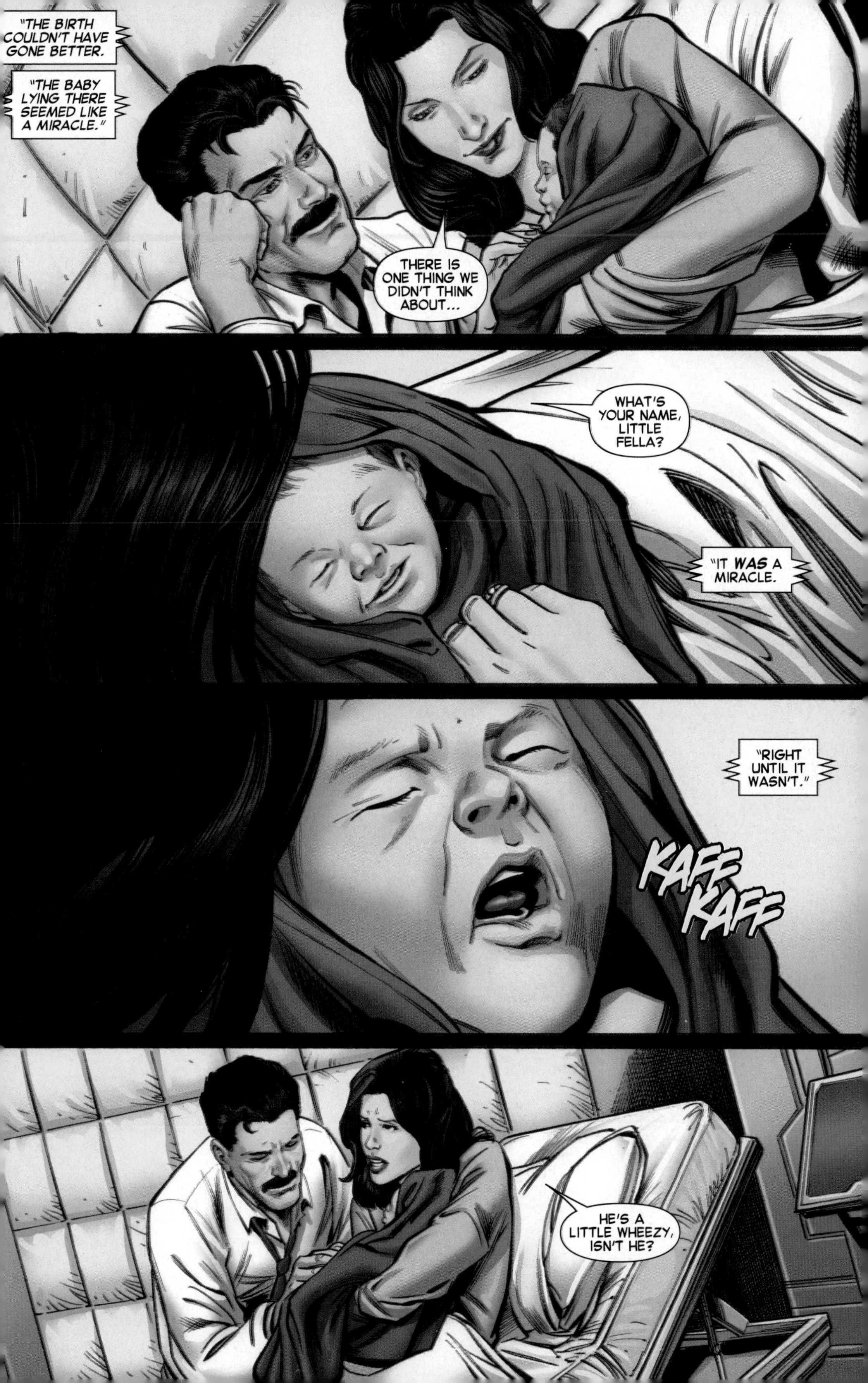
"THE BIRTH COULDN'T HAVE GONE BETTER.
"THE BABY LYING THERE SEEMED LIKE A MIRACLE."
THERE IS ONE THING WE DIDN'T THINK ABOUT...
WHAT'S YOUR NAME, LITTLE FELLA?
"IT *WAS* A MIRACLE.
"RIGHT UNTIL IT WASN'T."
KAFF KAFF
HE'S A LITTLE WHEEZY, ISN'T HE?

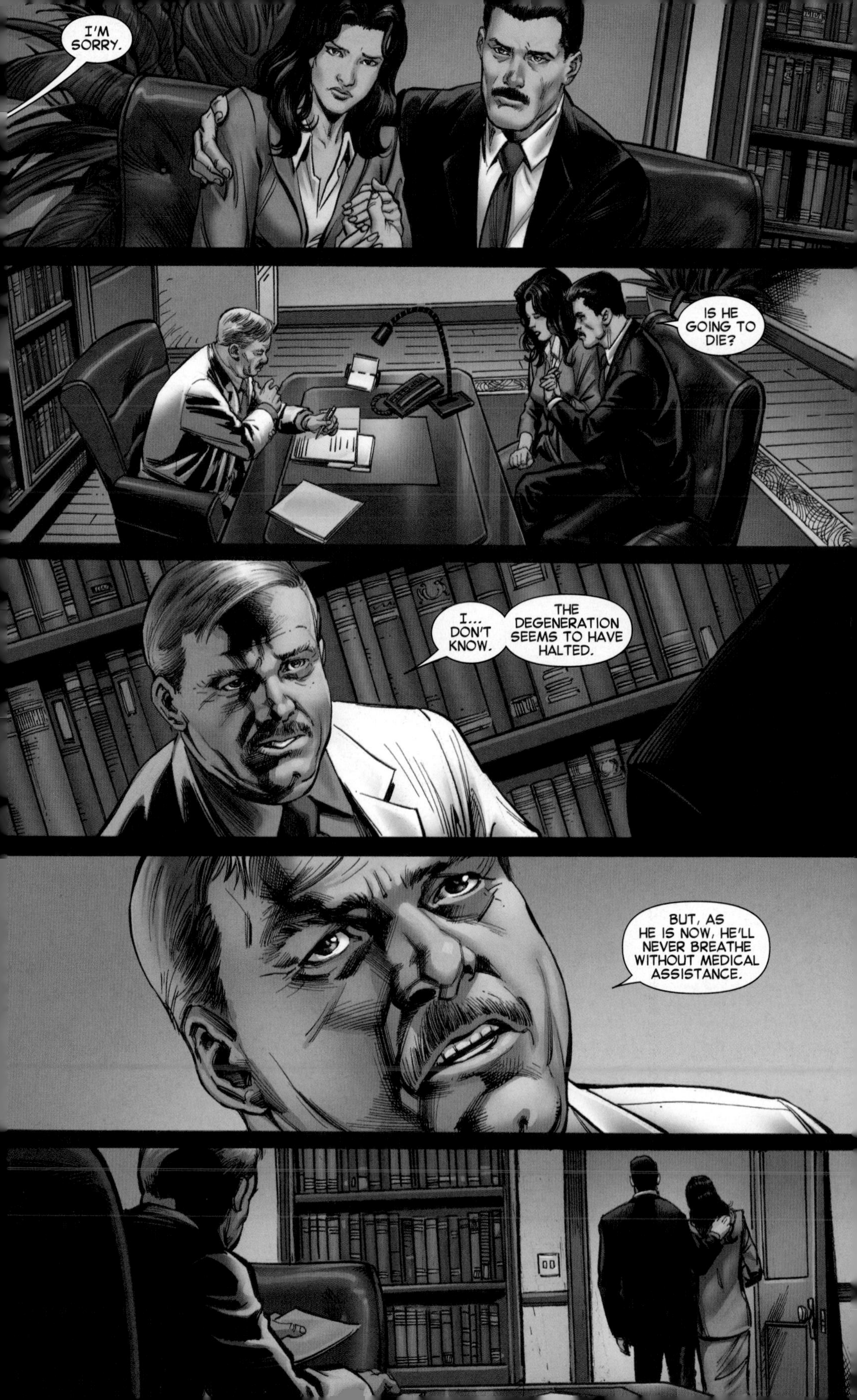
I'M SORRY.
IS HE GOING TO DIE?
I... DON'T KNOW.
THE DEGENERATION SEEMS TO HAVE HALTED.
BUT, AS HE IS NOW, HE'LL NEVER BREATHE WITHOUT MEDICAL ASSISTANCE.

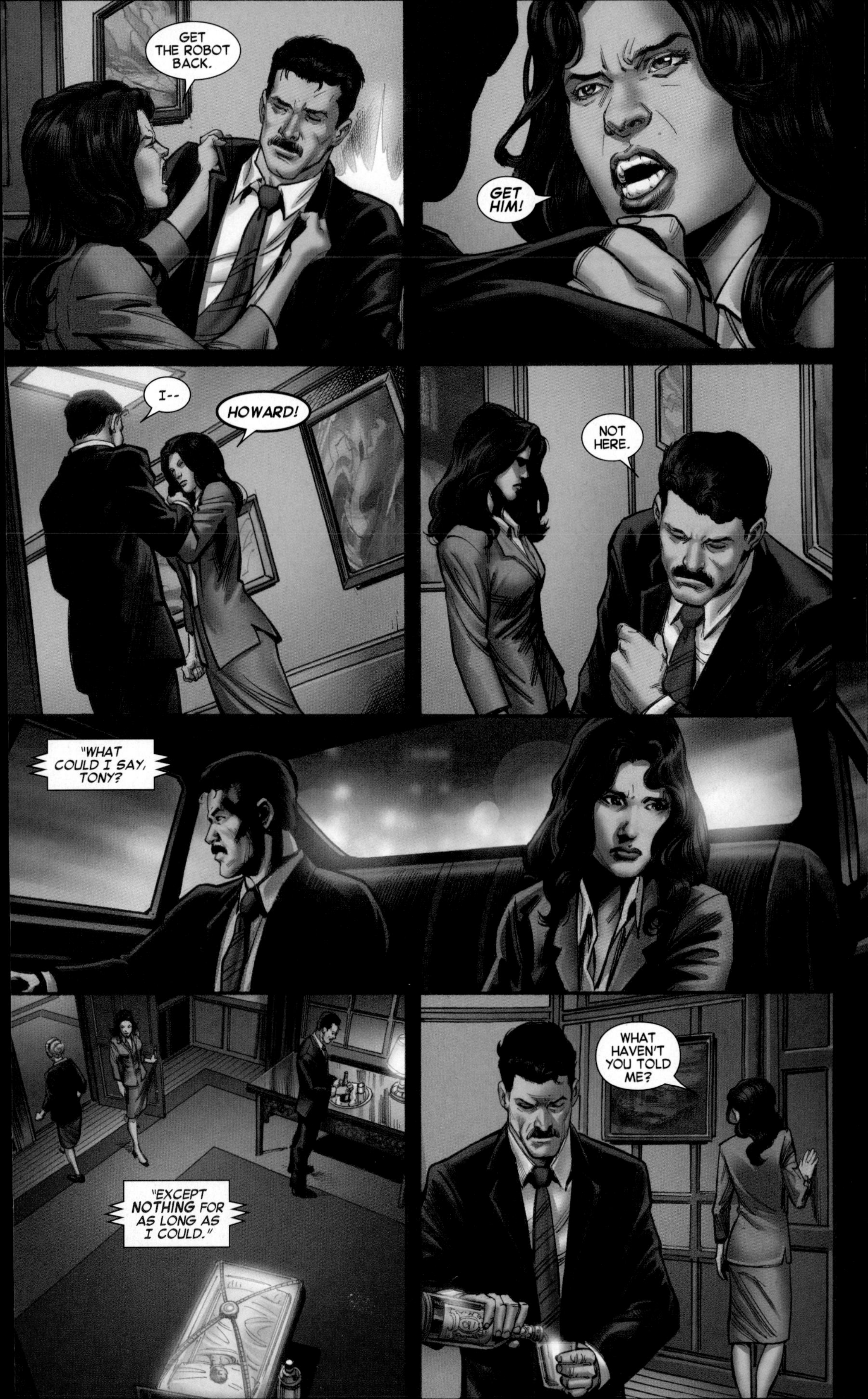
GET THE ROBOT BACK.
GET HIM!
I--
HOWARD!
NOT HERE.
"WHAT COULD I SAY, TONY?
"EXCEPT NOTHING FOR AS LONG AS I COULD."
WHAT HAVEN'T YOU TOLD ME?

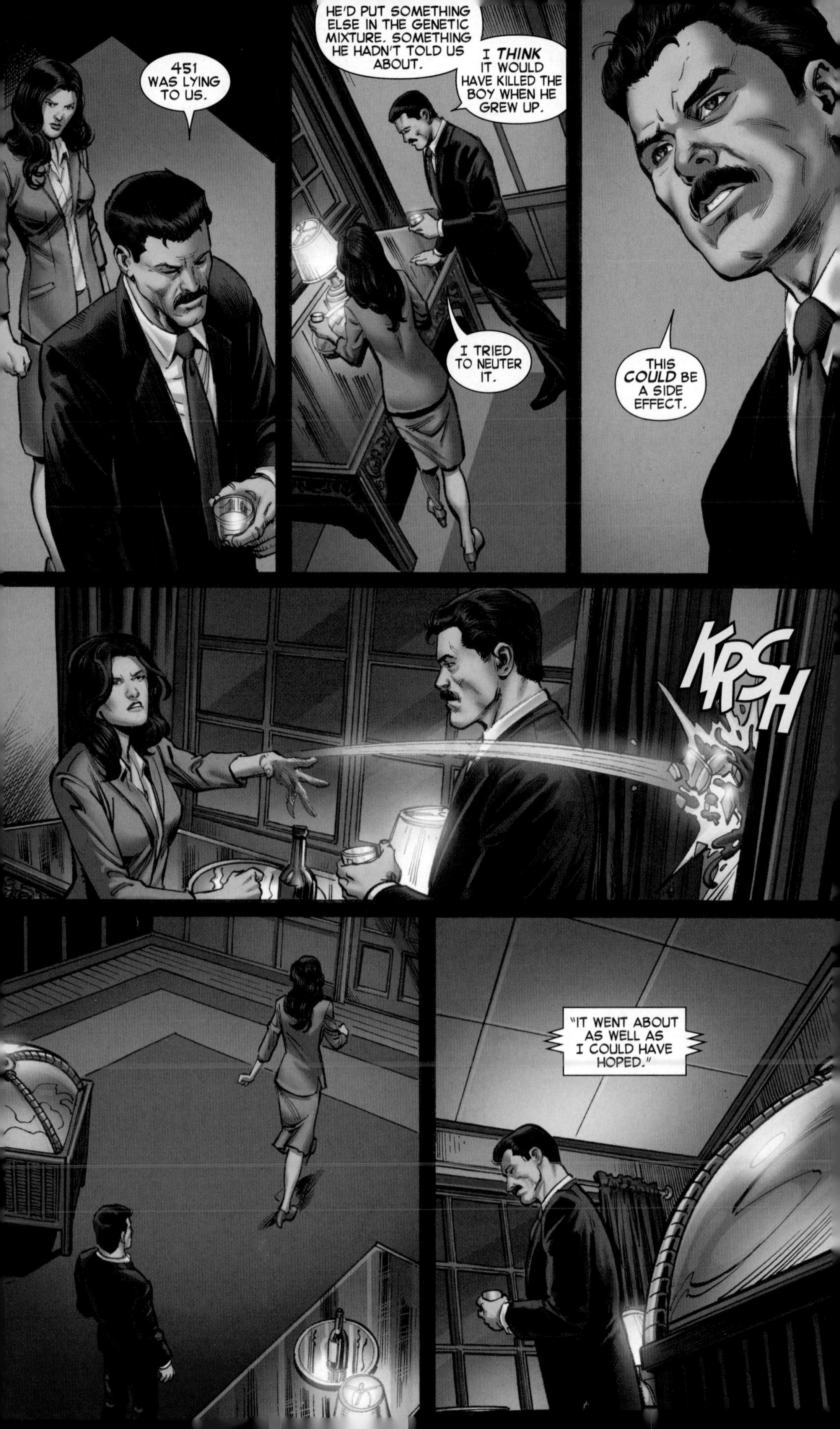
451 WAS LYING TO US.
HE'D PUT SOMETHING ELSE IN THE GENETIC MIXTURE. SOMETHING HE HADN'T TOLD US ABOUT.
I *THINK* IT WOULD HAVE KILLED THE BOY WHEN HE GREW UP.
I TRIED TO NEUTER IT.
THIS *COULD* BE A SIDE EFFECT.
KRSH
"IT WENT ABOUT AS WELL AS I COULD HAVE HOPED."

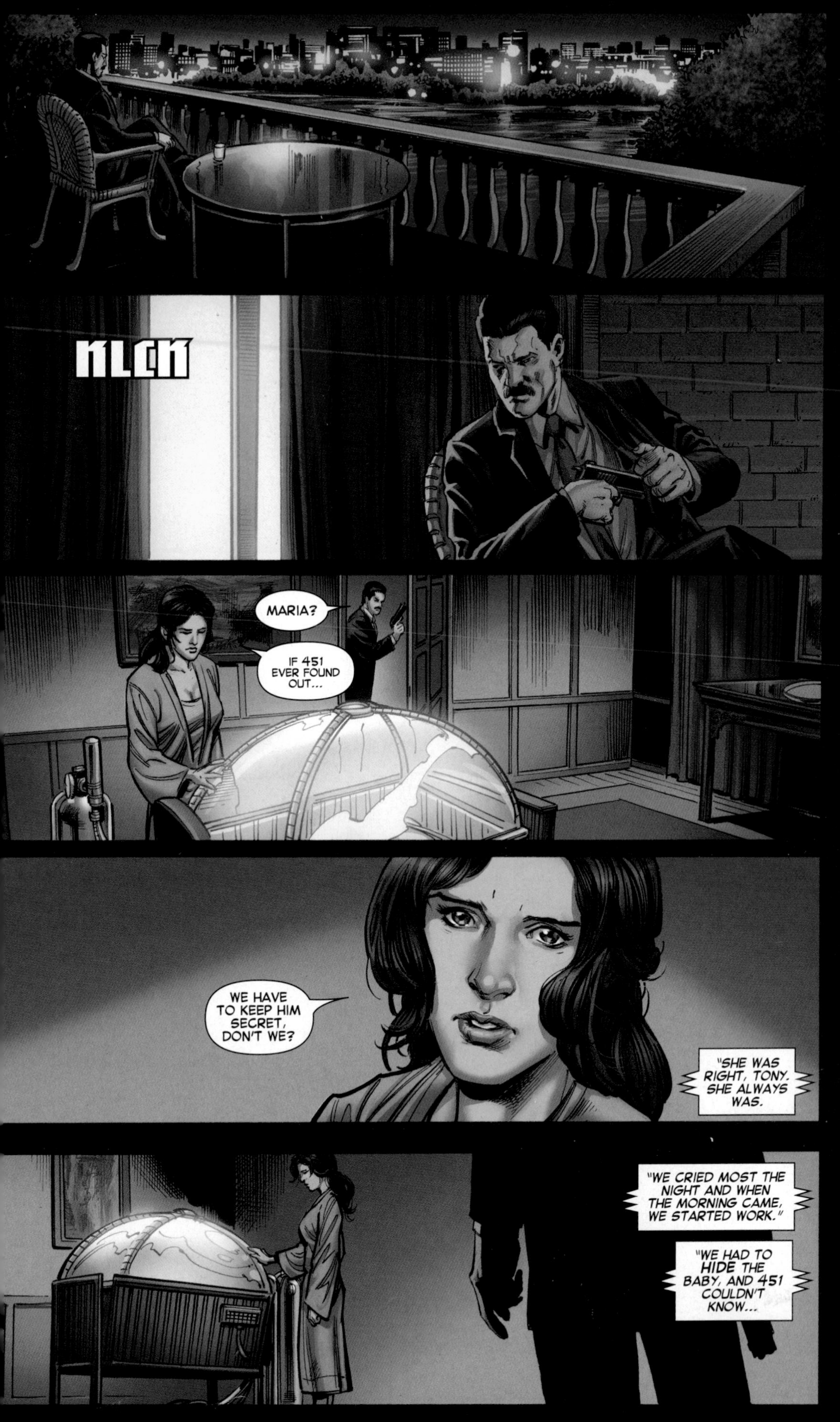
KLICK
MARIA?
IF 451 EVER FOUND OUT...
WE HAVE TO KEEP HIM SECRET, DON'T WE?
"SHE WAS RIGHT, TONY. SHE ALWAYS WAS.
"WE CRIED MOST THE NIGHT AND WHEN THE MORNING CAME, WE STARTED WORK."
"WE HAD TO HIDE THE BABY, AND 451 COULDN'T KNOW...

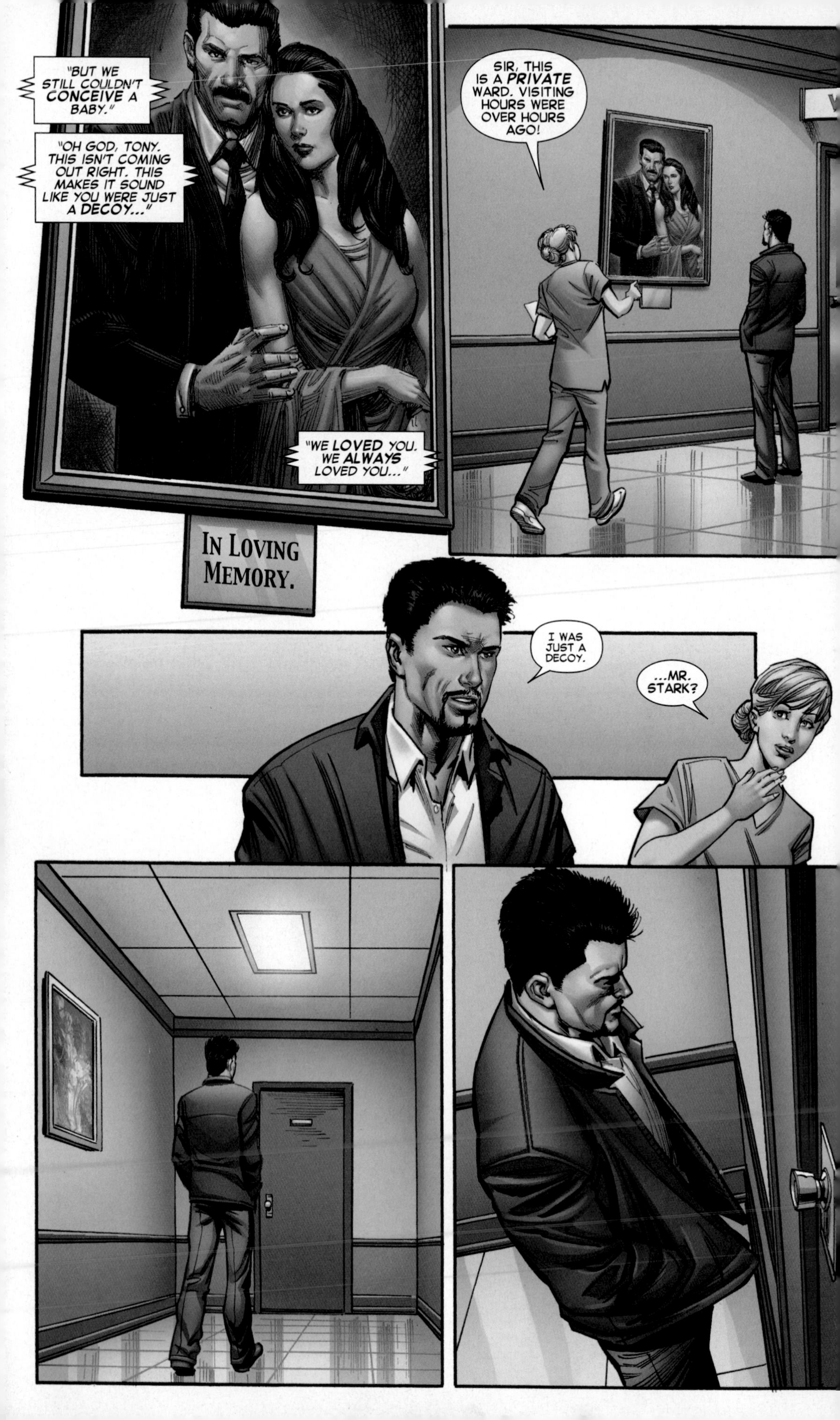

"BUT WE STILL COULDN'T CONCEIVE A BABY."
"OH GOD, TONY. THIS ISN'T COMING OUT RIGHT. THIS MAKES IT SOUND LIKE YOU WERE JUST A DECOY..."
"WE LOVED YOU. WE ALWAYS LOVED YOU..."
IN LOVING MEMORY.
SIR, THIS IS A PRIVATE WARD. VISITING HOURS WERE OVER HOURS AGO!
I WAS JUST A DECOY.
...MR. STARK?

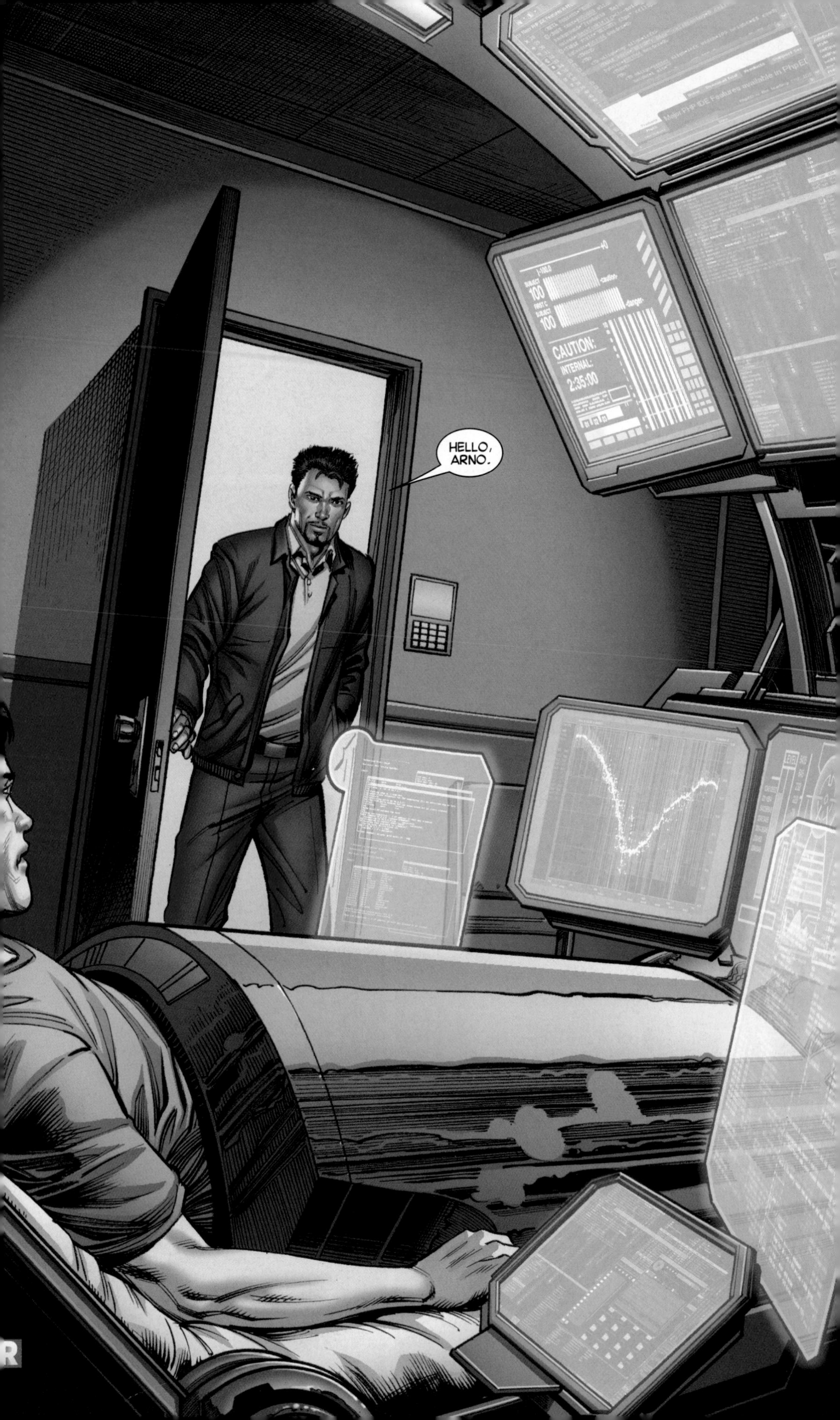
CAUTION:
INTERNAL:
2:35:00
HELLO, ARNO.

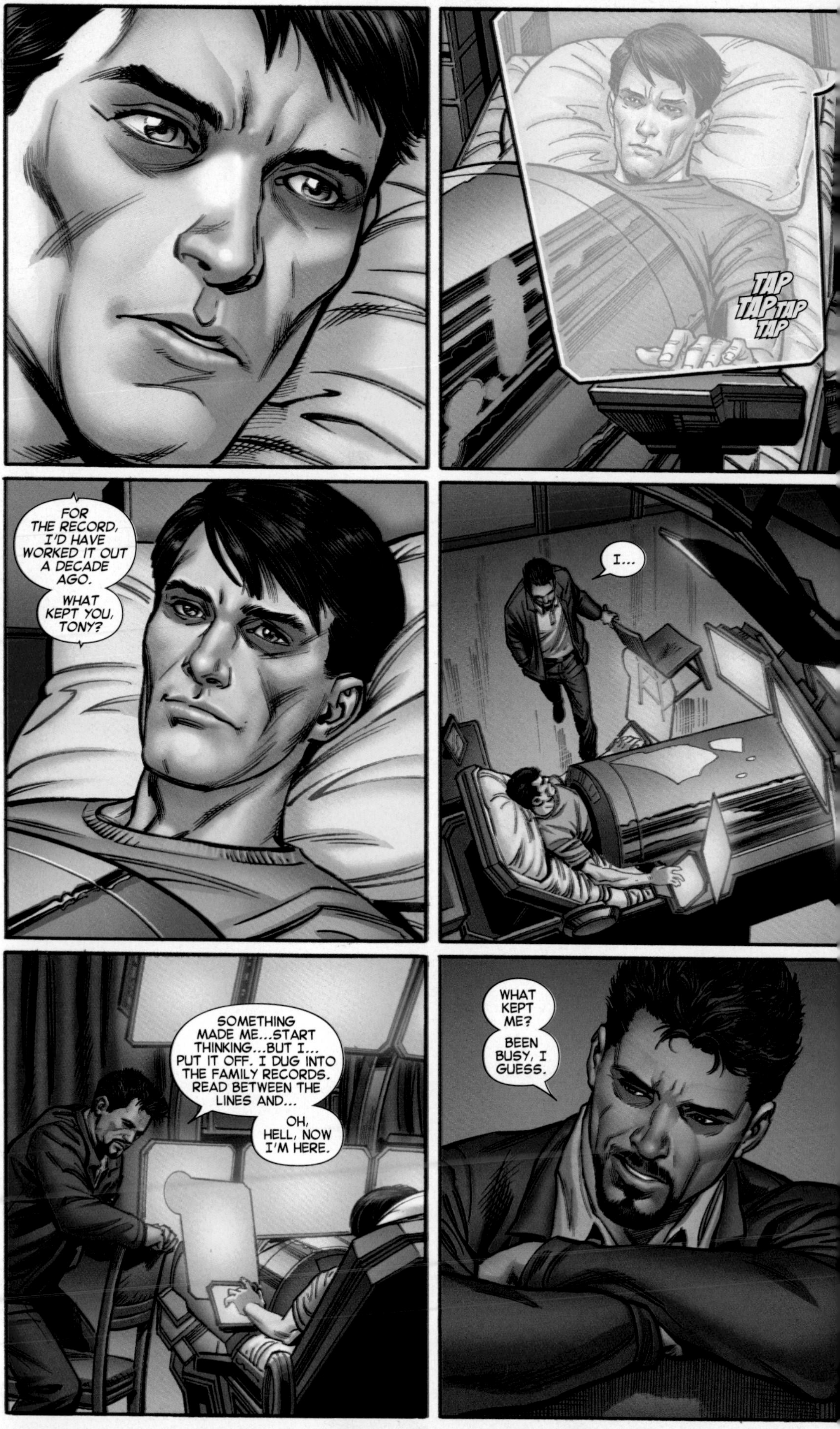
TAP TAP TAP TAP
FOR THE RECORD, I'D HAVE WORKED IT OUT A DECADE AGO.
WHAT KEPT YOU, TONY?
I...
SOMETHING MADE ME...START THINKING...BUT I... PUT IT OFF. I DUG INTO THE FAMILY RECORDS. READ BETWEEN THE LINES AND...
OH, HELL, NOW I'M HERE.
WHAT KEPT ME?
BEEN BUSY, I GUESS.

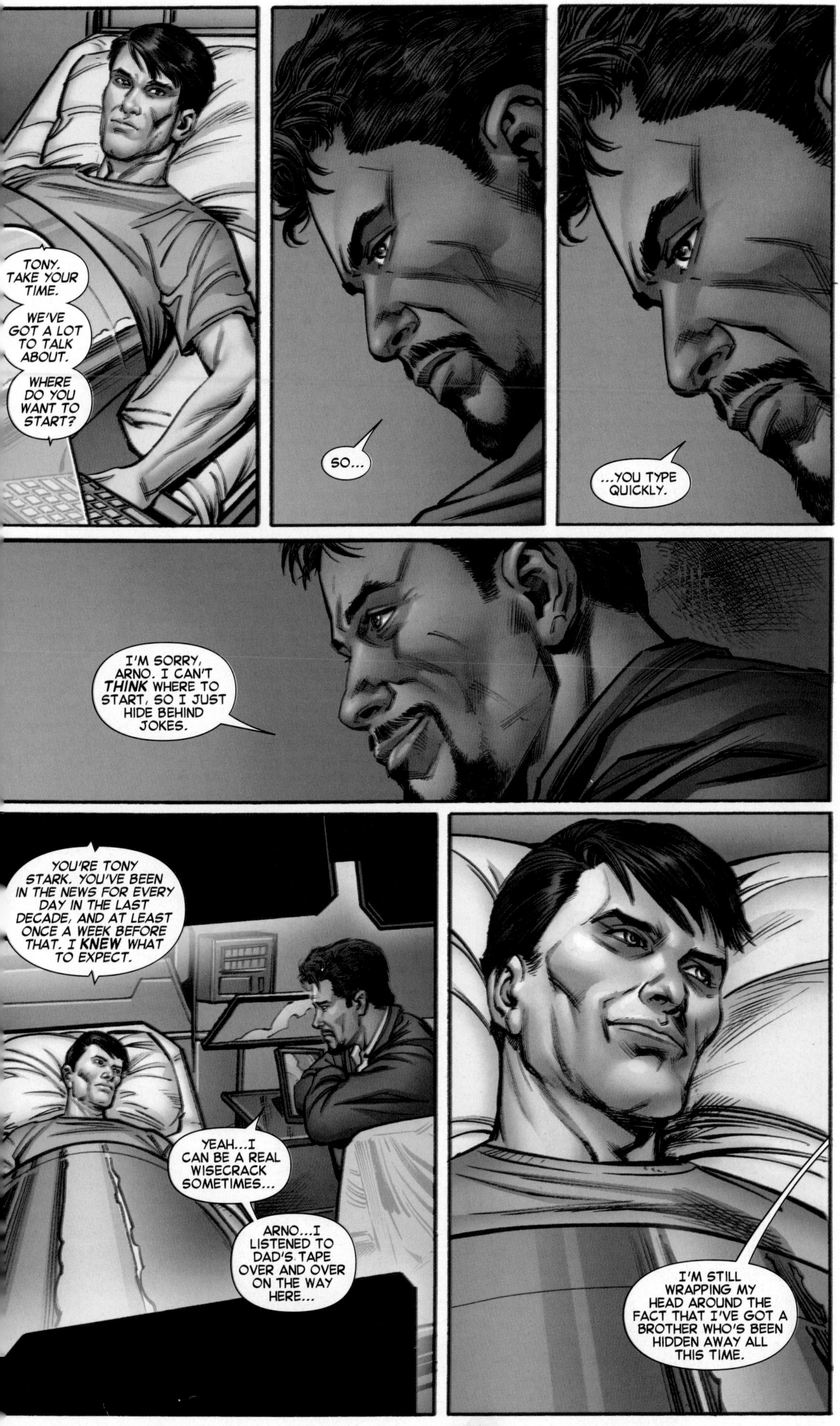
TONY. TAKE YOUR TIME.
WE'VE GOT A LOT TO TALK ABOUT.
WHERE DO YOU WANT TO START?
SO...
...YOU TYPE QUICKLY.
I'M SORRY, ARNO. I CAN'T THINK WHERE TO START, SO I JUST HIDE BEHIND JOKES.
YOU'RE TONY STARK. YOU'VE BEEN IN THE NEWS FOR EVERY DAY IN THE LAST DECADE, AND AT LEAST ONCE A WEEK BEFORE THAT. I KNEW WHAT TO EXPECT.
YEAH...I CAN BE A REAL WISECRACK SOMETIMES...
ARNO...I LISTENED TO DAD'S TAPE OVER AND OVER ON THE WAY HERE...
I'M STILL WRAPPING MY HEAD AROUND THE FACT THAT I'VE GOT A BROTHER WHO'S BEEN HIDDEN AWAY ALL THIS TIME.

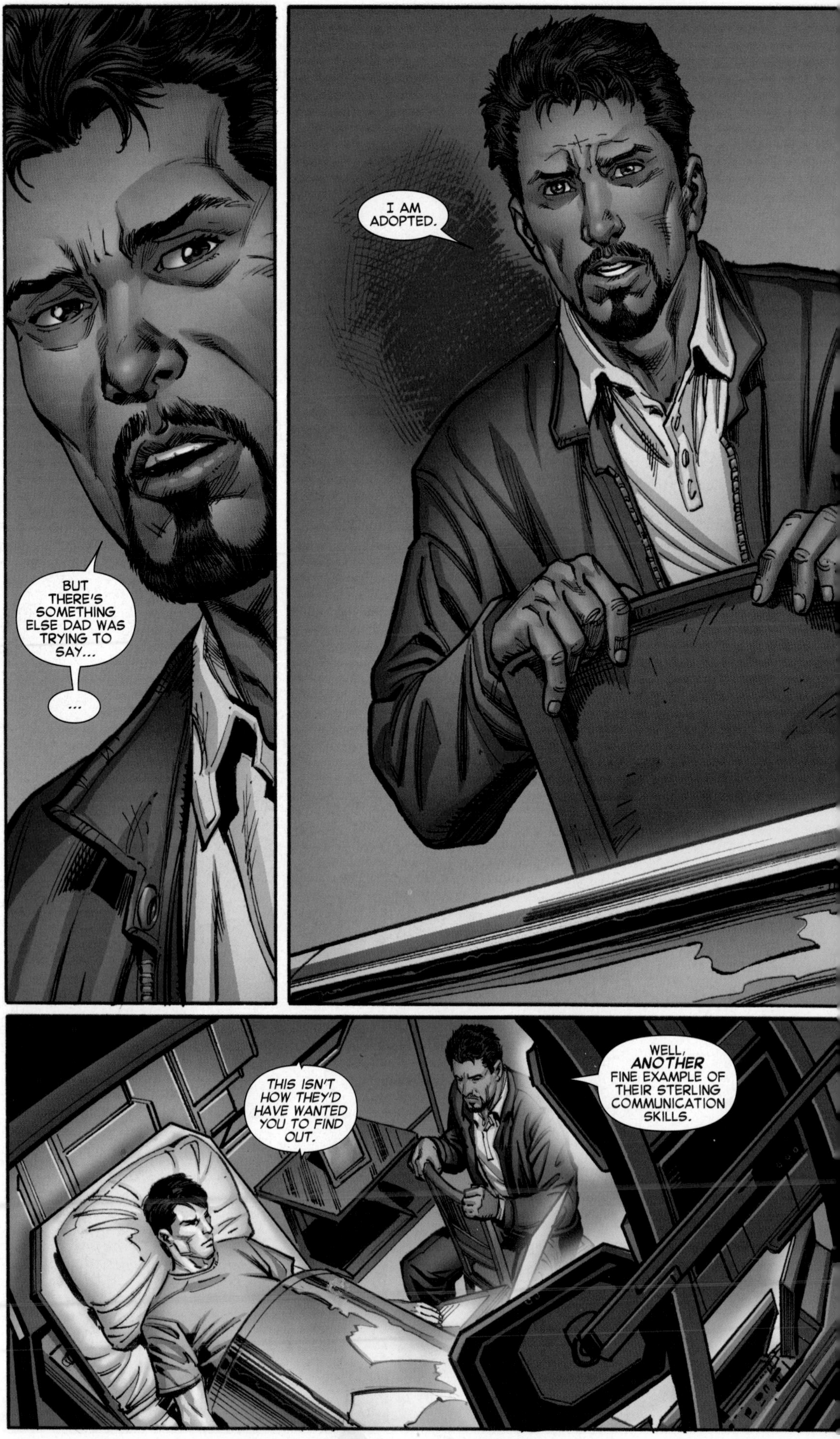
BUT THERE'S SOMETHING ELSE DAD WAS TRYING TO SAY...
...
I AM ADOPTED.
THIS ISN'T HOW THEY'D HAVE WANTED YOU TO FIND OUT.
WELL, ANOTHER FINE EXAMPLE OF THEIR STERLING COMMUNICATION SKILLS.

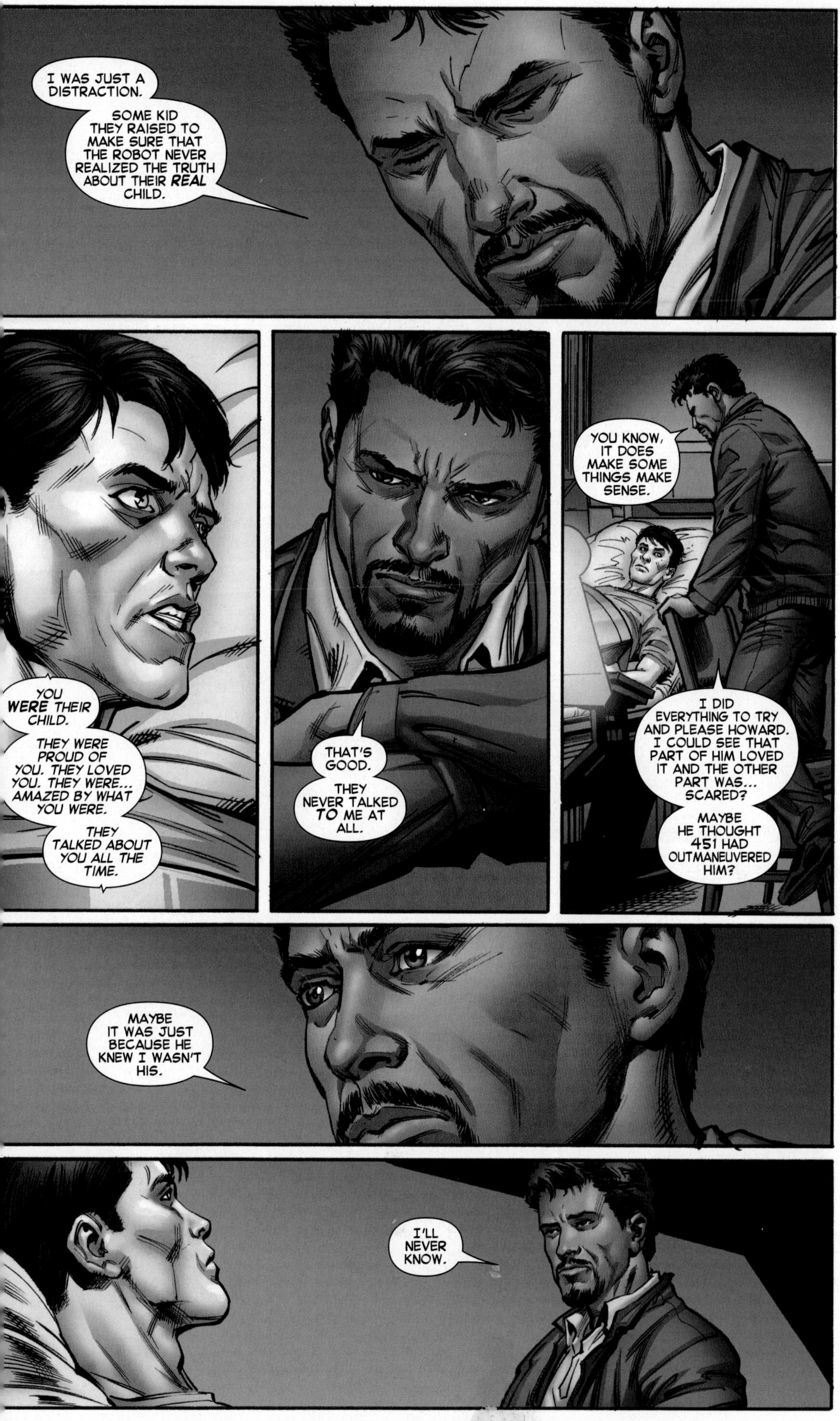
I WAS JUST A DISTRACTION.
SOME KID THEY RAISED TO MAKE SURE THAT THE ROBOT NEVER REALIZED THE TRUTH ABOUT THEIR REAL CHILD.
YOU WERE THEIR CHILD.
THEY WERE PROUD OF YOU. THEY LOVED YOU. THEY WERE... AMAZED BY WHAT YOU WERE.
THEY TALKED ABOUT YOU ALL THE TIME.
THAT'S GOOD.
THEY NEVER TALKED TO ME AT ALL.
YOU KNOW, IT DOES MAKE SOME THINGS MAKE SENSE.
I DID EVERYTHING TO TRY AND PLEASE HOWARD. I COULD SEE THAT PART OF HIM LOVED IT AND THE OTHER PART WAS... SCARED?
MAYBE HE THOUGHT 451 HAD OUTMANEUVERED HIM?
MAYBE IT WAS JUST BECAUSE HE KNEW I WASN'T HIS.
I'LL NEVER KNOW.

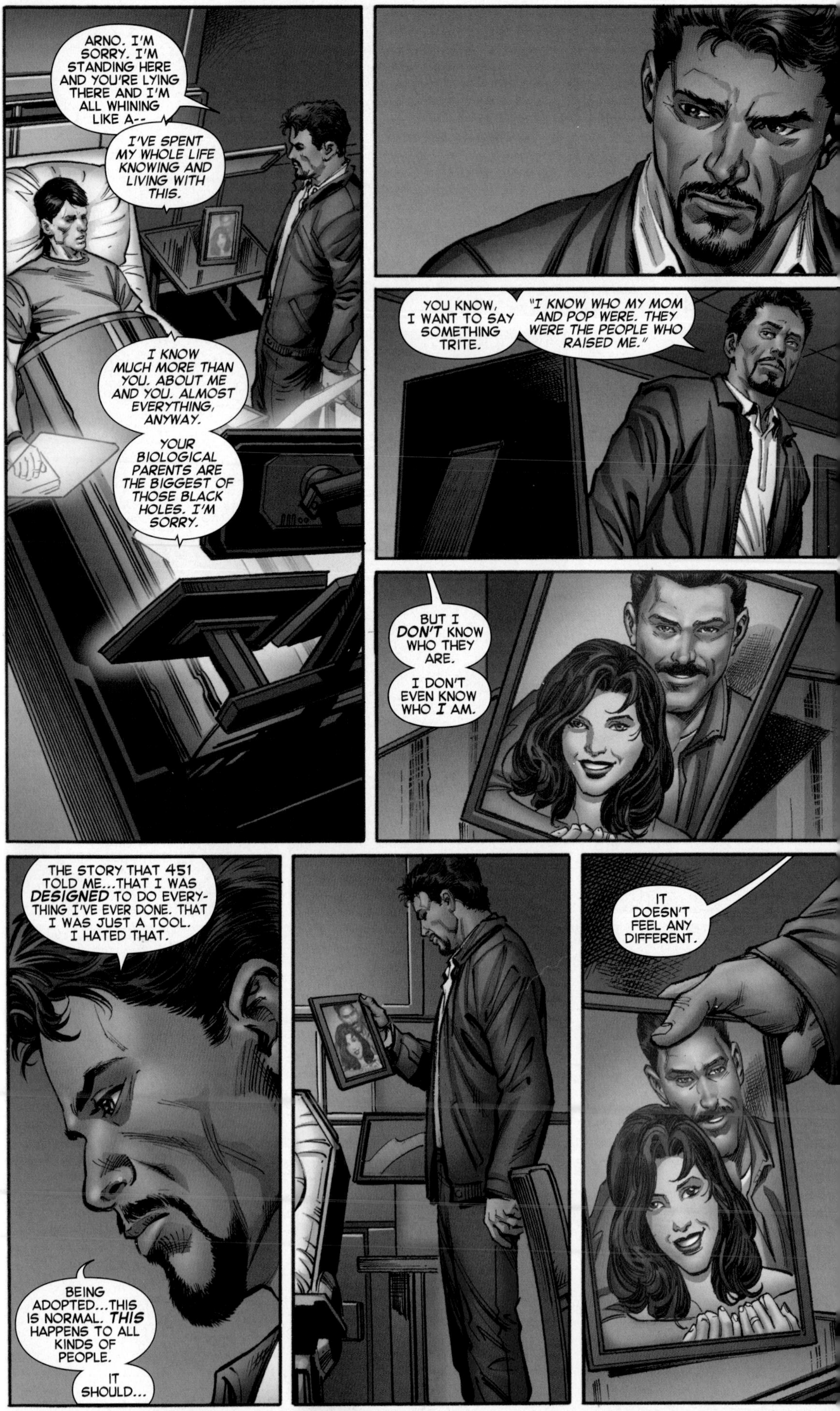

ARNO. I'M SORRY. I'M STANDING HERE AND YOU'RE LYING THERE AND I'M ALL WHINING LIKE A--
I'VE SPENT MY WHOLE LIFE KNOWING AND LIVING WITH THIS.
I KNOW MUCH MORE THAN YOU. ABOUT ME AND YOU. ALMOST EVERYTHING, ANYWAY.
YOUR BIOLOGICAL PARENTS ARE THE BIGGEST OF THOSE BLACK HOLES. I'M SORRY.
YOU KNOW, I WANT TO SAY SOMETHING TRITE.
"I KNOW WHO MY MOM AND POP WERE. THEY WERE THE PEOPLE WHO RAISED ME."
BUT I DON'T KNOW WHO THEY ARE.
I DON'T EVEN KNOW WHO I AM.
THE STORY THAT 451 TOLD ME...THAT I WAS DESIGNED TO DO EVERY-THING I'VE EVER DONE. THAT I WAS JUST A TOOL. I HATED THAT.
BEING ADOPTED...THIS IS NORMAL. THIS HAPPENS TO ALL KINDS OF PEOPLE.
IT SHOULD...
IT DOESN'T FEEL ANY DIFFERENT.

I CAN'T BELIEVE YOU NEVER CONTACTED ME.

I NEEDED TO STAY HIDDEN IN PLAIN SIGHT. IF 451 EVER SUSPECTED ANYTHING, GOD KNOWS WHAT HE'D HAVE DONE TO EARTH...

WHAT ABOUT A CURE?

IF IT WAS EASILY DONE, DON'T YOU THINK I'D HAVE DONE IT?

EVEN IF I HAD ALL YOUR RESOURCES, IT'D BE LIKE TRYING TO FIX YOUR IRON MAN SUIT WITH A STONE HAMMER.

SO I WAITED. IF I WAS FOUND? THAT'S ONE THING. BUT TO GO OUT THERE WHEN 451 COULD BE WAITING WAS TOO BIG A RISK F--

451 ISN'T A PROBLEM ANYMORE. HE'S GONE.

OH GOD. I'M FREE.

YES, ARNO. YOU'RE FREE.

TONY! I'VE SPENT MY LIFE HERE THINKING.

EARTH HAS PROBLEMS. I'D LIKE TO WORK ON SOLUTIONS.

I HAVE... IDEAS.

OH, I'M SURE YOU DO.

I'M NOT JOKING, TONY.

I'M NOT JOKING EITHER.

I NEED THIS. GIVE ME SOMETHING TO DO, ARNO, OR GIVE ME A BOTTLE.

BECAUSE REALLY?

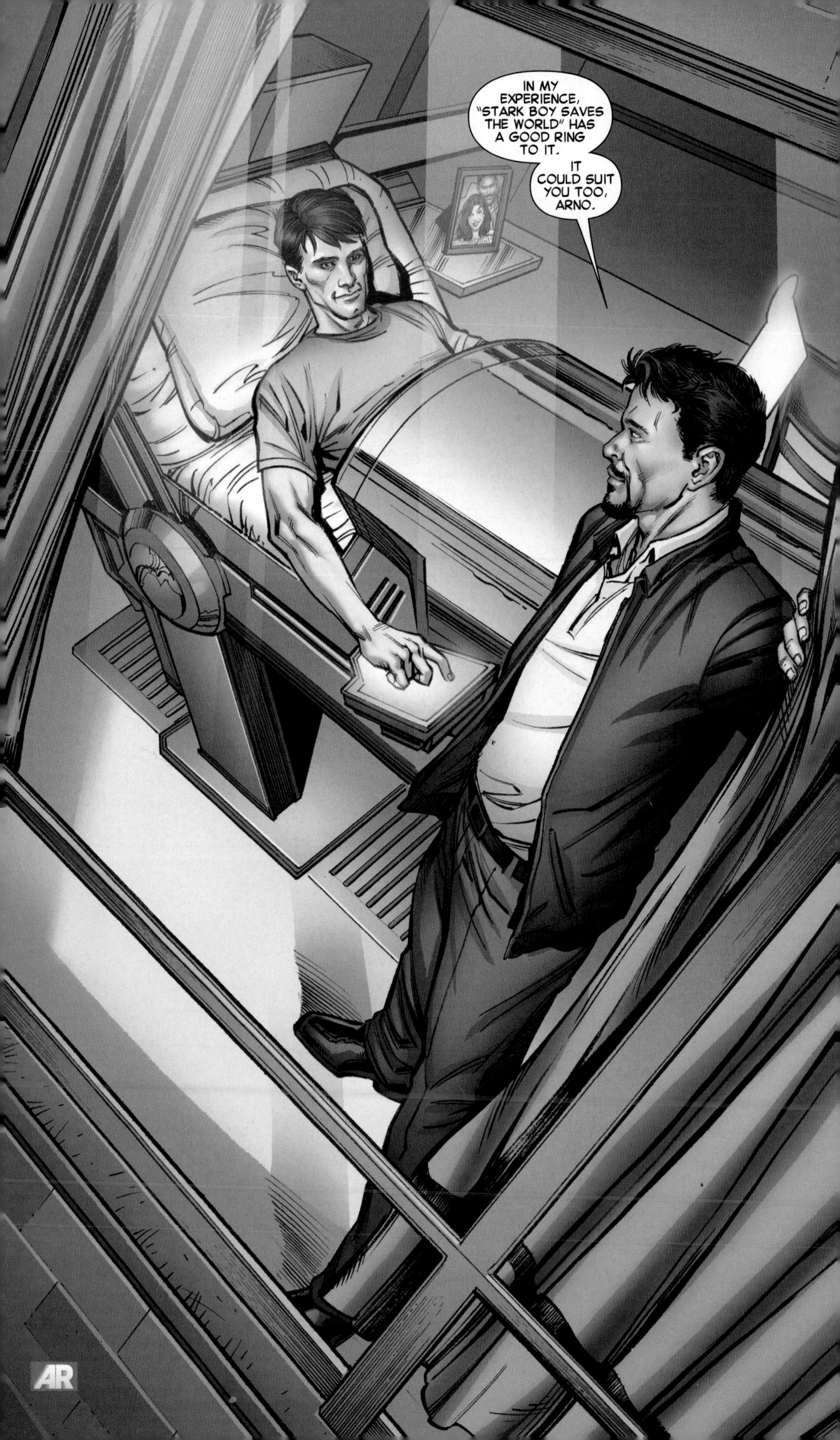
IN MY EXPERIENCE, "STARK BOY SAVES THE WORLD" HAS A GOOD RING TO IT.
IT COULD SUIT YOU TOO, ARNO.

nd so ends the first year of Iron Man.

ack in issue one, I wrote that I didn't really have a destination in mind for the book. I suspect at this oint, you may start to think I was lying to you.

lease. As if I'd do that to you. I only lie to editors.

Vhen I wrote that intro, I had just finished the first arc, which I knew had to work as sort of a thematic verture of the whole run. I knew that when Tony took off for his journey into space, everything had o change. Tony was the Grail Knight, searching for knowledge. I knew whatever that would be, it'd be eismic. He'd come back changed forever.

got the idea for the core origin in Gatwick airport, on the way to DICE comic con. I had an e-mail from Mark, talking about the possibilities for the third arc. He suggested that as it was the 50th anniversary, 'd be good to have something that harked back to the early days of Iron Man.

thrust my phone in my pocket, immediately angry. Really?

s I've talked about previously, I had a different original plan for Iron Man – a sort of hard-science ction Deadwood on the moon. When the idea of Tony joining the Guardians at the Marvel summit ppeared, I realised two things...

This is clearly a great idea, and should be done. It's great for Tony, it's great for the Marvel Universe nd it's great for the Guardians.

I can't do hard-science fiction stories at the same time. I need to set fire to all my plans.

was right on both counts. In the end, the core idea of that run is happening in a poppier form over in ne *Iron Man: Fatal Frontier* infinite comic, but back then, I just thought it was a sacrifice of the great itar of Iron Man's Better Future. Anyway — I'd done that, spent five issues setting up Tony going into pace, and had just turned IRON MAN into a sister-book to Guardians of the Galaxy...

nd now Mark seriously thought I was going to find a way to do a story about Earth fifty years ago?

stomped along, snarling. How the hell are you going to do that? I'd have to do something like...

urn Tony Into A Living Weapon Created By An Alien Conspiracy To Upgrade Earth For Nefarious urposes.

stumbled, a little shocked by the complete audacity of the idea. I shook my head. I couldn't do that.

couldn't do that for lots of reasons. Marvel wouldn't let me, for one. But more importantly, it would nnihilate the core of a character. Tony's belief he is a self-made man, who has built everything with is own two hands is completely core to him. It would destroy everything that made Tony who he is. I ouldn't do that.

took another few steps, and then stumbled again, almost laughing.

o, I couldn't do that. But that it was such an existential threat to Tony's existence made it perfect for different sort of story. One of those core parts of drama is to remove the supporting pillars, and have character face what they most fear. The idea of making Tony think he's just a machine — an Iron Man – and have to deal with who he is after you remove that egotistical heart struck me as full of potential. nat there was obviously enough evidence to support a fairly convincing conspiracy theory was the ther plus. It wasn't out of the blue. On some perverse level, it almost made sense.

ollowing that line of thinking let me strip away Tony's sense-of-self, and allowed him to have that dd moment in the Godkiller when he realised he'd rather be wiped out of existence than let anyone se suffer. Tony Stark is a living ego, but if it came to it, it's more important to save people. It's more nportant to be a hero. He's arguably the most flawed of the first-rank of Marvel's heroes, true. At least or me, that makes him all the more heroic.

didn't know exactly that I'd end up there when I was walking through Gatwick, but I knew that I'd have o go somewhere like it.

o, if Tony wasn't this child, who was?

nd Arno was there. Instantly.

got on the phone to Mark just before boarding, and threw the molten core of the story at him, only ccasionally glancing around to make sure no comic reader was eavesdropping. This felt like a story orth telling. Mark agreed. After a lot of battles, we were able to tell it.

hope you feel the need to re-read the run at this point. There's been a lot building to this point that nay now be clearer. And more importantly, I hope you feel the need to see what the Stark Brothers do ext. It's been a long road to get here.

nanks for joining me.

eron Gillen

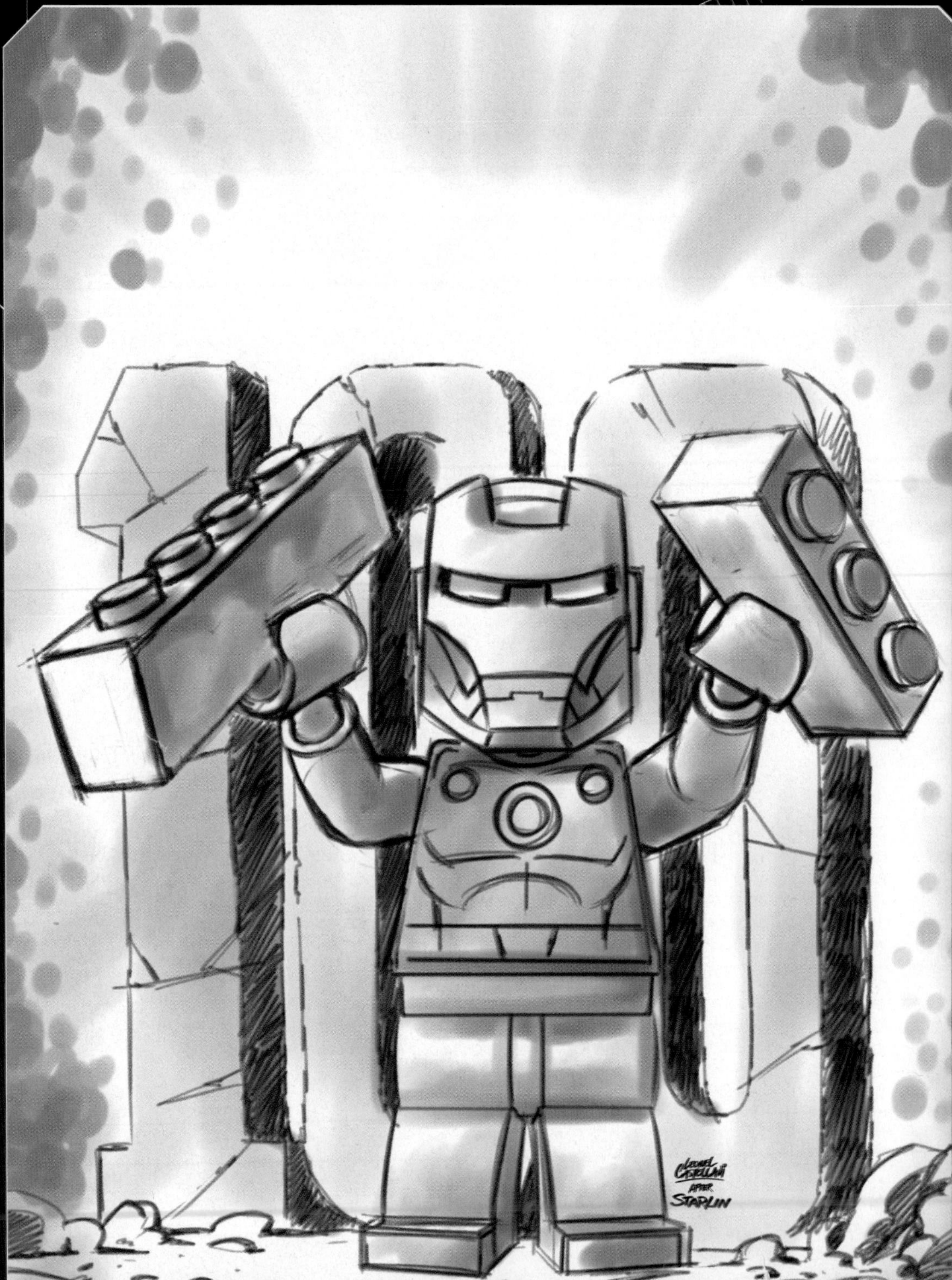
LEONEL CASTELLANI
AFTER
STARLIN

#17 LEGO SKETCH VARIANT BY LEONEL CASTELLANI

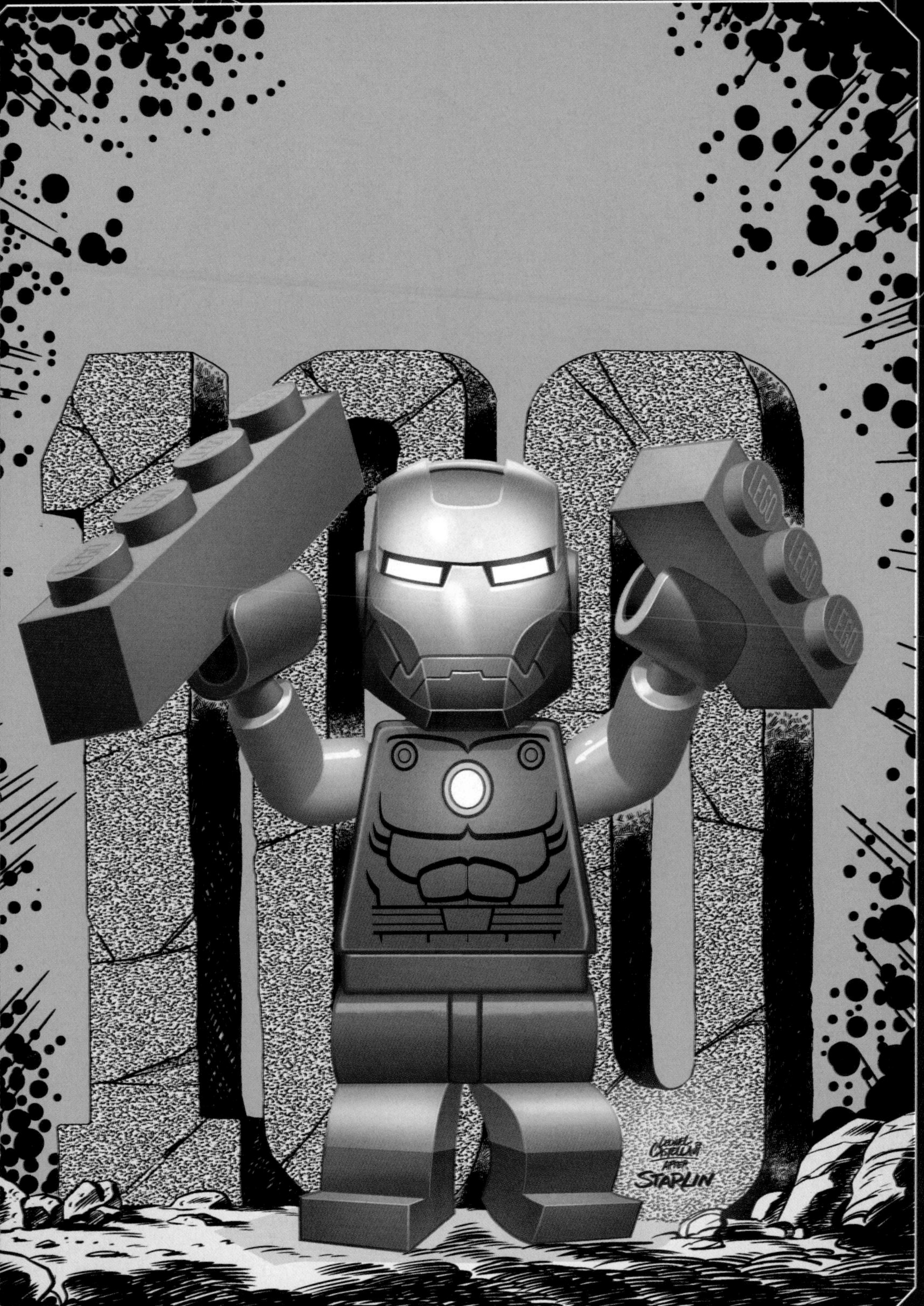
LEGO
LEGO
LEGO
LEONEL CASTELLANI AFTER STARLIN

#17 LEGO VARIANT BY LEONEL CASTELLANI

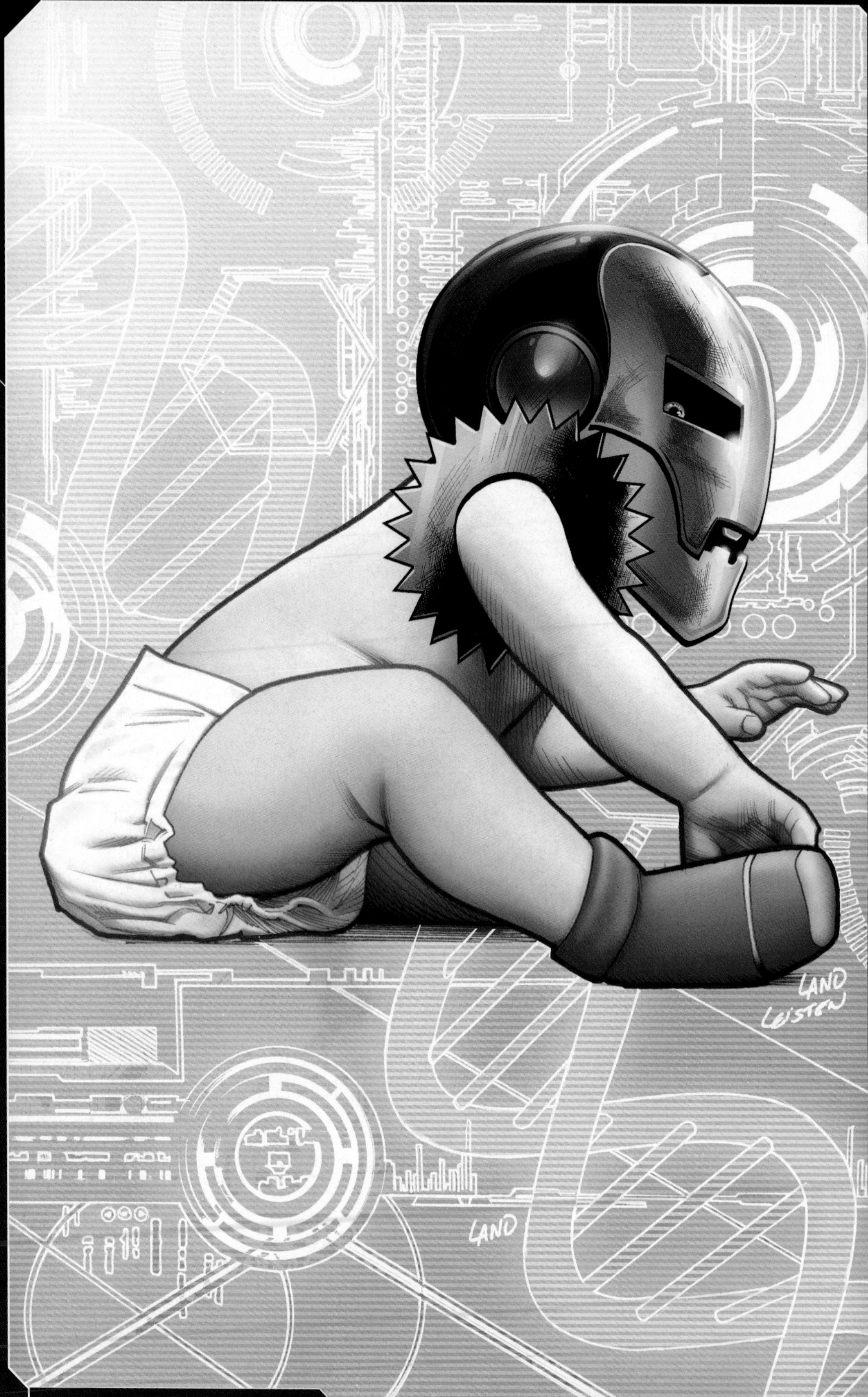
LAND
LEISTEN
LAND

#17 VARIANT BY GREG LAND & JAY LEISTEN

"..I COULDN'T THINK OF A BETTER WRITER TO HANDLE TONY STARK THAN (KIERON) GILLEN." – *AcomicBookBlog.com*

ON MAN VOL. 2: THE SECRET ORIGIN OF TONY STARK BOOK 1 PREMIERE HC
978-0-7851-6834-8 • MAY130719

"...A GREAT JUMPING-ON POINT" – *TalkingComicBooks.com*

© 2013 MARVEL

TO ACCESS THE FREE *MARVEL AUGMENTED REALITY APP*
THAT ENHANCES AND CHANGES THE WAY YOU EXPERIENCE COMIC

1. Download the app for free via
marvel.com/ARapp
2. Launch the app on your camera-enabled
Apple iOS® or Android™ device*

3. Hold your mobile device's camera ov
any cover or panel with the AR gra
4. Sit back and see the future of comics
in action!

*Available on most camera-enabled Apple iOS® and Android™ devices. Content subject to
change and availability.

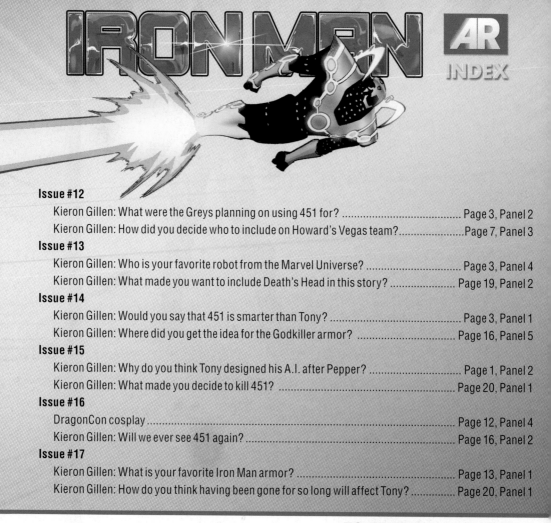

IRON MEN — AR INDEX

TO REDEEM YOUR CODE
FOR A FREE DIGITAL COPY:

1. GO TO MARVEL.COM/REDEEM.
   OFFER EXPIRES ON 12/4/15.
2. FOLLOW THE ON-SCREEN INSTRUCTIONS
   TO REDEEM YOUR DIGITAL COPY.
3. LAUNCH THE MARVEL COMICS APP TO
   READ YOUR COMIC NOW!
4. YOUR DIGITAL COPY WILL BE FOUND
   UNDER THE *MY COMICS* TAB.
5. READ & ENJOY!

YOUR FREE DIGITAL COPY WILL BE AVAILABLE

MARVEL COMICS APP
FOR APPLE® iOS DEVICES

MARVEL COMICS AP
FOR ANDROID™ DEVIC

Digital copy requires purchase of a print copy. Download code va
one use only. Digital copy available on the date print copy is ava
Availability time of the digital copy may vary on the date of release
© Marvel & Subs. Apple is a trademark of Apple Inc., registered in th
and other countries. Android is a trademark of Google Inc.